No

CW00409149

In an important departure from current theories of causation, David Owens proposes that coincidences have no causes, and that a cause is something which ensures that its effects are no coincidence. In *Causes and coincidences*, he elucidates the idea of a coincidence as an event which can be divided into constituent events, the nomological antecedents of which are independent of each other. He also suggests that causal facts can be analysed in terms of non-causal facts, including relations of necessity. Thus, causation is defined in terms of *coincidence*, and *coincidence* without reference to causation.

David Owens challenges ideas associated with Hume, Davidson and Lewis, constructing a theory which distinguishes nomological necessity and sufficiency from their logical counterparts. He is able to offer novel solutions to the major problems of causation, including the direction of causation, the logical form of causal statements, the problem of deviant causal chains, and the relationship between psychological and physical causation.

CAMBRIDGE STUDIES IN PHILOSOPHY

*Causes and coincidences*

# CAMBRIDGE STUDIES IN PHILOSOPHY

*General editor* ERNEST SOSA

*Advisory editors* J. E. ALTHAM, SIMON BLACKBURN, GILBERT HARMAN,
MARTIN HOLLIS, FRANK JACKSON, JONATHAN LEAR, WILLIAM LYCAN,
JOHN PERRY, SYDNEY SHOEMAKER, BARRY STROUD

JAMES CARGILE *Paradoxes: a study in form and prediction*
PAUL M. CHURCHLAND *Scientific realism and the plasticity of mind*
N. M. L. NATHAN *Evidence and assurance*
WILLIAM LYONS *Emotion*
PETER SMITH *Realism and the progress of science*
BRIAN LOAR *Mind and meaning*
J. F. ROSS *Portraying analogy*
DAVID HEYD *Supererogation*
PAUL HORWICH *Probability and evidence*
ELLERY EELS *Rational decision and causality*
HOWARD ROBINSON *Matter and sense*
E. J. BOND *Reason and value*
D. M. ARMSTRONG *What is a law of nature?*
HENRY E. KYBURG JR. *Theory and measurement*
MICHAEL H. ROBINS *Promising, intending and moral autonomy*
N. J. H. DENT *The moral psychology of the virtues*
R. A. DUFF *Trials and punishments*
FLINT SCHIER *Deeper into pictures*
ANTHONY APPIAH *Assertion and conditionals*
ROBERT BROWN *Analyzing love*
ROBERT M. GORDON *The structure of emotions*
FRANÇOIS RECANATI *Meaning and force*
WILLIAM G. LYCAN *Judgement and justification*
W. D. HART *The engines of the soul*
GERALD DWORKIN *The theory and practice of autonomy*
DAVID O. BRINK *Moral realism and the foundations of ethics*
PAUL MOSER *Knowledge and evidence*
D. M. ARMSTRONG *A combinatorial theory of possibility*
MICHAEL TYE *The metaphysics of mind*
CARL GINET *On action*
MARK RICHARD *Propositional attitudes*
JOHN BISHOP *Natural agency*
J. CHRISTOPHER MAHONEY *The mundane matter of mental language*
GERALD GAUS *Value and justification*
MARK HELLER *The ontology of physical objects*
JOHN BIGELOW AND ROBERT PARGETTER *Science and necessity*
ANDREW NEWMAN *The physical basis of predication*
DAVID OWENS *Causes and coincidences*

# Causes and coincidences

## David Owens

British Academy Post-Doctoral Research Fellow
Department of Philosophy, University of Cambridge

CAMBRIDGE
UNIVERSITY PRESS

Published by the Press Syndicate of the University of Cambridge
The Pitt Building, Trumpington Street, Cambridge CB2 1RP
40 West 20th Street, New York, NY 10011–4211, USA
10 Stamford Road, Oakleigh, Victoria, 3166, Australia

First published 1992

Printed in Great Britain at the University Press, Cambridge

*A catalogue record for this book is available from the British Library*

*Library of Congress cataloguing in publication data*

Owens, David (David J.)
Causes and coincidences/David Owens.
p.    cm. – (Cambridge studies in philosophy)
Includes bibliographical references.
ISBN 0-521-41650-7
1. Causation.  2. Coincidence.  I. Title.  II. Series.
BD541.084 1992   122–dc20   91–30562 CIP

ISBN 0 521 41650 7 hardback

TO MY PARENTS

# Contents

*Preface*                                                                    *page* xi
Introduction                                                                      1

1  THE INEXPLICABILITY OF A COINCIDENCE                                            6
   What is a coincidence?                                                          6
   The inexplicability of a coincidence: agglomerativity                         11
   The inexplicability of a coincidence: transitivity                            15
   Explanation and laws                                                          20

2  CAUSES AND LAWS                                                               23
   Causal and nomological relations                                             24
   Some Humean theses                                                           27
   Laws                                                                         32
   An argument for necessity?                                                   38
   Conclusion                                                                   40

3  EVENTS AND NON-CAUSAL EXPLANATIONS                                            41
   Davidson                                                                     42
   Lewis                                                                        49
   Causation as causal explanation                                             60

4  CAUSAL EXPLANATION                                                            63
   Empirical content                                                            63
   Causal explanation                                                           68
   Non-causal explanation                                                       71
   Constitutive explanation and event constitution                             77

5  THE DIRECTION OF CAUSAL EXPLANATION                                           82
   Causal forks                                                                 84
   Coincidences and the direction of causation                                  94

ix

Dummett's apple                                              98
Experience and causation                                    102
Some objections                                             105
Knowledge and time                                          110

6  LEVELS OF CAUSATION                                      114
The primacy of physics                                      115
Reductionism and causal pervasion                           121
Reduction                                                   124
Autonomy and reduction                                      132
Autonomy and causal pervasion                               137

7  DEVIANT CAUSAL CHAINS                                    143
The causal theory of perception                             143
Perception and physiology                                   152
Perception and teleology                                    155
The causal theory of memory                                 158

8  CAUSATION IN ACTION                                      163
The causal theory of action                                 163
Is decision theory empirical?                               167
The autonomy of psychology                                  170
Deviance in action                                          173

Conclusion: WHITHER CAUSAL REALISM?                         178

*Bibliography*                                              182
*Index*                                                     186

# Preface

This book was written during my tenure of a Research Fellowship at Girton College, Cambridge. My greatest debt is to the Mistress and Fellows of Girton for electing me to that fellowship, without which this book could not have been written. During the last year of my stay in Girton, I held a British Academy Post-Doctoral Research Fellowship and I am grateful to the Academy for enabling me to complete the work.

Parts of this book derive from a D.Phil thesis submitted to Oxford University in 1988. Paul Snowdon was my thesis supervisor and the present work has greatly benefited from his patience, insight and intellectual generosity. Jennifer Hornsby first directed my attention to many of the issues discussed herein and, though we rarely agreed, her demand for clarity and her anti-reductionism have had their effect. Susan Hurley introduced me to decision theory and made me aware of its philosophical implications.

As to the current text, the person who has influenced it most is Michael Martin. He read every part of the manuscript at least once and his comments necessitated extensive revisions. Roger Teichmann forced me to think seriously about ontology and the material on events is the result. Discussions with Andrew Jack changed my ideas on supervenience, modality and psycho-physical causation, among other things. I have also benefited from the comments of Simon Blackburn, Nicholas Denyer, Peter Lipton, Hugh Mellor, David Papineau, Tom Pink, Roland Stout and Sydney Shoemaker. I would like to thank Richard Sorabji, Nicholas Denyer and Kathy Wilkes for their help and encouragement at various points. Finally, the technical advice willingly offered by Andrew Jack and Michael Martin was invaluable to someone at sea with his own word processor.

I am grateful to the Editor of the Australasian Journal of Philosophy for permission to reproduce a passage from M. Davies – 'Function in Perception' *AJP*, 61, and to Cambridge University Press for permission to reproduce a passage from S. Blackburn – 'Losing One's Mind: Physics, Identity and Folk Burglar Prevention', published in ed. J. Greenwood *The Future of Folk Psychology* (1991). Passages from D. Dennett's 'True Believers' which appeared in ed. A. Heath *Scientific Explanation* (1981), from C. Peacocke's *Holistic Explanation* (1979) and from my own 'Levels of Explanation' *Mind*, 98, are reproduced by permission of Oxford University Press.

# Introduction

A cause ensures that its effects are no coincidence. That is the central claim of this book and it is, at first sight, a familiar one. If the trespasser left the field a moment ago because he had just observed the entry of a bull, then his leaving the field at that moment was no coincidence. The arrival of the bull ensured that he would leave the field without delay. On the other hand, had the trespasser failed to spot the bull prior to his departure from the field then, as far as the presence of the bull goes, it is a complete accident that he chose that moment to leave – here it is a coincidence that the bull's arrival at $t(1)$ preceded the trespasser's departure at $t(2)$, so one who thinks it no accident that the trespasser left at $t(2)$ can't cite the bull's entry as his reason.

Philosophers have found the causal relation deeply perplexing. To say that the bull's entry caused the trespasser's exit appears to commit one to a *sui generis* relation connecting the earlier event and the later one, the existence of which enables the bull's arrival to explain the trespasser's departure. But what is this relation? How do we come to know of its existence? Surely all we actually witness is the bull's arrival preceding the man's departure, but the bull may arrive and then the trespasser may depart without the one event causing the other. So what more is there to causation? Re-telling the bull story in terms of the notion of coincidence does not appear to help here.

A popular answer to these questions is that a cause is an event that is (a) necessary and (b) sufficient (in the circumstances) for its effect. So the bull's entry caused the trespasser's exit because (a) without the bull's entry the trespasser would not have left and (b) given the bull's entry, the trespasser would leave wouldn't he? We believe (a) and (b) because we have observed the behaviour of other trespassers in similar circumstances and know that when no bull appeared they did not leave, but when a bull did appear, they left.

Now many difficulties have been raised for this account of causation

1

but I wish to focus on three. First, one event may be necessary and sufficient for another without being causally necessary and sufficient. My moving to the left of you is necessary and sufficient to put you to the right of me, but my moving to the left of you does not cause you to go to the right of me. How are the genuinely causal relations to be distinguished from these other relations?

Second, 'being a necessary and sufficient condition for' is a symmetric relation. If the bull's arrival is necessary and sufficient for the trespasser's departure, the trespasser's departure is necessary and sufficient for the bull's arrival. But the trespasser's exit does not cause the bull's entrance, rather the bull's entrance causes the trespasser's exit. How is this fact to be explained?

Third, many philosophers hold that every event (whether physical or not) has a purely physical necessary and sufficient condition. But they do not wish to hold that every event has a purely physical causal explanation. On the contrary, there appear to be many events, psychological and social among them, which do not admit of a physical explanation. But if causes are just necessary and sufficient conditions then every event has a purely physical cause. How then could any of these events fail to have a physical explanation?

I believe we can make an important advance in the theory of causation simply by taking my first sentence literally. A cause ensures that its effects are no coincidence – so whatever is a coincidence necessarily has no cause. Our popular theory is committed to denying this, as can be seen from the following example. Just as the sight of an English bull drives a trespasser from an English field, across the world an antipodean bull provokes a similar response from someone trespassing in an Australian field. Surely none could deny that the simultaneous departure of these trespassers is a coincidence – even though there is a bull to explain why each of them left at the moment he did. But the bulls' simultaneous arrival is both necessary and sufficient for the trespassers' simultaneous departure. So an adherent of the theory must conclude that this collective departure, this coincidence, has a cause after all, namely the bulls' simultaneous arrival.

In the pages that follow, I shall plead the case for saying that the simultaneous departure of the trespassers has no cause, despite having a necessary and sufficient condition. Furthermore, I shall urge that the three problems outlined above can be solved if we accept this verdict. There follows a brief sketch of how this will be done.

In chapter 1, I elucidate the notion of a coincidence and contend that coincidences are inexplicable. A coincidence is an event which can be analysed into constituent events the nomological antecedents of which are quite independent of one another. To explain such a combination of events we must find some common nomological antecedent of its components, or some nomological connection between them. Since there is none, the combination is an accident and, as Aristotle urged, such accidents have no explanation.

Chapter 2 suggests that causal facts be analysed in terms of non-causal facts, among them relations of necessity and sufficiency: 'causation' can be defined in terms of 'coincidence', and 'coincidence' can be defined without reference to causation. Nevertheless, to analyse 'coincidence', we must speak of necessity and sufficiency, and necessity and sufficiency cannot be analysed in amodal terms – so some sort of modality will be taken for granted in our account of causation.

This leaves us with a problem. Any adequate theory of causation must distinguish nomological necessity and sufficiency from their logical counterparts, which are presumably irrelevant to causation. One option is to use the Humean shibboleth that causes are only contingently necessary and/or sufficient for their effects to make this distinction. But since it is impossible to analyse causation, except by taking some sort of modality for granted, one cannot demonstrate the contingency of these modal relations by reducing them to some amodal and clearly contingent relations. Furthermore, Hume's direct argument for the contingency of laws, from the fact that we can imagine their not holding, fails to establish its point and the problem remains.

The next beacon of hope is the Humean doctrine that causes must be distinct from their effects. This has been construed, by several modern philosophers, as the doctrine that causes and effects are objects which may stand neither in the relation of parthood nor in the relation of identity. Chapter 3 concludes that this idea cannot help us to distinguish causal explanations from those explanations, arising out of our logical or linguistic practices, which depend on non-nomological connections between events.

In chapter 4, I move from the conclusion that coincidences have no causal explanation, to the further conclusion that they have no cause *tout court*. In fact, I define a cause as something which explains its effects, which ensures that its effects are no coincidence. I then confront the question: why does my moving to your right not cause you to move to my left? The answer is there is no other event, *a priori* independent of your moving to my left, such that my moving to your right ensures that the co-occurrence of that event and your moving to my left is no coincidence. So we are at last in a position to distinguish those relations of necessity and sufficiency which give rise to causation from those which do not.

In chapter 5, I criticise a number of attempts to account for the fact that causes precede their effects. These attempts rely on the assumption that each event is necessary for more subsequent events than it has antecedents sufficient for it. As they stand, these efforts fail, but they can be made to succeed provided the role of a cause is to ensure that the co-occurrence of different effects is no coincidence. For, given the above mentioned assumption, there will be far fewer coincidences if causation runs from past to future than if it goes against the grain of time: that is why causal explanation flows from earlier to later events. Once we have a theory of the direction of causation along these lines, we can distinguish events related as cause to effect from causally unconnected events which possess a common cause. Other theories find this distinction hard to make, since events with a common cause may be both necessary and sufficient for one another.

Chapter 6 considers events which have economic, but not physical, explanations. These economic events are physical in that they are entirely composed of physical events, but the innumerable physical explanations which are required to account for the occurrence of all of these physical components cannot be combined to yield an explanation for the economic event which they compose. This economic event is a physical coincidence – it ceases to be a coincidence only when we take account of its economic causes. I show that these facts undermine various reductionist and non-reductionist proposals about the relationship between the physical sciences and the special sciences, and then formulate my own view of the connection between these different levels of explanation.

In chapter 7, I apply the theory of causal explanation, expounded in the rest of the book, to the problem of deviant causal chains. This problem arises in the context of causal analyses of perception, memory and action. For instance, it is said that a visual experience of a certain object must be caused by that object, but it quickly becomes apparent that not any old causal chain from object to experience will do. Several philosophers have made suggestions as to how the unwanted, deviant causal chains might be characterised and ruled out, and I aim to show that these suggestions are, in fact, an application of points about causal explanation established earlier on in this book.

Chapter 8 is taken up with the role of causation in human action. The causal theory of action is introduced and it is argued that those laws which govern human decision making and action may be causal laws. Next, I apply the model of the relationship between the physical and non-physical sciences, sketched in chapter 6, to resolve a tension which many have felt between the claims of psychology and those of physiology to explain human action. Finally, the resurgent problem of deviant causal chains is dealt with for the case of action.

Throughout this book, I shall speak in terms of necessary and sufficient conditions. This terminology might be considered rather quaint in the light of the probabilistic turn taken by modern physics. Philosophers, at least in the last fifteen years, have bent over backwards to allow for causation without determinism. Indeed, they have gone further and attempted to analyse the notion of causation itself in probabilistic terms. Now I have nothing against these developments which seem to me entirely sensible. Nevertheless, I do not think that our treatment of the problems considered in this book would be enhanced by reformulating the issues in probabilistic terms. All the traditional difficulties philosophers have faced with deterministic causation can be restated in the new probabilistic vocabulary and after this reformulation the problems are no less intractable.

For expository convenience, I assume throughout the book that determinism is true. Nothing rests on this assumption. A reader used to probabilistic treatments may follow a simple translation procedure. Whenever I say '$p$ is sufficient for $q$', read '$p$ raises the probability of $q$', and whenever I say '$p$ is necessary for $q$' read 'The falsity of $p$ lowers the probability of $q$'. Necessity and sufficiency are just the limiting cases of these probabilistic relations. For instance, a coincidence may be defined as an event analysable into two components such that the factors which raise the probability of one component occurring (or which would lower this probability were they absent) are probabilistically independent of the factors which raise the probability of the other component's occurring (or which would lower this probability were they absent). My analysis could just as well proceed in terms of this probabilistic notion of a coincidence.

# 1

## The inexplicability of a coincidence

### WHAT IS A COINCIDENCE?

As I write, it rains outside. It has been raining all week. Tomorrow is my wedding day and I crave fine weather, but the forecasters give me little grounds for hope. In desperation I pray for fine weather and, sure enough, tomorrow dawns clear and bright. Those sceptical of the power of prayer will dismiss this as a coincidence, while many of the faithful will insist it was no coincidence. I shall not attempt to adjudicate this dispute. My aim is to discover exactly what is at stake here: what is it for an event to be a coincidence?

The sceptics will enlarge on their interpretation of events as follows: 'your prayer's being answered is an event which is composed of two other events – (a) your praying for fine weather (b) your getting fine weather. The meteorological processes which brought about the fine weather were quite independent of those which brought about your prayer, therefore it was a coincidence that your prayer was answered.'

The faithful will reply as follows: 'we agree that your prayer's being answered is an event with two components, but we refuse to believe that these components are independent of one another. Either your prayer caused the weather to be fine because God heard your request and granted it, or else your prayer and the state of the weather had a common cause in God who set up the world at the beginning of time so that your praying one day would be followed by fine weather the next.'

It should now be clear what is at issue. The sceptics say that the answered prayer is a coincidence, by which they mean that it is a conjunction of two separate events, each produced by quite independent causal processes. The faithful say that the answered prayer is no coincidence, by which they mean that its components are either causally interrelated or have some common cause – they are not causally independent of one another.

6

Coincidences are not confined to the realm of human or divine action. For instance, the sun's exploding during an eclipse would most likely be a coincidence. It would be a coincidence because eclipses and explosions are causally independent. The intentions of a powerful being might have linked these events and ensured that the outcome was no coincidence, but an inanimate natural force would have served this purpose just as well.

Hart and Honore characterise the ordinary notion of coincidence as follows:

> We speak of a coincidence whenever the conjunction of two or more events in certain spatial or temporal relations is (1) very unlikely by ordinary standards and (2) for some reason significant or important, provided (3) that they occur without human contrivance and (4) are independent of each other. (Hart and Honore, 1959:74)

In defining a coincidence simply as any event whose constituents are produced by independent causal processes, I have accepted (4) and, by implication (3), since human contrivance would act as a common cause. But (1) and (2) have been omitted from my notion of a coincidence, thus stretching the ordinary concept in at least two directions.

First, I have not insisted that coincidences be significant or striking. The conjunction of my now driving a green car and the Queen's beginning a visit to France in exactly a year's time is a coincidence. More salient coincidences include the eclipsed explosion or my unwittingly booking myself onto the same cruise as my long lost enemy. But the universe abounds in coincidences which are of no interest to human beings. My insistence that many perfectly uninteresting events are coincidences does involve a certain departure from ordinary usage, but I would argue that such extensions of a familiar concept are perfectly permissible if they aid the task of understanding other familiar concepts such as causation.

Still someone may object to this liberality on the philosophical grounds that not every conjunction of two events is itself an event and genuine events alone can be coincidences. This point has force only if we regard events as like material objects, concrete particulars which we cannot amalgamate at will to form genuine new particulars – as we cannot fuse your hand and my book into a single self-standing entity. In chapter 3, I shall urge that an event, what explains and is explained, is expressed by a sentence and is not some concrete object to which a singular term might refer. So 'It is a coincidence that' is a sentential operator which may be tacked onto the front of sentences like 'My prayer was answered' and not a predicate of a concrete particular denoted by expressions like 'the answering of my prayer'. And surely we may conjoin sentences to form new sentences to our heart's content.

There is a second respect in which my definition of 'coincidence' constitutes a departure from the ordinary concept. Coincidences do not have to be unlikely, surprising, unpredictable or improbable (Mill, 1906:345–8). I may pray for the sun to rise tomorrow, in which case it is highly probable that my prayer will be answered. Nevertheless, so long as my prayer is independent of the causal factors which lead to its being answered, this is a coincidence. The rationale for this stipulation is again a theoretical one. I shall urge that *explanation* is the key to causation and, as we shall see, explanation does not go hand in hand with either prediction or high probability.

So far, I have given the impression that being a coincidence is an all or nothing matter – either an event is a coincidence or it is not. According to the sceptic, my prayer's being answered is a complete coincidence since meteorology has nothing whatever to do with psychology.[1] In the eyes of the faithful, it is completely non-coincidental since what is intentionally brought about (by God or anyone else) is no coincidence at all. But there are many events, partial coincidences, whose components share some, but not all, of their causal ancestors.

Consider the fact that I'm on the same cruise as my old enemy. This might be a complete coincidence – perhaps a full explanation of why I am on that cruise will have nothing in common with a full explanation of why he is on that cruise. But this is unlikely. Suppose that I am cruising partly because the weather is hot and I wish to escape to the cool sea – this may well be why he is cruising also. So there is at least one causal factor which is relevant both to my presence and to his presence on the liner. But if our meeting is not a complete coincidence neither is it likely to be wholly non-accidental. He is on that particular boat partly because it is calling at ports adjacent to antiquities which would bore me, but he has not heard of the liner's well-known jazz band which I am looking forward to hearing. So there are causal factors which are relevant to my presence but not to his, and *vice-versa*. I conclude that our meeting is a partial coincidence. How much of a coincidence it is will depend on the

---

[1] In fact, there are some common elements among the conditions necessary for the prayer and for the fine weather, for example the presence of oxygen in the earth's atmosphere. If the big bang hypothesis is true then there are common elements among the conditions necessary for any pair of events, so nothing is a *complete* coincidence.

weight and salience of the causes shared by its components relative to those of the causes which are not shared.

Coincidences are often contrasted with lawlike regularities. For instance, it is a law that all unsupported bodies fall to the ground, but it is a coincidence (let us suppose) that all hunks of gold are less than one mile wide. This usage of the word 'coincidence' is different from, but related to, my own. On this usage, a coincidence is an accidental correlation or regularity and what makes it a coincidence is the absence of any natural law which might explain the correlation. Both the correlation and the law would be expressed by eternal sentences, without tense or date.

My coincidences are events whose occurrence is expressed by a time-indexed sentence (for example 'The prayer was answered today') and what makes an event non-coincidental is another event, namely a cause. This 'singular' notion of a coincidence is obviously connected to the 'general' notion. It is no coincidence in my sense that an unsupported object falls to the ground – its being unsupported combines with its mass and gravity to cause the fall in the way dictated by a covering law. But, in general, it is a coincidence if a hunk of gold is less than one mile wide because, there being no law connecting size with golden constitution, usually a thing's being gold is causally independent of its size.

Until now, I have assumed that both coincidences and the subjects of explanation are to be expressed by true sentences. But it would be better to say that they are to be expressed by true sentences as used in a given context. Van Fraassen asks us to consider the following request for an explanation:

(i) Why did Adam eat the apple?

It may seem perfectly clear what the question is asking for, but that is only because we assume the sentence will be uttered in a context which will determine which of the following questions is intended:

(ii) Why was it *Adam* who ate the apple (rather than somebody else)?
(iii) Why was it *the apple* Adam ate (rather than some other fruit)?
(iv) Why did Adam *eat* the apple (rather than throwing it)?

The context of utterance will comprise the interests and the beliefs knowingly shared by the speaker and the hearer. For instance, the questioner may take it as read that it was Adam who ate a fruit – he may already have accounted for the fact that Adam and eating were involved, or else he may not be interested in these aspects of the situation. What he is not taking for granted is that Adam ate an apple rather than a pear, so our explanation must not presuppose this fact, it should explain it (Van Fraassen, 1980:126–9).

We can represent our interpretation of the why-question by specifying the intended contrast class. The contrast class will contain those statements which appear in the bracketed 'rather than' clause. Once we have specified the contrast class, we have also specified which statements the speaker is taking for granted, which he is not requiring an explanation of, when asking his question, namely those statements entailed by both sides of the contrast.

Van Fraassen's point applies to the examples already considered. For instance, I said that the summer heat might provide a partial explanation of why my enemy and I took the same cruise. But, strictly speaking, what the heat partially explains is why my enemy and I *both went on the cruise* (as opposed to taking a simultaneous trip up the Amazon). It does not help to explain why *both I and an enemy of mine* went on the same cruise (as opposed to some long lost friend). His being a long lost enemy of mine played no part in getting him on the cruise. So, while the fact that two people caught up in a hot English summer both went on a cruise is a partial coincidence, it is a complete accident that I met an enemy of mine on the cruise.

Someone may conclude from this that an event is a coincidence only in the eye of the beholder. It was no coincidence when everyone went off to the polls today – they all heard the election announcement – but it was a great coincidence that they all tried to vote at exactly the same time. How can the same situation be objectively coincidental from one point of view and yet not from another?

There is no mystery here. The coincidence is that certain sentences are true, sentences which we might try and fail to explain the truth of. As I shall argue in the next section, we may be able to explain why everyone went to the polls today, yet be unable to explain why they all appeared at exactly the same time of day. But, once we have determined precisely what we want explained, it is up to the world to decide whether a suitable explanation can be given. Similarly, while it is up to us to choose which true sentence (in a given context) we want explained, it is up to the world to decide whether the truth of that sentence is a coincidence.

## THE INEXPLICABILITY OF A COINCIDENCE: AGGLOMERATIVITY

We left the sceptics and the faithful in deadlock over the status of my answered prayer. One group brand it a coincidence, the others regard it as no coincidence. The faithful might support their view of events by claiming only they can explain why my prayer was answered and surely we should prefer a full explanation to no explanation at all. This leaves the sceptic with two options. Either he accepts that the answered prayer is inexplicable and shrugs off this consequence, or he denies that it is inexplicable. I would recommend the former reply, but let us first explore the alternative.

On the sceptical hypothesis, what determines that my prayer is answered is a combination of independent causal conditions – those psychological factors which led me to pray today and those meteorological conditions which ensure fine whether tomorrow. Cannot the sceptic explain why my prayer was answered by reference to this combination of conditions? He can explain why I pray today and he can explain why there will be fine weather tomorrow, so has he not done enough to explain why the prayer I say today is answered tomorrow?

But the faithful will question this move from '*p* explains *q*' and '*r* explains *s*' to '*p* and *r* explain *q* and *s*'. To put it another way, they will deny that 'explains' is *agglomerative*.[2] Surely we cannot explain why *both* *q* and *s* occur merely by composing independent explanations of *q* and of *s*. For example, there is more to explaining why both I and my enemy board the cruise on the same day than merely explaining why he boards on Saturday and explaining why I board on Saturday. And it would be disingenuous to remark that we joined the cruise on the same day because we independently booked the previous day (Sorabji, 1980:10–11).

The faithful's request for an explanation of our meeting should be carefully distinguished from the demand for an unconditional explanation of our meeting. An unconditional explanation is one that does not rely on any set of prior initial conditions whose co-occurrence is itself unexplained. Our meeting could be no coincidence, and thus perfectly

---

[2] Someone may object to agglomerativity on the following grounds: we cannot infer that '*p* and *r*' explains '*q* and *s*' from '*p* explains *q*' and '*r* explains *s*' because *p* and *r* may not be independent of one another. Perhaps *p* is incompatible with *r*, either logically or as a matter of empirical fact, so that if *p* were the case, *r* would not be the case and *vice versa*. This is true enough, but I do not wish to rest my case against agglomerativity on this point. For the purposes of my discussion, it may be presupposed that *p* and *r* are independent of one another in the required fashion.

explicable, and yet there be no unconditional explanation of why it happened because the combination of causal factors needed to bring it about was itself a coincidence. It is fatal to confuse the thesis that coincidences have no explanation with the thesis that coincidences cannot explain (because the only true explanations are unconditional explanations).[3]

Say that there were two causes of my decision to join the cruise today: the heat of yesterday's sun and the announcement of a special offer on cruises. It was a coincidence that the offer was announced on a very hot day, but it was the combination of these factors which caused me to book, neither factor would have sufficed by itself. Does this mean that it was a coincidence that I booked today? Surely not. These two factors united to bring about the event of my booking – they were not separately relevant to different parts of the booking, rather they were each relevant to the whole of my booking. So even though the co-occurrence of the events which brought about my booking was a coincidence, my booking itself was no coincidence.

Similarly, the fact that my prayer is answered may cause me to become a Catholic. Someone who believes it was a coincidence that my prayer was answered might well acknowledge that it was no coincidence that I became a Catholic. Rather, the coincidence explains my conversion – the answered prayer cannot be analysed into components separately relevant to different elements of my conversion, so its coincidental character is irrelevant.

This point is so important that it bears repeating with a different example. Say that I am sitting in my garden reading a book when the cargo door of an airliner passing overhead falls off the aircraft and onto me. It is a coincidence that I was sitting at the spot where the cargo door fell – this event can be analysed into two events (a) my sitting at place A and (b) the cargo door's landing at place A, events which have quite independent causal histories but it is no coincidence that, given that the cargo door landed where I sat, I was killed. My death cannot be analysed into two parts to one of which the impact of the cargo door alone is relevant and to the other of which my seating arrangements alone are relevant. Therefore, my death is explained by this (coincidental) combination of factors and is itself no coincidence.

---

[3] This important point is implicit in Richard Sorabji's discussion of the inexplicability of coincidences. See especially his airline crashes example in Sorabji, 1980:10–11.

A coincidence is an event which can be divided into components separately produced by independent causal factors. I think the faithful are right to maintain that coincidences cannot be explained. To explain each of the parts of an event is not necessarily to explain the whole event. To explain the whole we must show that its parts share a common cause, however complex and heterogeneous the elements of that common cause may be. *Nevertheless* coincidences may explain, they may render other events non-coincidental. Explanation should not be equated with unconditional explanation.

I have acknowledged that coincidences come in degrees, and a similar point must be made about explanation. An event may be totally inexplicable, the causal histories of its components may have almost nothing in common. This is what the sceptic should say about my answered prayer. On the other hand, there may be a complete explanation of an event, one which cites a causal factor whose components (if any) are each individually necessary for every part of the outcome and which are jointly sufficient for that outcome. This is what the faithful should say about my answered prayer.

But other possibilities exist. One can do something to explain why my enemy and I join the same cruise: we were both overwhelmed by yesterday's heat and we both heard of the special offer. But perhaps there were other factors necessary for our decisions which differed from, and were independent of, one another. Perhaps I am trying to escape some onerous duty while my enemy is attempting to forget his mother's death. So it is impossible to provide a complete explanation of why we boarded the same cruise. Our meeting can be given only a partial explanation. We may sum up the position as follows: the more of a coincidence an event is, the less amenable it is to explanation, and a complete coincidence is completely inexplicable.

So where does all this leave the sceptic? He must admit that, on his view, my answered prayer is completely inexplicable. I think he ought to accept this conclusion with equanimity. Surely many events *are* pure coincidences and my prayer is just another of those. We should not be moved to adopt the otherwise unsupported and possibly unintelligible hypothesis of an omnipotent omniscient necessary being just in order to avoid being landed with more coincidences. Perhaps for the theist there are no coincidences at all – every event, however complex, has its place in God's plan, and so the God-hypothesis can explain away all apparent coincidences. But an hypothesis should not be adopted just because it explains a lot and regardless of its intrinsic plausibility.

Hume hovers between the two options open to the sceptic:

> Add to this that in tracing an eternal succession of objects it seems absurd to inquire for a general cause or first author... In such a chain, too, or succession of objects, each part is caused by that which preceded it, and causes that which succeeds it. Where then is the difficulty? But the whole, you say, wants a cause. I answer that the uniting of these parts into a whole, like the uniting of several distinct countries into one kingdom, or several distinct members into one body, is performed merely by an arbitrary act of the mind, and has no influence on the nature of things. Did I show you the particular causes of each individual in a collection of twenty particles of matter, I should think it very unreasonable should you afterwards ask me what was the cause of the whole twenty. This is sufficiently explained in explaining the cause of the parts. (Hume, 1948:59–60)

Hume is wrong to think that the only genuine objects or causes are small things. He is also wrong to think that explaining the existence of each particle suffices to explain the existence of them all. But, as he says, we should not expect the members of an arbitrary set of twenty particles to share a common cause. It is unreasonable to insist on an explanation of everything.

Very often we explain one similarity (or difference) by reference to another similarity (or difference), and no less often the events whose similarities (or differences) concern us are causally quite independent of one another. Does this not constitute an objection to my thesis that coincidences are inexplicable?

For instance, we can explain why *both* Jones and Smith contracted AIDS by reference to the fact that they are *both* intravenous drug users, even though the fact that Jones uses drugs is quite unconnected with the fact that Smith uses them. Here it is a coincidence that both Smith and Jones use drugs. Furthermore, their individual drug use separately brings about their infection with the HIV virus. So should not the fact that they both have AIDS be an inexplicable coincidence on my view?

What we are doing here is explaining Smith and Jones' similarity in respect of whether they have AIDS by reference to their similarity in respect of whether they use drugs. Now its being a coincidence that Smith and Jones are similar in respect of whether they use drugs need not undermine our explanation, provided that this fact cannot be analysed into components which separately explain different parts of the explanandum. And I would claim that it cannot. Smith and Jones' being similar in respect of drug use is not at all the same thing as Smith's using drugs and Jones' using drugs. Smith and Jones would be similar in respect of drug use if neither of them used drugs. Since this similarity cannot be analysed into components, it can serve as a common cause ensuring it is no coincidence that Jones and Smith are similar in respect of whether they have AIDS.

Furthermore, we can explain why Jones has AIDS and Brown does not by reference to the fact that Jones does use drugs and Brown does not, even though Jones' indulgence is quite independent of Brown's abstinence. Here, Jones and Brown differ in respect of having AIDS because they differ in respect of whether they use drugs – a point which would apply equally if Brown used drugs and Jones did not. Therefore the relevant causal factor, their difference in respect of drug use, cannot be analysed into Jones's using drugs and Brown's not using drugs, conditions which separately bring about Brown's health and Jones' illness.[4]

## THE INEXPLICABILITY OF A COINCIDENCE: TRANSITIVITY

Until now, I have concentrated on events whose parts are not themselves causally related, though they may be connected by some common cause. But, as Hume observes in the above quotation, the same questions arise when we consider a causal chain. Is the occurrence of a whole causal chain a coincidence or not? I have argued that explanation is not *agglomerative*: we cannot infer that $p$ and $q$ explains $r$ and $s$ from '$p$ explains $r$' and '$q$ explains $s$'. But can we infer '$p$ explains $r$' from '$p$ explains $q$' and '$q$ explains $r$'? To put it another way, is explanation *transitive*?

Consider this well-known nursery rhyme:

> For want of a nail the shoe was lost,
> For want of a shoe the horse was lost,
> For want of a horse the rider was lost,
> For want of a rider the battle was lost,
> For want of a battle the kingdom was lost,
> And all for the want of a horseshoe nail.[5]

Presumably, each stage in this causal chain is explained by the conditions which obtain at the previous stage. But can we infer that the

---

[4] These explanations of similarity and difference play a key role in Mill's canons of causal inference. See his discussion of the Method of Agreement and the Method of Difference in Mill, 1906: book III, chapter 8. See also Hume, 1978:174.
[5] I take this example from Lowe, 1980:50–2.

lack of a nail explains the loss of the kingdom? The question at issue is whether we may infer that the lack of a nail explains the loss of the kingdom from the fact that the lack of a nail explains something which in turn explains something... which in turn explains the loss of the kingdom. It seems clear that the lack of a nail is, in these circumstances, necessary and sufficient for the loss of the kingdom. The relevant circumstances are those which ensure that the shoe will not remain on the horse without an extra nail and those which ensure that the horse will be disabled if it lacks a shoe, right down to those which ensure that a single military defeat is sufficient to undermine the whole kingdom. But this does not entail that the lack of a nail causally explains the national disaster.

In my view, the fact that all the events in this causal chain occur together is a coincidence, since the factors which are needed to explain the occurrence of some members of the chain will be distinct from, and quite independent of, those required to cement other links in the chain. To put it another way, the different parts of the chain have no common explanation. But if the occurrence of the chain is a coincidence, the occurrence of its first element can hardly explain the occurrence of its last element to the same degree as it explains much earlier elements. It requires a succession of accidents in order to keep the chain going, and the first element can only fully explain the second.

To see this more clearly, consider our example. We assume that the lack of a nail explains why the shoe was lost in virtue of the causal background in which it occurs. But the elements of this background which are operative in ensuring that the lack of a nail brings about the loss of the shoe will not be sufficient to ensure that the loss of the shoe disables the horse. In order to explain this we will need to invoke new features of the causal background, features which obtain quite independently of those we have already mentioned and which are irrelevant to the causal process leading up to the loss of the shoe. In general, the background conditions required to forge any given link in this causal chain will differ from and will obtain quite independently of those needed at other stages of the chain.[6]

The joint occurrence of the events in the chain is not a complete coincidence. There is at least one set of causal factors which are necessary

---

[6] This point gets made on pages 447–53 of Hempel, 1965. He appears to conclude that 'explains' is not a transitive relation, since, on his view, explanation requires a covering law and in these examples there is no law covering the whole chain. See also Hornsby, 1980a:86–7.

for all of them, namely the original lack of a nail and the other conditions which led to the loss of the shoe. If it had not been for that little event and the conditions relevant to its occurrence, none of the more important events would have happened. And later events on the chain and their associated background conditions are each necessary for all succeeding events. This is why we do get some explanatory insight from the story – it is not just a list of accidents. Nevertheless, the element of coincidence is very large and the explanatory illumination correspondingly small.

But someone who concedes what I have said about the non-agglomerativity of 'explains' may still insist that the lack of a nail, given a suitable background, does explain the loss of the kingdom. We know there are conditions which, when combined with the lack of a nail, are necessary and sufficient for the loss of the kingdom, and these conditions are not separately relevant to different parts of that loss. So why do they fail to explain this disaster?

The objector is right to point out that agglomerativity may be abandoned while transitivity is retained. The chain-explanation of the kingdom's loss satisfies a condition which is not met by those purported explanations of coincidences considered earlier – the elements of its *explanans* are each causally relevant to the whole of the *explanandum*. However, reflection on the notion of a coincidence should lead us to deny that 'fully explains' is transitive.

A coincidence is an event which cannot be explained. I have tried to show that purported explanations of coincidences can be analysed into sub-explanations which perform their explanatory task more or less independently of one another. When these sub-explanations are combined, the illumination they yield is diminished in proportion to the degree of their mutual independence. Thus, combining independent explanations of the different parts of a coincidence will not explain that coincidence. But equally, combining (partially) independent explanations of the different parts of a temporally extended process which leads to a certain end-result will not (fully) explain that result. In both cases, the factors invoked to explain the outcome do not mesh with one another in such a way as to provide an explanation for it – they do not unite to produce it – so the outcome inherits the coincidental character of the combination of processes which brought it about.

It may now be thought that while 'fully explains' is a non-transitive relation, 'partially explains' or 'explains to some degree' is transitive. After all, the loss of the nail partially explains the loss of the shoe which partially explains ... and is it not also true that the loss of the nail partially explains the loss of the kingdom? But this is an artifact of the particular example. The causal chain described in the nursery rhyme starts with a necessary condition for the fall of the kingdom and describes the gradual formation of a sufficient condition as more and more causal factors come into play. But there are causal chains in which the earlier events switch from being unnecessary for the outcome to being necessary for it and from being sufficient for the outcome to being insufficient for it as time goes by. Once a factor's causal role is allowed to vary in this way, we can construct chains of partial explanation whose first member does not explain their last member.

Say that I contract a disease which will kill me sometime in the course of the next six months. The only possible way of treating the disease is to take a certain drug 1. This drug cures the disease but has side effects which will kill me in six months to a year's time. So taking the drug ensures that I shall die in the second half of the year rather than the first. I take drug 1. After nine months, my doctors happen to discover a quite different drug 2 which both cures the disease and clears up the side effects of drug 1. I take drug 2 and live beyond the end of the year. Question: Does my taking drug 1 partially explain why I live beyond the end of the year?

In the conditions in which drug 1 was administered, it was sufficient to kill me within a year and certainly not necessary for my surviving beyond the year. This, by itself, establishes that my taking drug 1 can be no part of an explanation of why I survived beyond the end of the year. Nevertheless, drug 1 was necessary for my surviving for nine months, and after nine months conditions had changed and drug 2 was then sufficient to cure me. So drug 1 did partially explain something which partially explained my surviving beyond the end of the year, although it did not itself explain my survival. We cannot infer from 'my taking drug 1 partially explains my surviving for nine months' and 'my surviving for nine months partially explains my surviving beyond a year' to 'my taking drug 1 partially explains my surviving beyond a year'.[7]

True, had I not survived, I could not have been cured, so the administering of drug 1 was necessary for my survival and partially explains it. But to my mind, it is no good if drug 1 is necessary for my survival only given a series of subsequent events quite unconnected with the adminstering of drug 1. It is a *complete* coincidence that my taking

---

[7] This example is a deterministic version of a type of example much discussed in the literature on probabilistic causation. See, for example, Eells, 1991:347–50.

drug 1 was followed by my survival beyond a year, and therefore the drug can do nothing to explain it: there is no factor which was causally necessary for my survival at every stage of the causal chain leading from the taking of drug 1 to my survival. The various explanations which link drug 1 to my survival have *nothing* in common, therefore we cannot combine them to generate even a partial explanation of why I survived in terms of my taking drug 1. By contrast, it was not a complete coincidence when the absence of the nail was followed by the loss of the kingdom – the nail's absence was something which remained necessary for this outcome at every stage of the causal chain which led up to it.

Causal chains in which the first event does fully explain the last event are liable to be less colourful than those we have considered so far. Let us say that such a chain consists of three events $x$'s having $P$, $y$'s having $Q$ and $z$'s having $R$, where each event explains the next event. For the first event to explain the last event, the feature of $y$ which ensures that it is necessary and sufficient for $z$'s having $R$, namely $Q$, must be the very feature, or must be nomologically determined by that feature, which ensures that $x$ was necessary and sufficient for $y$ to be $Q$, namely $x$'s being $P$. So, in this case, there must be a law which ensures that $P$s are necessary and sufficient for $Q$s, and a law which ensures that $Q$s are necessary and sufficient for $R$s.

There are relatively few causal chains which meet the exacting conditions necessary for their first member to (fully) explain their last member. It is only within isolated causal systems in a state of equilibrium, such as the solar system or a wrist watch, that we find causal chains which are like mathematical series in that we can predict all later members of the series just on the basis of a knowledge of how its first members are generated. Where the system is not isolated, the course of events will be influenced by numerous causal factors of various kinds at different stages of the process. The laws which generated the initial stages of the chain will need to be supplemented by new laws to describe its later evolution. As we have seen, a series of such diverse explanations does not add up to one big explanation, so we should not be surprised if an historical understanding of an event in terms of the processes which lead up to it differs from a scientific explanation which invokes its proximal causes alone (Popper, 1960:117).

## EXPLANATION AND LAWS

I have argued that 'explains' is neither transitive nor agglomerative, something which accounts for the evident fact that coincidences are inexplicable. Coincidences could be explained only if we were allowed to infer complex explanations from more simple ones in ways which would be licensed by the assumption that explanation is agglomerative or transitive. But such patterns of inference are illicit.

Someone might respond to this point by agreeing that I can use 'explanation' in my restrictive sense if I like, but still maintain that I have given no reason why it *must* be so used. Why not say, in the traditional way, that to explain an event is to cite necessary and sufficient conditions for it? The answer is that my more restrictive notion is necessary for making several distinctions which the standard notion of causal explanation is normally used to make. So my notion of explanation is theoretically fruitful and indeed essential for the tasks which that notion is usually supposed to perform.[8]

The 'other distinctions' I am thinking of are (a) the distinction between a causal explanation and a non-causal explanation of a given phenomenon (b) the distinction between the direction of causation and its converse (it is often said that causation runs past-to-future because past events explain future events and not *vice versa*) (c) the distinction between different levels of explanation (it is often said that there are sciences other than physics because there are non-physical explanations which cannot be stated in physical terms) (d) the distinction between deviant and non-deviant causal chains in the philosophy of perception, memory and action (it is often said that an action must be causally explained by the reasons for it, that an object seen must causally explain an experience of it, that an object remembered must causally explain a memory of it). I shall argue that none of these distinctions can be made while we hang onto the broad notion of explanation which would allow coincidences to be explained. We need my narrow notion of explanation to perform this

---

[8] This is how I would respond to philosophers who claim that the events which I call coincidences are no coincidence because they do have necessary and sufficient conditions (Neander and Menzies, 1990:461–2). I do not deny that there is a sense of 'explanation' in which such events can be explained and a sense of 'coincidence' in which such events are no coincidence given a full specification of their antecedent necessary and sufficient conditions. I just hold that there is also a theoretically important sense of these terms in which this is not so, however fully the relevant nomological antecedents are described.

function and that is as good a reason as I can think of for recommending it.

What would lead a philosopher to resist this conclusion? One worry can be quickly dismissed. My conclusion punches no holes in the causal nexus which should concern a scientist. For a start, I have argued only that coincidences have no explanation, it is a separate issue whether coincidences have causes. But even if, as I shall urge in chapter 4, coincidences do not have causes, this does not produce worrying gaps in the causal nexus. All the parts of a coincidence will have a causal explanation, and no reasonable scientist should expect an arbitrary conjunction of events to have a causal explanation, so he should not be surprised when such inexplicable conjunctions occur.

However, there is an influential model of what an explanation is which presents a more serious obstacle to acceptance of my point. This is the well-known deductive–nomological model of explanation put forward by Hempel. Hempel asserts that to explain an event is to show that the sentence $p$ which states that it has occurred is entailed by a true lawlike generalisation $l$ and a certain set of true singular initial condition statements $c$ but not by $c$ or $l$ alone. $l$ will say that the truth of $c$ is necessary and sufficient for the truth of $p$. (Hempel, 1965:333–75).

A typical deductive–nomological explanation would go as follows: we wish to explain why a certain billiard ball accelerates at a certain rate (why $p$ is true) and we do this by invoking Newton's second law which says that an object's acceleration is a function of its mass and the force which it experiences. We explain the truth of $p$ by deriving it from this law together with a statement $c$ telling us what the mass of the ball and the force applied to it are.

Now, according to one school of thought, a law is any true generalisation which supports predictions and counterfactual suppositions (Goodman, 1983:20–2). This view of laws and the deductive–nomological model of explanation together entail that if a generalisation supports predictions and counterfactual suppositions then it also explains why its consequent is instantiated, given the instantiation of its antecedent. To be able to predict an event from certain initial conditions and make counterfactual suppositions about what would happen were different initial conditions to obtain, is to be able to explain what actually did occur.

However, if what I have said about explanation is correct, a generalisation may support predictions and counterfactual suppositions without explaining the instantiation of its consequent. Say that our billiard ball is yellow and there is a law which tells us that yellow things reflect light of a certain wavelength. Then there is a true generalisation which will enable us to predict its total behaviour: $(x)$ if $x$ has mass M, experiences force F and reflects light of wavelength W, it will accelerate at rate A and appear to be yellow. This generalisation supports counterfactual suppositions – it tells us how the acceleration of the object or its colour would have varied with variations in its reflectance, or in the mass or the force it experienced.

On my account, this generalisation could not explain why the object both accelerated at rate A and looked yellow. The process of acceleration and the creation of a certain chromatic effect are quite independent occurrences brought about by quite independent features of the ball: its mass and its reflectance. So it is a coincidence that the ball both accelerates at rate A and looks yellow, and this generalisation can do nothing to explain it.[9]

To accept that coincidences have no explanation is to accept that there is more to explaining an event than merely citing nomologically necessary and sufficient conditions prior to the event, knowledge of which enables us to predict the occurrence of the event with certainty. Given this, we must either modify our notion of a law by requiring that laws explain as well as predict, or else abandon the deductive–nomological model of explanation (Sorabji, 1980:16–17).

---

[9] This example supports the thesis, argued for on different grounds in Owens, 1989a, that the class of laws is not deductively closed, *pace* Lewis, 1983b:368 and Hempel, 1965:346.

# 2

# Causes and laws

In chapter 1, I took causation for granted. A coincidence was defined as an event naturally divisible into two parts with independent causal histories. So 'cause' was used to analyse 'coincidence'. Given this, 'cause' appears the more fundamental notion and the analysis of causation must proceed without regard to the explicability of a coincidence. Of course, the inexplicability of a coincidence sets a limit on causal explanation – if coincidences cannot be explained, they cannot be explained causally either. But this may have more to do with the nature of explanation than with that of causation.

Such reflections led me to think that causation must be firmly distinguished from causal explanation: coincidences have no causal explanation, nevertheless they are caused (Owens, 1989b:71–2). This reaction sits well with the work of philosophers such as Davidson and Lewis who have their own reasons for distinguishing causation from causal explanation and for analysing the causal relation, if at all, without reference to explanation. I now think that this reaction was misguided: causation should be tied to causal explanation (Sorabji, 1980:11). In fact the following is my analysis of causation: a cause is an event which ensures that its effects are no coincidence.

I arrived at this conclusion by considering two problems which confront all analysts of causation. First, some way must be found of distinguishing causal explanations from the awkwardly similar but importantly different quasi-logical explanations to be considered in chapters 3 and 4. No analysis which fails in this task can be deemed adequate. Secondly, the analyst must make room for the direction in causation, for the fact that causes are asymmetrically related to their effects – if $c$ causes $e$ then $e$ does not cause $c$. This issue occupies chapter 5. But before going any further, I must provide a definition of 'coincidence' which does not invoke the notion of causation.

## CAUSAL AND NOMOLOGICAL RELATIONS

Here is a definition of 'coincidence' which does not mention causation and fits the examples discussed in chapter 1: an event is a coincidence if, and only if, it can be naturally divided into parts which are such that the (temporally prior) conditions necessary and sufficient for the occurrence of one part are independent of those necessary and sufficient for the occurrence of the other. The bracketed phrase can be dropped once the work of chapter 5 has been completed. Later, we shall need a broader notion of coincidence, one which allows that the prior conditions need not be both necessary and sufficient for the outcome: a coincidence may have parts with mutually independent sufficient conditions or else with mutually independent necessary conditions. But for now, I shall operate with the narrower notion just defined.

As I pointed out in the introduction, we could get along with an even weaker, probabilistic notion of coincidence. We could stipulate that an event is a coincidence if, and only if, it can be analysed into components such that either (a) it is the presence of quite independent conditions which raises the probability of each component or (b) it is the absence of quite independent conditions which would lower the probability of each component. 'Sufficiency' and 'necessity' are just the limiting cases of these probabilistic relations – a sufficient condition raises the effect's probability to 1, the absence of a necessary condition lowers it to 0. For expository convenience, I consider only these deterministic relations.

The notions of 'necessity' and 'sufficiency' are to be elucidated by certain conditionals. The fact that my prayer for fine weather was followed by fine weather was a coincidence because atmospheric conditions were those necessary and sufficient for the sunshine and they were quite independent of the psychological conditions necessary and sufficient for the prayer. What does it mean to say that the air pressure's being $n$ was necessary for the sunshine? What it means is that if the air pressure had not been $n$ pounds per square inch then the weather would have been different. What does it mean to say that the level of the air pressure was sufficient for the sunshine? It means that given that the air pressure was $n$, the sun would be shining. And what does it mean for the air pressure to be independent of the psychological precursors of the prayer? What it means is that the air pressure's being $n$ and the psychological state of the supplicant are not connected by such conditionals.

24

The obvious response is to enquire into the grounds on which these conditionals are asserted, perhaps by requesting an account of what makes them true or false. Unfortunately, these issues are far too difficult to be treated adequately here. I can only gesture at the lines along which an account sufficient for my purposes must run. By giving such a sketch I shall at least indicate the sort of conditional on which I am relying and how such conditionals may be used to determine the causal facts, not be determined by them.

In chapter 1, I noted that laws of nature characteristically support counterfactual suppositions. One of the features which distinguishes a law such as 'all ravens are black' from a contingently true generalisation like 'all people in this room speak English' is that the law supports 'if this dove were a raven, it would be black' while the truth of our generalisation should not tempt us to believe 'if Mr Gorbachev were in this room, he would speak English'. So, any viable account of the assertibility or truth conditions of these conditionals must spell out their relation to laws of nature.

Many laws of nature merit the label 'causal laws' in that they postulate causal relations between events instantiating their antecedent and events which instantiate their consequent. Does this not pose a problem for an *acausal* account of the conditionals which they support? We can hardly define causation by reference to a class of conditionals which is, in the end, singled out by the relation these conditionals bear to *casual* laws.

Take Snell's law. Snell's law assures us that when a ray of light passes through an isotropic medium, the angle at which it passes through the medium (the angle of refraction) will be a certain function of the angle at which it hits the medium (the angle of incidence). Now one could treat Snell's law as a causal law which informs us that the light's angle of incidence will produce a certain angle of refraction. But one could also regard Snell's law as stating a purely functional relationship between the two angles – one which enables us to infer the angle of refraction from the angle of incidence, *or vice versa*. On this reading, the law says nothing about which angle determines which, it just puts a constraint on their relative values. Such a functional relationship, unlike causation, is perfectly symmetric.

Snell's law ensures that if the light had not hit the medium at an angle of $n°$ (to the normal) it would not have proceeded through it at an angle of $m°$ (to the normal). Equally, the law tells us that if the light was refracted by $m°$, it must have hit it at $n°$. And Snell's law also ensures that, given an angle of incidence of $n°$, we shall get an angle of refraction of $m°$ and that, if we do not get an angle of $m°$, the angle of incidence was not $n°$. In brief the angle of incidence is, in the presence of the law, both necessary and sufficient for the angle of refraction, *and vice versa*. But the law, as we are now construing it, says nothing about causal relations.

I take it that all laws of physics could be read in this minimalistic way and some must be so construed.[1] For instance, the Boyle–Charles law tells us only that the pressure, volume and temperature of a (ideal) gas are related by the formula 'Pressure × Volume = Temperature × k' (where k is a constant for a given mass of gas). It does not describe any asymmetrical causal relation between changes in one of these variables and changes in the others. And yet it gives us all the materials we need to support counterfactual suppositions about what would have happened had the pressure of the gas changed while its volume remained constant etc. I conclude that we may excise the causal element from laws of nature and still be left with generalisations supportive of the required conditionals.[2]

I hope, in this section, to have shown that I may define 'coincidence' in terms of 'necessary condition' and 'sufficient condition' without surreptitiously employing the notion of causation. Thus we are free to use 'coincidence' in the analysis of causation. If such an analysis succeeds, we shall have demonstrated that the causal facts about the world are fixed by the non-causal facts, including acausal laws. However, there is a great problem lurking here. Logical and analytical truths and their associated conditionals ensure that one state of affairs is necessary and sufficient for another. Yet such truths do not support causal assertions. How are the relations of necessity and sufficiency which underwrite causation to be distinguished from these others?

There are three ways to make this distinction. First, one could claim that logical and analytical connections have a metaphysical status quite different from that of nomological connections. This suggestion occupies

---

[1] Russell thought that all any law of an advanced science does is to lay down an acausal functional relationship between states of the universe. See Russell, 1953:183–4.

[2] Several philosophers have recently argued that no logical kind is picked out by the grammatical classification 'subjunctive conditional'. Specifically, they have urged that certain conditionals in the indicative mood must receive the same semantic treatment as subjunctive conditionals (Bennett, 1988). If these philosophers are right, my conclusion must be modified somewhat: the conditionals used to define 'coincidence' are not subjunctive conditionals alone, but rather any member of that class of conditionals which are to be found in the same semantic box as subjunctive conditionals.

me in the rest of the present chapter. Secondly, one could claim that what distinguishes causal from logical connections is not the metaphysical status of these connections so much as that of the causally related entities and the non-causal relations between them. Chapter 3 looks into the views of Davidson and Lewis on this point. Finally, in chapter 4, I shall urge that it is the epistemic status of nomological generalizations which makes them different from logical and analytical truths. This difference in epistemic status derives from the very thing that makes the nomological generalizations support causal assertions: they resolve coincidences. So 'coincidence' is analytically prior both to 'causation' and to 'natural law'.

## Some Humean theses

One of David Hume's greatest intellectual achievements was to pull apart causal from logical relations. By doing so, he laid the foundation-stone of empiricism, grounding scientific knowledge firmly in observation and experience. It is worth quoting the relevant passage of Hume's first *Enquiry* in full, since it contains the original formulation of three theses about causation which I wish to discuss.

When I see, for instance, a billiard ball moving in a straight line towards another; even suppose motion in the second should by accident be suggested to me, as the result of their contact or impulse; may I not conceive, that a hundred different events might as well follow from that cause? May not both these balls remain at absolute rest? May not the first ball return in a straight line, or leap off from the second in any line or direction? All these suppositions are consistent and conceivable. Why then should we give the preference to one, which is no more consistent or conceivable than the rest? All our reasonings *a priori* will never be able to show us any foundation for this preference.

In a word then, every effect is a distinct event from its cause. It could not, therefore, be discovered in the cause, and the first invention or conception of it, *a priori*, must be entirely arbitrary. And even after it is suggested, the conjunction of it with the cause must appear equally arbitrary; since there are always many other effects, which, to reason, must seem fully as consistent and natural. In vain, therefore, should we pretend to determine any single event, or infer any cause or effect, without the assistance of observation and experience. (Hume, 1975:29–30; see also Hume, 1978:650–1).

When Hume wrote this passage, he may well have thought of himself as making a single assertion about the causal relation in several different ways. However, the modern reader will discern at least three distinct claims in the passage:

(1) Causes are only contingently sufficient for their effects.
(2) Causal connections are discoverable only *a posteriori*.
(3) Causes must be distinct from their effects.

These three theses have had enormous influence on subsequent discussion. They have been detached from Hume's scepticism about induction and incorporated into received wisdom on the subject. Only once we are clear about (1), (2) and (3) can we tackle the many examples which philosophers have produced of non-causal explanatory relations, relations hard to distinguish from causal relations. I shall deal with (1) in this chapter, (3) in chapter 3 and (2) in chapter 4.

Hume's (1) is not the uncontroversial thesis that any cause event might have occurred without its accompanying effect. This thesis is uncontroversial because one event will bring about another only given certain conditions, and it will generally be a contingent fact that these conditions obtain. So, even when the cause occurs, the existence of the effect will be a contingent fact. But what concerns Hume is not this, but rather the contingency of the connection between events which do find themselves in conditions propitious for causation. Hume's point is that these events, even though they actually do fall under causal law and engage in the prescribed causal action, might not have behaved in accordance with the law.

What is Hume's argument for thesis (1)? It goes as follows: take any given cause and effect which fall under a causal law, we can always conceive or imagine the cause having occurred without the effect's occurring *in the very circumstances that obtain*, therefore it is possible to have the cause without the effect in those circumstances, therefore it is only a contingent fact that causes like this are sufficient for effects like that. A similar argument would show that causes are only contingently necessary for their effects. In the *Treatise*, Hume claims he can perfectly well imagine an event's happening spontaneously without any cause at all (Hume, 1978:78–82), thus advancing the even stronger thesis that an event might be engendered in a completely irregular way. But I am asking whether the law concerned might have been different, and not whether there might have been no law at all.

What is the principle underlying Hume's argument? He appears to assume that imaginability or conceivability establishes possibility. But (a) people knowingly entertain the thought that *p* in the course of a *reductio ad absurdum* proof, a proof which shows that *p* could not possibly be true

(b) people mistakenly believe that $p$ could be true when $p$ is impossible, as is shown by the effort put into squaring the circle. These facts demonstrate that our ability to entertain the proposition $p$ does not, by itself, establish that $p$ might be true (Hart, 1988:15).

This is not to deny that we can, by thought, determine whether $p$ might be true. *Reductio ad absurdum* is one method of acquiring such modal knowledge, a method particularly effective when it shows that $p$ entails a contradiction. There are surely other cognitive routes to more positive modal knowledge, methods which perhaps involve the 'modal intuitions' of necessity and contingency appealed to by many essentialists. But I have no *a priori* intuition that Newton's laws might not hold, and the mere fact that I can entertain the supposition that Newton's writ no longer runs is no evidence for its possibility.

However, Hume may insist that he was relying, not on the faculty of conception but rather on the sensuous imagination. To sensuously imagine that $p$ is at least to imagine having an experience as of its being the case that $p$. Hume's reasoning here may be as follows: if we can imagine having such an experience then such an experience is possible; but if it really is possible to have an experience as of $p$'s being the case, then $p$ itself might possibly be true; so the sensuous imagination can establish the possibility of $p$'s truth (Peacocke, 1985:31).

This line of thought is quite persuasive. Experience is the primary indicator of what is actually the case. Having an experience as of a dog in a kennel may not conclusively establish that the dog is in the kennel, but it lends support to this proposition. So why should not the possibility of that experience be *prima facie* evidence for the possibility of the state of affairs experienced? True, certain experiences represent the world as containing states of affairs which could not possibly obtain (for example those induced by Escher drawings) but that no more undermines experience's role as a guide to possibility than the existence of illusions undermines empirical inquiry.

Hume's argument, thus construed, does not claim to prove that laws are contingent; it just points to defeasible evidence in favour of their contingency. We can sensuously imagine phenomena governed by non-Newtonian laws, therefore an experience as of such a phenomenon is possible, and the possibility of that experience is at least *prima facie* evidence for the possibility of such a phenomenon. This evidence may be overridden by the results of reflection and inquiry, but our imagination puts the burden of proof on those who think that laws of nature are necessary truths. Since I do not know of any decisive argument in favour of the necessity of laws, this weaker conclusion would establish the point.

But Hume has got this far only because we granted that one can sensuously imagine non-Newtonian phenomena. Now sensuous imagination derives its authority about what might obtain from the authority which experience has about what actually does obtain. We can simply imagine a scene governed by a non-Newtonian physics only if we can simply experience it. But what would an experience as of such a scene be like? One can certainly have an experience as of one billiard ball's hitting another and the other's failing to move, but this is not an experience as of a piece of non-Newtonian behaviour. In order to get that, we have to embellish the experience with a commentary which asserts that there are no other Newtonian forces at work on the second ball, forces which might explain why that ball did not move, that the mass of the second ball is not so great that its movement was imperceptible etc. etc. In the absence of such a commentary, the experience counts neither for nor against the truth of Newton's laws.

This distinction between the experience and the theoretical commentary on it is crucial.[3] The commentary by itself has no more power to determine what is and is not possible than the cognitive entertainings and suppositions considered above. Potential experience, as revealed in imagination, is supposed to be the source of modal knowledge. If the necessary commentary could be included in the representational content of the experience itself, then Hume would be home and dry. But it is hard to see how it could be. What element of the content of the experience would correspond to the absence of friction, or of a magnetic field?

Hume may respond by expanding the experiential base to include the results of all sorts of tests which we might carry out on our two balls in an effort to detect interfering forces, or other factors exercising an influence over the second ball. But while such evidence will certainly bear on our decision as to whether to abandon Newton's laws or not, no course of experience, *however veridical*, can *entail* the falsity of Newton's laws solely in virtue of its content. It is just not possible to have an experience which is such that if it were veridical, Newton's laws would not hold.

All Hume is really entitled to is this: we can imagine having an experience as of a state of affairs which constitutes evidence for the

[3] A similar distinction is made in Peacocke, 1985:24–6 and in Williams, 1973:30–1. It is also implicit in Anscombe's discussion of Hume's argument (Anscombe, 1981a).

hypothesis that Newton's laws do not hold, therefore such an experience is possible, therefore the evidence, the state of affairs, which it is an experience as of is possible. In other words, it is possible to discover evidence which counts against Newton's laws. But this is just the point made by Hume's (2), that natural laws are known *a posteriori*; they could hardly be empirical laws if it was impossible to imagine experiential evidence which would count against them. By contrast, Hume's (1) claims that statements of law are, if true, contingently true, and to support this we must be able to experience in imagination the obtaining or non-obtaining of a law of nature.

I suspect that Hume found his argument for (1) cogent because he thought that laws concerned observational properties of things, properties we can simply see a thing has, at least in favourable conditions. So the paradigmatic law of nature would be something like 'all square things are yellow.' Now certainly, such a generalisation, if true, would appear to be contingently true, because one can clearly imagine having an experience as of a red square, and the content of this experience falsifies the generalisation. But I cannot think of a single generalisation, basic or otherwise, connecting *purely* observational predicates, which a serious science has put up for lawhood. (Statements like 'there is no perfectly transparent white surface' are presumably not contingent truths).

Some readers will doubtless consider that the above discussion was predicated on a false assumption. The distinction between theoretical and observational statements, between the content of experience and the interpretation put upon it, has been roundly rejected. According to many philosophers, there is no significant division between states of affairs which one simply sees and those which one postulates in order to account for these observations (Churchland, 1979: chapter 2). I happen to think these philosophers are wrong and that a viable distinction can be drawn but I will not attempt to establish the point here.[4] My present target is Hume's argument for the contingency of natural laws, and that argument has little force unless there is some way of separating experience from interpretation. We have seen that we cannot tell what is possible in nature from what is not by using our capacity for theoretical speculation alone; laws of which we can conceive may be quite impossible. And if theory completely permeates experience, sensuous imagination is no better at revealing possibility than the thought behind it.

[4] For two rather different ways of drawing the distinction, see Peacocke, 1983: chapter 4 and Fodor, 1990: chapter 10.

In fact, few philosophers think Hume's direct defence of (1) is successful. Nevertheless, the view that statements of natural law are only contingently true is still very widespread. The most popular way of establishing the contingency of laws of nature is to urge that laws of nature hold in virtue of certain non-nomological facts, facts which are obviously contingent. I shall argue that either the cited facts are contingent but cannot ground laws of nature, or else they cannot be specified in law–neutral terms and thus to assert their contingency is to beg the question; so while causal facts are fixed by non-causal facts, nomological facts are not fixed by anything else. This conclusion does not entail that laws of nature are necessary truths, of course, but it does mean we cannot argue for their contingency from the contingency of something else. And in the absence of any more direct and cogent argument, Hume's (1) must be left on one side.

## LAWS

Consider the following generalisations

All solid spheres of uranium (U235) have a diameter of less than one mile.

and

All solid spheres of gold (Au) have a diameter of less than one mile.[5]

I take it everyone would acknowledge that while both generalisations may be true, only the former counts as a law of nature and any adequate theory of law must account for this difference. It is a mere accident that gold has nowhere come together to form a lump a mile wide, while facts about the critical mass of radioactive substances ensure that no such hunk of uranium could exist. But what exactly does this difference amount to? One obvious thought is that a law of nature must support subjunctive conditionals while an accidentally true generalisation will not. The uranium law supports the assertion that if we tried to create a big hunk of uranium we would not succeed, while the truth of the gold-generalisation is, by itself, no obstacle to such a counterfactual project.

There is wide agreement that laws do support subjunctive conditionals, but rather less consensus about how this relationship should be understood. Some philosophers hold that laws support subjunctive conditionals by entailing them. Others have thought that if laws entailed

---

[5] This example comes from Van Fraassen, 1989:27.

subjunctives, that would make laws into necessary truths and so we should construe their relation to subjunctives in some other way. Yet others have maintained that laws can entail subjunctives while remaining contingently true.

Rather than review all the possible options here, I shall concentrate on one particular account of laws and subjunctive conditionals, that constructed by Lewis. Lewis is a regularity theorist about laws of nature, that is he believes 'It is a law of nature that all $P$s are $Q$s' and 'all (actual) $P$s are (actually) $Q$s' are logically equivalent. Since 'all (actual) $P$s are (actually) $Q$s' appears to be a contingent truth, the truth of the regularity theory would seem to imply the contingency of natural laws. However, any satisfactory regularity theory must demonstrate how the supposedly contingent facts which make statements of law true also enable those statements to support subjunctive conditionals. We shall find that Lewis' theory can succeed in accommodating such conditionals only by diluting the contingency of the facts which make law statements true. And what is true of Lewis' theory is going to be true of any theory which attempts to specify contingent truth conditions for statements of law. So the contingency of laws cannot be demonstrated in this fashion at least.

First of all Lewis provides us with a semantics for subjunctive conditionals (Lewis, 1973: chapter 1). He says that the conditional 'if $p$ had been the case, $q$ would have been the case' is true if and only if (a) $p$ is necessarily false or (b) $q$ is true in the most similar possible world to our own (actual) world in which $p$ is true. Thus, a counterfactual is non-vacuously true when, and only when, it takes less of a departure from actuality to make the consequent true along with the antecedent than to make the antecedent true without the consequent. Where $p$ is actually true, the conditional as a whole is true if, and only if, $q$ is also true.

Say that a match is lit by striking. Here, the striking of the match is necessary for the lighting because, if the striking had not occurred, the lighting would not have occurred either. And that subjunctive is true because the most similar possible world in which the striking did not occur is one in which the lighting did not occur either. Where there is actually no striking but the striking would have been followed by the lighting, this is because the most similar world in which the striking occurs is a world in which the lighting occurs also.

Now we are clear about what makes subjunctive conditionals true, we can ask how laws support these conditionals. The answer is that the laws support counterfactuals via the similarity relation between worlds. One feature of a world which will help to determine its similarity relations are the laws true at that world. For example, the worlds most obviously relevant to the question whether this match would have lit without the striking are those with the same laws as the actual world. And laws are more important in the similarity stakes than mere true generalisations. A law for Lewis is a contingent generalisation which 'appears as a theorem (or axiom) in each of the true deductive systems that achieves a best combination of simplicity and strength' (Lewis, 1973:73).

How will this criterion of lawhood apply to the generalisations considered above? It is reasonable to suppose that the generalisation about uranium will be a deductive consequence of a general theory about radioactive substances, and that this theory will in turn be derived from a yet more general account of the behaviour of sub-atomic particles. Thus, to abandon the uranium generalisation would be to disrupt our systematic description of the world quite considerably – worlds in which this generalisation was false are rather dissimilar to our own. Admitting that there was a hunk of gold more than a mile in diameter would not cause a comparable disturbance since the statement that no such hunk exists plays no part in any system of generalisations. Therefore, worlds with an incredibly large hunk of gold could be reasonably similar to our own.

To sum up: laws support subjunctive conditionals because they are important (though not the sole) determinants of inter-world similarity. If it is a law that all $P$-events are $Q$-events, then this law will usually be true at the closest world with a $P$-event, thereby ensuring that this closest world also contains a $Q$-event. But, on Lewis's view, laws like 'all $P$-events are $Q$-events' do not always support conditionals of the form 'if $x$ had been a $P$, it would have been a $Q$'. Other factors, such as exact similarity in respect of particular fact between worlds, may override nomological similarity in selecting the possible world relevant for the evaluation of a given conditional. To put it another way, laws do not *entail* their associated subjunctive conditionals. Therefore, in order to explain how laws support subjunctive conditionals, we need not treat a law as anything other than a contingently true generalisation which states that, as a matter of actual fact, all $P$-events are $Q$-events.

Lewis seeks to ground both laws and the conditionals they support in contingent facts. He hopes to do this by expanding the set of contingent facts to include those which hold in worlds other than the actual world and then claiming that these facts will determine a similarity relation between different worlds, a relation which provides the conditionals with their truth conditions. Various objections might be raised here. One question is how we could possibly know that a certain subjunctive is true if it is made true by facts to which we have no epistemic access. Another question is how Lewis' semantics can be made to yield plausible truth conditions for sufficiency as well as necessity subjunctives. Finally, many will simply deny that a law could fail to support its corresponding subjunctive. I shall not pursue any of these points here. What I shall suggest is that Lewis is not entitled to assume that the facts which underwrite the relevant conditionals within his semantics are contingent facts.

Lewis states that we should decide whether 'if $p$ then $q$' is true by looking to see whether $q$ is true in the most similar possible world to our own in which $p$ is true. But whenever the notion of similarity is used, we may ask: similarity in what respect? In what respect must this actual stationary billiard ball which has not been hit be similar to a possible accelerating billiard ball which has been hit in order for the acceleration of the possible ball at a certain rate to make it the case that if the actual billiard ball had been hit it would have accelerated at that rate? One obvious answer is that these balls must be similar in respect of their mass. But mass is a dispositional term, one which can be used of an object only if certain subjunctive conditionals are true of it. To say that two balls have the same mass *entails* that if they experience the same force they will accelerate at the same rate.

One might suppose that our ball has the mass that it does only in virtue of a non-dispositional property, a property which does not entail that the ball will accelerate when it is hit by another. In that case, this entailment would be no more than a product of the way we describe the situation – if we describe the balls in non-dispositional terms, if we cite their intrinsic non-dispositional character, only contingent connections remain. Indeed, several philosophers have suggested that when one ascribes a certain mass to a ball, all one is saying is that it has some non-dispositional property in virtue of which it accelerates when a force is applied to it, a property which, unlike mass, is only contingently connected to this acceleration. 'Mass' is a mere place-holder for the name of this property (Mackie, 1973: chapter 4).

The weakness in this proposal is that it is impossible to specify any non-dispositional property which could serve as the categorical basis of mass. The only plausible candidates (gravitational mass?) seem every bit as dispositional as inertial mass. And the same is true of other physical quantities. Temperature might be reduced to kinetic energy, but the kinetic energy of a molecule is constitutively connected with its mechanical behaviour. And if the magnetisation of a load-stone can be explained in terms of the possession of a certain electrical charge, what is to serve as the non-dispositional basis of the electrical charge? What more could there be to having a certain charge than behaving in certain ways in relation to other charged bodies? In view of this, it is difficult to maintain that, whenever we speak of a physical quantity, we are committing ourselves to the existence of some underlying non-dispositional property (Mellor, 1974).

To avoid the charge of circularity, Lewis must find some way of describing his actual and his possible ball, which both does not entail that subjunctive conditionals are true of them and also brings out the similarities relevant to the truth of those very conditionals. To put it another way, he must find some way of formulating the laws true at a world without using dispositional predicates. I simply cannot see how this might be done.[6]

There is a quite general problem here for any attempt to argue that laws of nature are contingent which proceeds by specifying facts meant to serve as the truth conditions of a statement of law. Such truth conditions must be (a) indisputably contingent (b) capable of grounding a connection between the law and the relevant subjunctive conditionals. But it is hard to satisfy both desiderata. In order to satisfy (b), we will have to employ the usual scientific language of quantities and substances. But facts described in such a language will serve this purpose only because our conception of physical quantities and substance is thoroughly dispositional. And, if we invent a language free of dispositional terms and without nomological presupposition, this language will not be of any use in formulating truth conditions for statements of law.

The regularity theorist might argue that he can use the language of science to specify the contingent regularities which make laws true. He will point out that no law of mechanics enters into our conception of mass, otherwise violations of those laws would be literally inconceivable. Rather our concept lays it down that a thing's having a certain mass must have some implications for its mechanical behaviour, how it accelerates under different forces etc., without going on to stipulate precisely how

---

[6] This objection to Lewis' analysis occurs on pages 157–60 of Stalnaker, 1984. I also heard it advanced by D.H. Mellor in lectures given before the publication of Stalnaker's book.

any massive object will behave. Empirical inquiry will then reveal the exact relationship between mass, force and acceleration and the regularity theorist can claim as contingent the fact that these quantities are so related, a fact grounded in the actual masses, forces and accelerations of actual objects. So we can use the dispositional language of science in order to state the contingent facts which make laws true.

But recall, the regularity theorist is arguing that *all* laws of nature are contingent, and the vaguely formulated laws which are part of the concept of mass, for instance the law that mass helps to determine acceleration, are laws no less than the mathematically precise ones we claim to have discovered. The general claim is particularly important for our purposes, since we want to distinguish relations of logical or analytical necessity and sufficiency from their nomological counterparts. If we can demonstrate only that contingency is a feature of some laws of nature, we will not have distinguished the class of laws and the causal connections which they lay down from those engendered by non-causal logical and analytical truths.

I noted at the outset that there are philosophers who reject the regularity theory of laws but still wish to maintain that statements of law are contingently true (Armstrong, 1983 and Tooley, 1987). The fundamental thought here is that there is a kind of necessity, nomological necessity, which is 'weaker' than logical necessity and which connects either the events which instantiate laws, or the universals mentioned in laws. Since a law asserts that these events or universals are (contingently) connected by a relation of necessitation, a relation stronger than mere constant conjunction, it is no longer so hard to explain how laws can support subjunctive conditionals.

Now some have questioned the very intelligibility of this notion of a nomological modality, hovering between the logically contingent and the logically necessary, while others suspect that theories of nomological modality simply assert and do not explain how a statement of law can both support subjunctive conditionals and be logically contingent. I suspect these doubts are well-founded, but I do not have the space for a full treatment of them here. For my purposes, it is enough to observe that these necessitarians are no better off than the regularity theorists. To demonstrate the contingency of laws of nature, they must be able to describe the relata of the necessitation relation, be they events or universals, in a fashion which does not in itself carry nomological implications. They are then free to assert (on whatever grounds) that

'$P$ necessitates $Q$' is a contingent truth. But if '$P$' and '$Q$' can be grasped only by someone who thinks of $P$-things and $Q$-things as entering into nomological relations with other specific phenomena, how can the contingency of all the laws involving $P$ and $Q$ be established?

## AN ARGUMENT FOR NECESSITY?

There is an argument against (1) which is often rehearsed and from which I wish to dissociate myself. I have urged only that (1) cannot be established by reducing nomological facts to contingent non-nomological facts because the subject matter of physical laws cannot be thought of except in nomological terms. Several philosophers have relied on the completely different point that the subject matter of physical laws will be unknowable unless physical kinds have their associated causal powers essentially.

For instance, Shoemaker argues as follows:

Suppose that the identity of properties consisted of something logically independent of their causal potentialities. Then it ought to be possible for there to be properties that have no potential whatever for contributing to causal powers ie., are such that under no conceivable circumstances will their possession by a thing make any difference to the way the presence of that thing affects other things or to the way other things affect it. Further, it ought to be possible that there be two or more different properties that make, under all possible circumstances, exactly the same contribution to the causal powers of the things that have them. Further, it ought to be possible that the potential of a property for contributing to the production of causal powers might change over time, so that, for example, the potential possessed by property A at one time is the same as that possessed by property B at a later time, and that possessed by property B at the earlier time is the same as that possessed by property A at the later time. (Shoemaker, 1984:214–15)

Shoemaker says, quite plausibly, that if these possibilities were actualised, we could never know that they were actualised. We learn about the nature of an object by causally interacting with it and can discriminate between different kinds of object by means of the different effects they have on us. As a result, we could never discover the causally inert property, we could never discriminate between the causally exactly similar properties and we could never know that property A and property B had swapped causal roles. More seriously, we cannot be sure that these possibilities are not *actually* realised and thus we cannot know many of the things we do take ourselves to know. For example, we cannot be certain that we have detected all of a thing's properties, however hard we look, and we cannot be sure that any two apparently identical properties are the same property.

However, if this line of reasoning is meant to support the conclusion that properties have their causal powers essentially, it has three serious flaws. First, just because we would not know that *p* were true if it were true, this does not mean that *p* is impossible. It is possible that I am a brain in a vat on the Moon being fed images of Cambridge, England, notwithstanding the fact that, if I were, I would not know that I was. The inconceivability of a certain state of affairs might be a good reason to believe that it is impossible, but the fact that it would be unknowable, were it to obtain, is not.

Secondly, Shoemaker's argument is just a special form of the general sceptical argument, and that argument has often be called into question. Suppose there is a city which looks exactly like Cambridge, England, but is located on a different planet. If I was transported unawares to that city, I would still believe that I was in Cambridge, England. Does this mean that, given that I am in Cambridge, England, I cannot know that I am in Cambridge, England? Similarly, one could say, the fact that there are different properties which look identical and identical properties which look different does not imply that, assuming I am not confronted with such properties, I am incapable of knowing whether two properties are the same or different (Nozick, 1981: chapter 3).

Finally, let us waive the first two points and suppose that (a) the nature of physical kinds must be such that we can always know about them and (b) that this knowledge must be proof against the above sceptical doubt. Still, we do not get the conclusion that a property's causal powers are essential to it. In order to rule out inert properties, we must stipulate that necessarily every property has some causal powers. In order to rule out causally similar properties we must stipulate that necessarily different properties have different causal powers. And in order to rule out the same property developing different causal powers, we must stipulate that, necessarily, identical properties have identical causal powers. But none of these stipulations entail that, for each property, there are some causal powers such that they are necessarily associated with that property – the stipulations entail only this: necessarily each property has some distinctive set of causal powers associated with it, an association which might be perfectly contingent. A useful parallel: we may suppose that, necessarily, each object has some spatio-temporal location, that, necessarily, distinct objects never share the same spatio-temporal location and that, necessarily, identical objects always share the same spatio-temporal location, but it does not follow from any of this that an object's spatio-temporal location is among its essential properties.

## CONCLUSION

I maintain that the causal facts about the world obtain in virtue of non-causal facts, but I do not hold that nomological facts obtain in virtue of non-nomological facts. If we are to specify the non-causal facts in virtue of which causal connections obtain, we must be able to distinguish between those connections forged by the laws of nature and those laid down by other logical and linguistic truths. I have argued that we cannot make this division by reference to the supposed contingency of the laws which underwrite causal connections. There is no imaginative proof of the contingency of natural laws, and it is impossible to pinpoint contingent non-nomological facts which could serve as the truth conditions of statements of law. I do not assert the necessity of natural laws, I just think that we cannot assume their contingency when analysing causation.

# 3

# Events and non-causal explanations

The task before us is to draw a line between causal and non-causal explanations, between the explanations delivered by natural science and those arising out of our non-scientific logical, legal and linguistic practices. Since I believe that causal facts can be reduced to non-causal facts, and in particular to relationships of necessity and sufficiency between events, we must find the source of this division in some further difference among these underlying relations. In chapter 2, I decided there was no way of establishing that the relations themselves differed in their metaphysical status: connections established by natural law might be no more contingent than those engendered by language, logic or the civil law. Now we must ask whether some other feature of their relata, present in one case and absent in the other, can do what is required.

According to Hume

(3) A cause must be distinct from its effect.

He may have intended this as no more than an alternative formulation of the other two theses I attributed to him in the previous chapter:

(1) causes are contingently sufficient for their effects.
(2) causal connections are discoverable only *a posteriori*.

However, modern philosophers such as Davidson and Lewis, who treat causes and effects as objects, have construed (3) as a further constraint on causation, telling us that causes are neither identical with, nor a part of, their effects. And nothing I have said so far touches on this requirement of distinctness.

In fact, Davidson and Lewis employ three analytical tools to deal with non-causal relations, all of which are available only to those who regard event-objects, concrete particulars, as the relata of the causal relation: they distinguish expressions which refer to genuine events from those which do not, they distinguish events and their relations from the descriptions which those events satisfy and they hold that events may stand in relations of parthood and identity, much as do objects. I shall ask whether these tools can do the job of distinguishing causal from non-causal explanations before trying to do the job without them.


## DAVIDSON

According to Davidson, when an ordinary material object has a certain property, or changes from having one property to having another, there is a further particular which is the possession or the change – an event. And this event, like an ordinary material object, may be described in quite diverse ways, so a single event might be the having of one property by one object and also the having of other properties by the same object or by different objects. Causation is a relation between these event-objects, best rendered by the two-place predicate 'cause', a relation to be distinguished from any explanatory connection between true sentences (Davidson, 1980a; Ducasse, 1951:121–7).

Thus, Davidson holds that singular causal statements such as

(4) The striking of the match caused the lighting of the match.

have the same logical form as

(5) The butcher's son married the baker's daughter.

The definite descriptions 'the butcher's son' and 'the baker's daughter' refer to individuals who satisfy the two-place predicate 'married'. If we substitute some co-referring expression for either of these descriptions, we shall arrive at a sentence with the same truth value as (5). For instance, the farmer's son may be the most ugly man in the village and the baker's daughter the most beautiful woman. These facts, together with (5) entail that the most ugly man married the most beautiful women. In Davidson's view, 'the striking of the match' and 'the lighting of the match' are definite descriptions referring to particular events; and these events may be redescribed while leaving the truth value of (4) unaffected. So, if the striking was the first event mentioned on page 3 of today's *Times* and the fire the second, the first event mentioned on page 3 of today's *Times* caused the second event there mentioned.

Davidson wishes to distinguish sentences like (4) from sentences like (6)

(6) The match lit, not because the match was struck but because the match was struck with such force.

According to Davidson, though (6) quantifies over events, it does not contain definite descriptions referring to events. It should be read as

(6a) There was a lighting of the match not because there was a striking of the match but rather because there was a hard striking of the match.

and *not* as

(6b) The match's lighting was caused not by the striking of the match but rather by the hard striking of the match.

In Davidson's eyes (6b) is false because the striking and the hard striking are identical; if one caused the lighting, the other did also. Nevertheless, (6), when construed as (6a), may be true. Since these events are not referred to (but only quantified over) in (6a) one cannot substitute co-referring descriptions of them, so (6a) may be true while (6b) is false. (6a) does not state that two concrete particulars are causally related, rather it tells us why 'The match lit' is true by giving us another true sentence 'The match was struck' (Davidson, 1980a:155–6 and Davidson, 1980b:135).

In chapter 1 (pages 7–8), I spoke about statements like (6). There, I failed to acknowledge the existence of event-objects at all and gave the term 'event' the quite different function of standing in for certain sentences. Should I have taken Davidson's views into account? Since my main interest is in causal explanation, Davidson's assertion that there is another causal idiom of which (4) is an example might seem to raise an issue that can safely be put to one side. But, in fact, Davidson's point bears on something which no theorist of causal explanation can afford to ignore: the problem of distinguishing causal from non-causal explanations. Were the problem soluble within Davidson's framework, this would provide a powerful reason for adopting it and re-writing chapter 1 accordingly.

The following statements are widely agreed to be non-causal explanations, under some interpretation of them, despite their formal similarity to (6).[1]

(7) Gauss was surprised because of the convergence of series S.

(8) I wrote my name, in part because I wrote 'D'.

(9) I broke the law because I parked on a double yellow line.

---

[1] Some of my examples are taken from Kim. See Kim, 1973:570–2 and Kim, 1974:41–52.

(10) I became an uncle yesterday because Mary gave birth yesterday.

(11) I built the second tree house because you built the first tree house.

(7) to (11) are each associated with suitable conditionals such as 'If the series had not converged, Gauss would not have been surprised', so a simple subjunctive analysis of causation could not rule them out. Nor can we appeal to the fact that the generalisations which support these subjunctives are necessary truths. As I urged in chapter 2, one cannot assume that natural laws are not necessary truths.

So far as I am aware, Davidson himself never directly addresses the problem of non-causal explanations. He has an ulterior motive for discerning a two-place predicate 'cause' (satisfied by pairs of event-objects) in ordinary causal statements, one which need not detain us.[2] But someone already working with this causal predicate might find a further use for it. They might apply the following test to candidate causal explanations: try to re-write such explanations so as to transform them into statements which assert that a causal relation obtains between a pair of event-objects. This re-writing can be done successfully if it can be done *salva veritate*, if it does not turn a true explanatory statement into a false causal statement or a false explanatory statement into a true causal statement. And, should the re-writing succeed, we will have demonstrated that the explanatory statement in question is a genuine causal explanation.

How should the re-writing go? Start with an explanatory statement like 'the match lit because the match was struck' which we suppose to be true. Then turn it into an hermaphrodite expression of the form 'the *e* occurred because the *c* occurred', here 'the match's lighting occurred because the match's striking occurred'. Finally, drop the occurrence-verb, swap the component sentences round and replace 'because' with a causal verb to get 'the match's striking caused the match's lighting'. We have now arrived at a causal statement which is plausibly true if, and only if, our original explanatory statement is true, so this particular explanation passes the test with flying colours: there is a suitable correspondent referring to two event-objects and stating that the causal relation holds between them, a correspondent which is true if, and only if, the explanatory statement itself is true. So 'the match lit because the match was struck' is a causal explanation.

---

[2] Davidson wishes to make causal idioms amenable to a certain style of semantic treatment, a treatment which requires that they be extensional: Davidson, 1984.

(7) would be unlikely to pass such a test as it stands. The obvious correspondent 'the convergence of series S caused the surprising of Gauss' will be rejected on the grounds that the description 'the convergence of series S' fails to refer to a real event-object. For genuine events, like genuine objects, have something which this 'event' lacks, namely a spatio-temporal location. If we wish to treat (7) as a causal explanation, we must re-write it as follows: Gauss was surprised because he discovered that series S converged. This statement's correspondent is 'Gauss' discovery that series S converges caused his surprise' a statement which is plausibly true if, and only if, the explanatory claim is true. But here it is Gauss' discovery which is the cause and that event does have a spatio-temporal location (Jackson and Pargetter, 1988:110–11).

(8) and (9) are faulted no less easily. Davidson can invoke Hume's dictum that causally related event-objects must be wholly distinct from one another – a cause event can be neither identical with nor a part of its effect. (8)'s correspondent is 'my writing of the letter 'D' caused my writing of my name'. Now, if my writing my name is an event-object with spatio-temporal parts, my writing the letter 'D' is surely one of them. So, given Hume's dictum, this statement cannot be true, despite the truth of (8), thereby showing up (8) as a non-causal explanation. Furthermore, Davidson's views about the individuation of actions commit him to saying that my parking on a double yellow line is the very same event-object as my breaking the law (Davidson, 1980c). So (9)'s correspondent 'my parking on a double yellow line caused my breaking of the law' cannot be true either, despite the truth of (9), so it too is a non-causal explanation.

Someone might suggest that we can get away without ascribing spatio-temporal parts to events by making use of the fact that the letter 'D' is a part of my name. But it would be wrong to generalise on this basis and adopt the thesis that a part of any object's having a certain property may never cause the whole object to have that property. After all, the whole apple may have become rotten because some part of it was rotten. What must be said is that the event-object of this part's being rotten cannot cause any event-object of which it is itself a part. Similarly, we cannot hope to deal with (9) by stipulating that an object's having one property may not cause that very object to have another property. Rubbing the apple will cause the apple itself to shine. Rather what must be said is that events-objects do not cause themselves (Thomson, 1977:63 and Swain, 1980:161–3).

What of (10)? Here the correspondent would be something like 'Mary's giving birth yesterday caused my assumption of unclehood yesterday.' Davidson provides no reason for thinking that 'Mary's giving birth' and 'my assumption of unclehood' fail to refer to genuine event-objects. Rather, what he will probably say is that, (10)'s correspondent may be false, despite the truth of (10), because Mary may be my sister. If Mary is my sister then 'Mary's giving birth' and 'my assumption of unclehood' will refer to the same event and no event can cause itself. So, in that case, (10) is not a causal explanation. Note, it does not follow that (10) could not express a causal explanation. If Mary is not my sister, but rather my sister's best friend, and Mary's giving birth somehow causes my sister to give birth, then (10)'s correspondent relates distinct events and (10) is a causal explanation.

But even if Mary is my sister, the event-identity claim may be questioned on the grounds that it is perfectly possible for Mary and I to be in quite different places when she goes into labour; in that case, the event of her giving birth will occur in a separate location from the event of my becoming an uncle and no single event can be wholly present in different places at the same time.[3] However, Davidson might simply deny that my assumption of unclehood occurs where I am. What it is to become an uncle is just for one of one's siblings or their partners to give birth. Hence the event of my becoming an uncle is just the event of one of these people giving birth. It would be strange to count two events here since there is no change in me when I become an uncle, though various things happen to my sister. Davidson could paraphrase (10) as, roughly, 'there was a giving birth by one of my siblings (or by their partners) because there was a giving birth by Mary' and when Mary is my sister, (10), so construed, is not made true by two distinct events in the domain over which it quantifies.

Davidson must take a different tack with (11). Surely, my building activities and your building activities *are* distinct events occupying different spatio-temporal regions. One is not a mere logical shadow of the other, nor is one a part of the other. Furthermore, there is an explanatory relation between the two component sentences in (11). Nevertheless, the truth of 'You built the *first* tree house' does not causally explain why, does not bring it about that 'I built the *second* tree house' is

---

[3] This objection to the identity-claim is made in Kim, 1974:42 during discussion of an analogous example. I am grateful to Michael Martin for suggesting a Davidsonian response to it – the rest of the paragraph is due to him.

true. (Here I use the emphasis markers introduced in chapter 1 (pages 9–10), to indicate that it is the temporal order of these events which is being explained). (11) supports the subjunctive conditional 'if your tree house had not been first mine would not have been second', but there is no implication that the firstness of mine causally produced the secondness of yours.

Someone may deny that the two component sentences in (11) quantify over real events. Perhaps the acquisition of a relational property, such as being first or second, cannot be a real event-object because relational properties are not real properties. I have little sympathy with this view: an object has many of its relational properties in virtue of the intrinsic properties had by it and by other objects (for example two things have the same colour in virtue of their colours) and if these intrinsic properties are real, it is hard to see how the relational properties which they fix could be any less real. But whatever the merits of this thought, it is not open to Davidson to claim that the sentences 'you built the first tree house' and 'I built the second tree house' do not quantify over genuine events. He must render (11) as 'there was a building of a second tree house because there was a building of a first tree house' and building activity is a perfectly real occurrence. For him, the expression 'my building the second tree house' and 'my building the tree house' refer to exactly the same event-object, as do 'my striking' and 'my hard striking'.

Is the correspondent of (11) namely 'your building of the first tree house caused my building of the second tree house' false? We have failed to find any reason to think so, for it states that a relation obtains between two wholly distinct event-objects; why should this relation not be the causal relation? Hume's (3) cannot help us. For all we have said, a true (11) has a true correspondent leading us to the false conclusion that (11) is a causal explanation. But, it may be objected, Hume's (3) was never meant to give a full analysis of causation. Surely there are plenty of distinct events which are not causally related and there must be some *other* way of distinguishing them from causally related events. For example, there might be a perfect vacuum between the two tree houses and our scientific consciences may recoil from hypothesising causal action across such a vacuum.

But it does not have to be like that. Suppose what got me to build is that I didn't want to be seen providing my children with poorer playthings than those you gave to yours. In this case, your building of a tree house causes my building of a tree house and, Davidson must say, your building of the first tree house causes my building of the second tree house. So (11)'s correspondent is here true. But this does nothing to show that (11) itself, the explanatory statement, is a causal explanation. The fact that your tree house was the first one in the whole world is causally irrelevant to mine's being the second.

(11) is one instance of a quite general problem: there is a many–one relationship between explanations and their Davidsonian correspondents, and whereas some of the explanations associated with a given correspondent are causal explanations, others will not be, yet Davidson lacks the resources to separate the two. For instance, the (we suppose) causal explanation 'your building the first *tree house* caused me to build the second *tree house*' shares the same correspondent as the (we suppose) noncausal explanation 'your building the *first* tree house caused me to build the *second* tree house'. So, by our Davidsonian criterion, they are either both causal or both non-causal, depending on the truth or falsity of our correspondent; they cannot be what they are, namely a mixed bag.

This difficulty originates in an essential feature of Davidson's theory, namely that causal relations obtain between event-objects however those objects are described. This fact forces him to distinguish statements of causal relation from statements of causal explanation. At the same time, it prevents our setting up a one-to-one correspondence between such statements. So, Davidson's causal relations between event-objects cannot help us tell causal and non-causal explanations apart.

However, they might still be of use in connection with Hume's second dictum. As I formulated it above, this said that causal connections are discovered only *a posteriori*. But Hume faces a difficulty: some true causal statements may be known *a priori*.

(12) The cause of the defeat caused the defeat.
(13) The fatal wound he received caused his death.

Now the assertion that (12) and (13) are knowable *a priori* must be qualified a bit. One could not know any of them without being made aware of some contingent facts (for example that there was a defeat) which could hardly be known *a priori*. The point is rather that the only generalisations needed to support (12) and (13) are *a priori* truths: that the cause of *x* causes *x*, that fatal wounds cause death. The fact that *a posteriori* known singular facts are also required to support the statement is neither here nor there.

Within Davidson's framework, we can reformulate Hume's second dictum so that (12) and (13) are not ruled false by it (Davidson, 1980d:223–4 and Davidson, 1980e:14). The event-objects referred to in (12) and (13) may be redescribed so as to reveal a causal dependence between them which is governed by a generalization with empirical content. The cause of the defeat might be the illness of the commander, the fatal wound might be the penetration of the heart, both of which are connected by an empirical generalisation to the relevant outcome. Hume's dictum can now be read as saying that a statement with a relational form is causal only if the events to which it refers can be described so as to instantiate an empirical generalisation.

However, it is hard to see how to reformulate Hume's dictum for causal explanations. One would like to say that an explanation is causal only if the events it quantifies over can be described so as to instantiate some empirical generalisation. But, as we have seen, such a proposal will not work. If it is a desire to keep up with the neighbours which leads me to build my tree house, there will be an empirical, psychological generalisation connecting your building activity with my building activity, but this will do nothing to make (11) a causal explanation. What one wants to say here is that the generalisation supporting the explanation should not be devoid of empirical content but we cannot construe 'supports the explanation' here as 'subsumes the events quantified over in the explanation (under some description or other)'.

## LEWIS

Davidson did not seek to tell us what the causal relation is, he did not seek to provide a full analysis of causal statements. Rather he attempted to exclude certain non-causal relations by laying down conditions necessary for any relation to be causal. Lewis is more ambitious and presents an analysis of causation in terms of subjunctive conditionals, perhaps the most illuminating yet propounded. But this analysis is unsatisfactory and, as a result, he cannot make the distinction between causal and non-causal explanations. Nor, as we shall see in chapter 5, can he give direction to causation.

Lewis sets out to analyse causation in terms of subjunctive conditionals (Lewis, 1986a). As I described in chapter 2, he provides us with a semantics for such conditionals. To recapitulate, the conditional 'if *p* had been the case, *q* would have been the case' is true if, and only if, (a) *p* is necessarily false or (b) $q$ is true in the most similar possible world to our own (actual) world in which $p$ is true. Thus, a counterfactual is non-vacuously true when, and only when, it takes less of a departure from actuality to make the consequent true along with the antecedent than to make the antecedent true without the consequent. Where $p$ is actually true, the conditional as a whole is true if, and only if, $q$ is also true (Lewis, 1973: chapter 1).

Lewis regards causation as a relation between particular event-objects (to be denoted by '$c$' and '$e$') and not between propositions, facts or sentences (denoted by '$p$' and '$q$'). He says that $e$ depends causally on $c$ if, and only if, the following conditionals are true: (a) if $c$ had occurred, $e$ would have occurred and (b) if $c$ had not occurred then $e$ would not have occurred. So $c$ causes $e$ if, and only if, the occurrence of $e$ depends on the occurrence of $c$. Thus, a causal claim of the form '$p$ because $q$' is true if, and only if, both '$q$' and '$p$' are of the form '$e$ occurred', or else '$e$ did not occur' and the two relevant subjunctives connecting $p$ and $q$ are true.

Where $e$ and $c$ actually occur (a) will be vacuously true and the truth of the causal claims will depend on the truth of (b). So the striking of the match caused the lighting because if the striking had not occurred, the lighting would not have occurred. And that subjunctive is true because the most similar possible world in which the striking did not occur is one in which the lighting did not occur either. Where there is actually no striking but the striking would have caused the lighting, this is because the most similar world in which the striking occurs is a world in which the lighting occurs also.[4]

As I observed in chapter 2, Lewis is a regularity theorist about natural laws, even though he is not a regularity theorist about causation. That is, he believes 'it is a law that all $P$s are $Q$s' is logically equivalent to 'all $P$s are $Q$s' while denying that '$c$ causes $e$' is equivalent to '$c$ is a $P$-event and $e$ is a $Q$-event and all $P$-events are $Q$-events' or some such thing. As we have seen, he provides an ingenious account of how laws support subjunctive conditionals and through them causal claims, without actually entailing them. But his insistence that laws do not entail subjunctive conditionals is no mere Humean whim. Lewis needs to hold that some laws do not support subjunctive conditionals in order to rule

---

[4] According to Lewis, the relation of causal dependence just defined is not quite the same as causation. It is a consequence of his semantics for subjunctive conditionals that causal dependence is non-transitive whereas causation is transitive, so he defines causation as the ancestral of the causal dependence relation.

out one set of non-causal relations which would otherwise be accounted causal on his subjunctive analysis.

Imagine that *e* and *f* have a common cause *c*. There are laws which ensure that events like *c* cause both events like *e* and events like *f*. One might reason as follows. If *e* had not occurred, that could only have been because *c* did not occur and if *c* had not occurred then *f* would not have occurred. Therefore, if *e* had not occurred then *f* would not have occurred and thus, absurdly, *e* is a cause of *f*. This last conditional is supported by a law of nature connecting *e* to *f*, a law derived from the laws connecting *c* to *e* and *c* to *f*.

Lewis evades this conclusion by denying that if *e* had not occurred, *c* would not have occurred. He says that the most similar possible world in which *e* does not occur is one in which *c* occurs anyway and causes *f*. This is a world in which the law connecting *c* to *e* is broken. The fact that in this world the events before *e* and their other effects remain the same matters more in the similarity stakes than the occurrence of a small miracle. Thus Lewis attempts to distinguish, as every satisfactory theory of causation must, the genuine effects of an event from those events which are effects of its causes. If, as I believe, laws of nature may be necessary truths, we cannot assume that there is any world, far or near, in which some law of nature is violated, so Lewis' clever manoeuvre is open to question. In chapter 5, I shall present my own solution to this problem.

There are some important similarities between Davidson's account and Lewis' account. Both hold that causation relates concrete particulars. Both think that if two such particulars are causally related, they are so related however described. Therefore, let us use Lewis as we used Davidson and require causal explanations to be underwritten by corresponding causal statements to see if this helps us with non-causal explanations. However, be warned, Lewis and Davidson individuate events rather differently and, as far as the problem of non-causal explanation is concerned, this difference is crucial.

Lewis begins by distinguishing a specification of an event-object by means of its accidental properties and a specification of an event-object by means of its essential properties (Lewis, 1986b). According to him, there is an event-object which is essentially a striking of this match and an event-object which is essentially a lighting of this match and the former causes the latter in that had the striking not occurred, the lighting would not have come about either. But the striking and the lighting may also be specified by means of accidental properties, as in the sentence 'the first event mentioned on page 3 of *The Times* caused the second event mentioned on page 3 of *The Times*' and this sentence is no less true for that.

Davidson acknowledges no such distinction between the accidental and essential properties of events. But once this distinction is in play it complicates the individuation of events and the ascription of causal relations. Consider a hard striking of the match. According to Davidson, when the match is struck hard there is one event-object, a striking which is hard, but, according to Lewis, at least two events happen: one which is essentially a hard striking of the match, and another which is essentially a striking but only accidentally a hard striking. The reason Lewis gives for discerning these two event-objects is that they differ in their causes and effects.

For instance, it is true that if the event-object which was essentially a striking had failed to occur, the lighting would not have occurred either. However, we should not assume that had the event-object which is essentially a hard striking not occurred (i.e. there was no hard striking but perhaps a soft striking), the lighting would not have occurred either. So these event-objects differ in their effects. Furthermore, it may be true to say that had I not moved my wrist with such vigour, the event-object which was essentially a hard striking would not have happened. But we cannot infer from this that the event-object which was essentially a striking would not have happened also. So these event-objects may differ in their causes. Of course, the striking and the hard striking will be intimately related. The occurrence of the hard striking will entail the occurrence of the striking, they occupy the same spatio-temporal region and share the same spatio-temporal parts. In fact, they differ only in their modal properties. But, in Lewis' view, it is these properties which fix their causal relations.

Take the statement 'the hard striking caused the noisy lighting'. Lewis will distinguish several different ways in which this statement may be read, not all of which make it a true statement. The two descriptions may each refer to strikings and lightings which are only accidentally hard and noisy, in which case the sentence says truly that the striking, which was in fact hard, caused the lighting, which was in fact noisy. On the other hand, the two descriptions may refer to strikings and lightings which are essentially hard and noisy, in which case the statement says truly that the hard striking caused the noisy lighting.

What we cannot do, without rendering the statement false, is to give it a certain mixed interpretation. There is no objection to treating 'the hard striking' as an accidental specification while construing 'the noisy lighting' as an essential specification, but falsity will result if 'the hard striking' refers to a striking which is essentially a hard striking, while 'the noisy lighting' refers to a lighting which is only accidentally noisy. For the essentially hard striking might have failed to occur without that preventing the occurrence of a lighting which is only accidentally noisy, provided some not so hard striking occurred in its stead. Therefore, on this reading the hard striking does not cause the noisy lighting.

Lewis, like Davidson, appears to assume that all causal statements are of the form 'the occurrence of $c$ causes the occurrence of $e$'. But may not the occurrence of $c$ affect the way $e$ happens without thereby causing it to exist? For instance, $c$ might cause $e$ to have a certain property $Q$, a property which is not essential to $e$, so that $e$ could have lacked $Q$ while still occurring (Mellor, 1987:126). Suppose that a hard striking causes the lighting to be noisy. Perhaps noisiness is an accidental property of the lighting. If so, the hardness of the striking may cause the lighting to be noisy without thereby causing the lighting, which is in fact noisy, to occur. For the lighting would still have occurred even if a soft striking had replaced the hard striking. Lewis cannot accommodate this causal idiom directly, but it is open to him to claim that every true causal statement, of whatever form, has a true correspondent of the form 'the occurrence of $c$ causes the occurrence of $e$'. 'The hardness of the striking caused the lighting to be noisy' will correspond to 'there is an event $c$ which is essentially a hard striking and there is an event $e$ which is essentially a noisy lighting and $c$ caused $e$'. Thus, we postulate an event-object which is essentially a noisy lighting whose occurrence does depend on that of the hard striking and then stipulate that, in our substitute statement, 'the noisy striking' refers to this event-object and not to any accidentally noisy event-object. By expanding his event-ontology, Lewis may aspire to assimilate every causal statement to one of the form 'the occurrence of $c$ causes the occurrence of $e$'.

Perhaps it is formally possible to abjure the idiom 'the $P$'s being $Q$ caused the $R$ to be $S$' in favour of 'the occurrence of $c$ caused the occurrence of $e$' but an advocate of the subjunctive theory of causation is then faced with the following question: is every property which might be mentioned in an accidental specification of one event part of the essence of some other event? If so, we are landed with a large number of very peculiar causal relations. If not, how do we draw the line between properties which can be part of the essence of some event and those which cannot?

Take 'the prince's afternoon fall from the saddle'; is there an event-object of which this is an essential specification? If the prince had fallen in the morning rather than in the afternoon, would some of the falls which took place have been different? Might all the same falls have happened to someone else? Might an unmounted prince have undergone all the same falls? On our answer to these questions hang the causal relations of the event-objects in question. For example, if there is a fall specified by the above description which could not have occurred except in the afternoon, then the rain which postponed the morning's polo was among the causes of that fall, but if all the same falls could have occurred in the morning, the rain is causally irrelevant to them all.

Now I have simply no idea how to go about resolving these issues, and when Lewis attempts to do so he relies on unexplained intuitions about causation, the very relation in question (Lewis, 1986b:249–51). But such metaphysical worries need not concern the man in the street, for the causal facts which supposedly hang on the outcome can be expressed in different terms. We may say, by using the idiom which Lewis abjures, that the ground's being wet *in the morning* caused the prince's fall to be *in the afternoon*, without inquiring into the essences of event-objects at all. This is because the statement is no more than a rewording of a causal explanation and does not assert any relation between objects. So there is every reason to regard statements of causal explanation as more fundamental than causal judgments expressed in terms of Lewis' event metaphysics.

The circularity implicit in Lewis' treatment of causation comes out most clearly when he is confronted with problematic non-causal explanations. Take (10). Lewis does not deny the truth of the conditional 'if Mary had not given birth yesterday I would not have become an uncle yesterday'. He also concedes that if this subjunctive relates events, they are wholly distinct event-objects. Nor does he follow Hume's lead and focus on the *a priori* nature of the connection between these event-objects. Rather, he claims that 'my assumption of unclehood yesterday' fails to refer to any genuine event-object and thus (10) has no causal corre-spondent and cannot be regarded as a causal explanation.[5]

[5] In attributing these opinions to Lewis, I am extrapolating from what he says about the analogous example of Xanthippe discussed on pages 262–6 of Lewis, 1986b.

Whether I am an uncle is a largely relational matter. Intrinsic properties like my sex are relevant, but the salient fact is my relation to my sister. So the event-description 'my assumption of unclehood' is formulated in terms of extrinsic properties. Furthermore, it is hard to see what intrinsic properties could constitute an essential specification of the supposed event-object of my becoming an uncle, after all my own intrinsic state has little to do with this change in my familial status. So Lewis concludes that this expression fails to refer to any genuine event-object; (10) is a non-causal explanation because one of its clauses cannot be construed as an existential quantification over events.

The metaphysical principle behind the conclusion is this: every genuine event-object can be specified by means of essential properties, and essential properties must be predominantly intrinsic properties; relational properties cannot play a large role in the essence of an event-object. However, Lewis does not want to exclude all relational properties from essential specifications, since he wishes to allow that facts about the spatio-temporal location of an event-object may help to determine which event-object it is (Lewis, 1986b:264). And this seems sensible in view of the fact that the spatio-temporal location of one event (the morning's rain) may causally determine the spatio-temporal location of another (the afternoon's fall). So we are left with a rather vague stipulation and, once again, our prior causal judgments must take up the slack.

Are (12) and (13) ruled out also by this metaphysical principle? It seems sensible for Lewis to suppose that 'the cause of the defeat' and 'the fatal wound' refer to genuine event-objects, objects with a predominantly intrinsic essential specification (for example 'the stab through the heart') and which stand in suitable relations of subjunctive dependence, however specified. So, Lewis should regard these descriptions as accidental specifications of event-objects which really are causes, and indeed as specifications of these event-objects in terms of their actual causes and effects. So (12) and (13) serve to make genuine causal statements.

Lewis has to adopt a slightly different tack with (11). As we observed above, the building activities referred to in (11) occur in distinct, non-overlapping spatio-temporal regions, and it is perfectly true to say that if you had not built the first tree house, I would not have built the second. Furthermore, 'your building of the first tree house' and 'my building of the second tree house' may be treated as accidental specifications of genuine event-objects, namely the building done by you and by me, which have other essential, predominantly intrinsic specifications. So Lewis cannot dismiss (11) as failing to quantify over genuine events.

Suppose the buildings are causally independent. Lewis may then deny that (11) is a causal explanation on the grounds that it has no correspondent of the form 'the occurrence of $c$ caused the occurrence of $e$'. For the following subjunctive will then be false: 'if the event which was in fact your building of the first tree house had not occurred then the event which was in fact my building of the second tree house would not have occurred'. So there is no correspondent of (11) which can be read as a true causal statement containing accidental specifications of the causally related event-objects. And Lewis assumes that the descriptions in (11) cannot be essential specifications of any event-object.

What if there is a causal connection between the building of the two tree houses? What if I built a tree house in order not to be shamed by your tree house? Then 'I built the second *tree house* because you built the first *tree house*' would be a causal explanation. As we saw when discussing Davidson, this does not entail that (11) is a causal explanation when (11) is construed, in the way intended, as an explanation of pure temporal order, as 'I built the *second* tree house because you built the *first* tree house'. The secondness of my tree house would still not be causally explained by the firstness of yours, even if I built my tree house because you built yours. So Lewis appears to be confronted with the very difficulty which defeated Davidson: he must assign the same correspondent to different explanations, one of which is causal and one of which is not.

However, unlike Davidson, Lewis has the resources to assign distinct correspondents to these two explanations. He may claim that, in the case of the causal explanation, we are treating 'your building the first tree house' and 'my building the second tree house' as accidental specifications of causally related events and so the relevant correspondent is true. Whereas, in case of the non-causal explanation, the relevant correspondent is one in which 'your building the first tree house' and 'my building the second tree house' are treated as essential specifications of these events – and this correspondent must be false. It must be false because these descriptions cannot be *essential* specifications of an event-object, being far too extrinsic.

But can Lewis stipulate that these descriptions fail to specify some genuine event objects essentially? As we have seen, Lewis allows that spatio-temporal location may play some role in the individuation of event-objects. So it is just not clear why the exact temporal order of the buildings may not help to individuate these building events. Once more, the suspicion is that we are forced to rely on our prior conviction that (11), so interpreted, is not a causal explanation in order to apply Lewis' metaphysical criteria correctly.

My fundamental objection has been that Lewis' account of causation cannot support but must look for support from our judgments about what constitutes a causal explanation. But there is a further worry: how does his event metaphysics cope with the mereology of event-objects? can it uphold the principles which I invoked on Davidson's behalf to deal with (8) and (9)? Lewis certainly believes he can attribute parts to event-objects, and he explicitly employs the maxim that causes must be wholly distinct from their effects in order to dispose of (8) (Lewis, 1986b:258–9). He might well follow Davidson in regard to (9) also and claim that 'my breaking the law' is just a more extrinsic specification of the event of my parking on a double yellow line and so (9) does not relate distinct events. However, the mereology of events makes problems for any theory which combines an analysis of the causal relation in terms of subjunctive conditionals with the thought that causation is a relation between event-objects.

Several philosophers have held it as obvious that for event-object $c$ to be the cause of another event-object $e$, $c$ must be the cause of every component of $e$ (Thomson, 1977:63, Swain, 1980:163). And, once one is speaking the language of event-objects, this does indeed seem to be obvious: how can one event bring about another event without bringing about every part of that event? True, I can bring a tree house into existence without bringing all its parts into existence, indeed without creating any of its components – I just need to arrange them in a certain way. But causing an event-object is not like creating an ordinary material object from pre-existing objects – one does not start the First World War by re-arranging pre-existing battles, rather bringing about the war just is bringing the battles which compose it into existence.

As we saw earlier, Lewis analyses the causal relation in terms of necessity conditionals: 'if the cause had not occurred the effect would not have occurred'. Was it the case that every event necessary for the occurrence of the First World War was also necessary for the occurrence of each of the battles which comprised it? Surely not. Forced to pronounce on the essence of the war, we would probably say that the First World War was essentially a general European conflagration, nothing which didn't involve most of Europe would have been the same war. Now it was necessary for this war to occur that most of the countries in Europe arm themselves to the teeth. However, this condition wasn't necessary for the occurrence of the Battle of Jutland – all that was necessary for that, in the way of armaments, was a naval build up involving Britain and Germany. Perhaps there are other events, the assassination of the Archduke Ferdinand, or whatever, which were, in the circumstances, necessary for both the battle and the war. But this does not undermine the claim that there were other events whose occurrence was necessary for the First World War, but not necessary for its component, the Battle of Jutland.

Two possible escape routes are open to Lewis. First, he might claim that the Battle of Jutland could not have occurred except as a part of the First World War. But this seems implausible. Suppose that Archduke Ferdinand's assassination led to all the declarations of war it actually did, but that Britain and Germany alone had the means necessary to fight and they had only a navy. Then the train of events at sea which led to a naval battle off Jutland in 1916 could have been much the same as it actually was, even though there was no European land war and thus no First World War. Surely this is a case of the Battle of Jutland occurring without the war occurring? In general, there will be some part of almost any event which can occur without the whole event occurring, and, so long as there are conditions necessary for the whole which are not necessary for the part, Lewis will be in trouble.

The second possible way out is to hold that the First World War would occur provided at least one of its component battles occurred. So the Battle of Jutland's occurrence would be sufficient for the whole war's occurrence. But again, this seems implausible. And it would be even more implausible to claim that the occurrence of any part of a given event, however trivial, is sufficient for the occurrence of the whole event. Yet only if the occurrence of each part is sufficient for the occurrence of the whole is it the case that any condition necessary for the whole must also be necessary for each part. It seems we must concede that there are some conditions necessary for the whole which are not necessary for each part.

At this stage, one might have the very sensible thought that Lewis' analysis of causation is unduly restrictive, since it takes no account of sufficiency conditionals. For example, I might express my opinion that a certain Polish man condemns sin because he is the Pope by means of the sufficiency conditional 'since he is the Pope, he would condemn sin wouldn't he?.' But it will not help us with the mereology of event-objects to analyse causation along the lines of: given the occurrence of the cause, the effect would occur.

I have urged that were causation really a relation between event-objects, a cause would bring about every part of its effect. Since we are regarding causes as sufficient for their effects, this implies that a cause of the whole must be sufficient for each of its parts. But, on a subjunctive analysis, all that being a sufficient cause of the whole entails is being a cause of every *essential* part of the whole, that is of every part without which the whole could not have occurred. The cause of the whole need not also be a cause of its accidental parts, the parts which it could have occurred without. So we might get a cause that is sufficient for an event without being sufficient for each of its parts.

Take the First World War once more. One of the parts of this war was the Battle of Jutland, but it would be implausible to claim that this war could not have occurred without the Battle of Jutland. Surely if the British and German fleets had missed one another in the fog, as they so nearly did, the same war would still have happened on land. So, to be sufficient for the First World War, it is not necessary to be sufficient for the Battle of Jutland. For analogous reasons it seems plausible to suppose that no individual battle was essential to the occurrence of the First World War. So a cause of the First World War need not be sufficient for any one of the individual battles which comprise the war. Perhaps all it need be sufficient for is grosser occurrences such as a general European land war.

At this point we might decide to depart from Lewis' declared position and say that the only parts of an event-object are its essential parts, those essential to its occurrence, thus evading the conclusion that one event-object can cause another without causing all of its parts, but this would lead us into difficulties with (8). Is writing the letter 'D' essentially a part of writing my name? Could I not have written my name even though I did not write the letter 'D' (i.e. if I had had a different name)? It does not seem at all strange to say that writing 'D' is only accidentally part of writing my name and thus no part at all on the current proposal. So, we are left without a reason to deny that (8) is a causal explanation.

I said earlier that these are weighty objections once we start to speak of event-objects and their parts as the relata of the causal relation. But, if we do not start, we can make perfect sense of the examples considered above.

There is surely a difference between being either necessary or sufficient for the truth of the statement 'There was a European war in 1914', and being either necessary or sufficient for the truth of the statement 'There was a naval battle off Jutland in 1916.' Why should anyone deny it? The difficulty arises only when we suppose that one event-object, an assassination in Sarajevo or whatever, brought about another event-object, a war, and that this 'bringing about' relation is to be analysed in terms of conditionals. By refusing to analyse causation as a relation between event-objects, we also escape intractable questions about which of its parts are essential to a given event and which are merely accidental. Again, all the causal facts can be stated without committing ourselves on such delicate metaphysical issues.

## CAUSATION AS CAUSAL EXPLANATION

In this chapter, we set out to tackle the problem of non-causal explanations by postulating event-objects and construing causation as a relation between these objects, a relation to be distinguished from the explanation of one sentence by means of another. The hope was that, by requiring every causal explanation to be underwritten by a causal relation between event-objects, we could separate genuine causal explanations from the impostors. This hope was not realised. I will now briefly argue that we need not follow Davidson, Lewis and many other philosophers in assuming that causal statements have a logical form quite distinct from that possessed by causal explanations.

In chapter 1, I hinted at a quite different treatment of causal statements, one which assimilates all such statements to causal explanations. Singular causal statements like (4) – the match's striking caused the match's lighting – are construed as follows: the match lit because the match was struck. So 'cause' is rendered by a sentential connective 'because', and does not denote a relation between event-objects. In general, a singular causal statement says that an object has one property at one time because some object had some property at another time.

Until now, when speaking on my own behalf, I have used the term 'event' not to refer to concrete particulars, but as a stand-in for the sentences which the causal 'because' connects. I was assuming that many of the expressions which apparently refer to event-objects, for instance 'the match's being struck', are just nominalisations of sentences like 'The match was struck' and thus should be treated as denoting what, if anything, the corresponding sentences refer to. This is all perfectly consistent with the following point: 'Events presumably are not linguistic entities ... Events and relations between events would exist even if there were no humans, or language, to describe them; there still would be earthquakes, collisions of particles, and expansions of metals caused by rising temperatures' (Kim, 1969:198). If there were no language, there would be no true sentences and no explanations could be given. Nevertheless, our sentences can be true of a world without language, so one phenomenon may causally explain another in the absence of any language.

When I say that causation is not a relation between event-objects, I do not mean to imply that no causal statement ever refers to event-objects. It *might* be best to construe 'the Second World War was long because Hitler was a fanatic' as saying that one object, a war, was long because another object, Hitler, was a fanatic – after all, 'war' is not easily read as a sentence nominal. But such an example gives us no reason to regard causation as a relation between event-objects; the causal facts are better expressed by a connective binding sentences which contain expressions referring to event-objects. Here a sentence ascribing one property to Hitler explains the truth of a sentence ascribing another property to a war. In what follows, the reader should keep in mind this distinction between 'events': the explanans and explananda of the explanatory relation and 'event-objects', the alleged relata of the two-place predicate 'cause'.

The following examples might be thought to present a difficulty:

(a) The war caused my death.
(b) What Brutus did on the Ides of March caused his downfall.[6]

Can these statements be construed without the aid of the two-place predicate 'cause'? Assuming that 'the war' in (a) refers to an event-object then (a) must be an elliptical statement, rather like 'Peter caused my death.' Were he confronted with 'Peter caused my death' Davidson would have to insist that the cause of my death is not Peter himself but some event involving Peter, such as Peter's firing a gun. I can make an analogous move with (a). It is not the war itself which explains the fact that I died, rather I died because the war spread to London, or whatever. So (a) is elliptical.

[6] I owe (a) and (b) to Michael Martin and Roger Teichmann respectively and I owe my treatment of (b) to Michael Martin.

In (b) 'what Brutus did on the Ides of March' is neither a nominalisation of a sentence nor a term denoting an event-object. Davidson would read it as a quantification over event-objects: 'there is an action $x$ such that Brutus did $x$ and $x$ was on the Ides of March and $x$ caused Brutus' downfall' (Davidson, 1980b). We might try to agree with Davidson that (b) quantifies over event-objects while rendering it as follows: Brutus fell because there was an action $x$ such that Brutus did $x$ and $x$ was on the Ides of March, or, more colloquially, Brutus fell because he did something on the Ides of March. Here the explanans sentence quantifies over event-objects, but there is no causal relation between event-objects, only an explanatory relation between sentences which quantify over event-objects.

Unfortunately, this construal of (b) does not capture the intended sense, since Brutus fell because of some specific thing he did on the Ides of March, and not just because he did something rather than nothing. What we need is a quantification into predicate position: Brutus acted in a certain way on the Ides of March, and he fell because he acted in that way. Such quantification into predicate position within an intensional context may be problematic, but we need to make sense of it in contexts which have nothing to do with causation or events: 'There's someone James believes to be a spy'. I see no reason why this general treatment should not then be applied to the cases which interest us.

To sum up, the way seems clear for us to treat all singular causal statements as of the general form '$p$ because $q$'. Nor is any advantage to be gained from bifurcating these statements into causal explanations of the form '$p$ because $q$' and causal statements of the form '$c$ causes $e$'.

# 4

# *Causal explanation*

In attempting an analysis of causation, I am traversing a terrain littered with the remains of other philosophical theories. Many of these theories foundered because they made a two-stage attack on the problem. They set out to define 'cause' in terms of 'law' in the hope of then explaining what a 'law' was in other terms, a task which turned out to be impossible. I shall tackle 'cause' and 'law' together by using the notion of a coincidence to analyse them both. The basic idea is that causes are events which ensure their effects are no coincidence. Laws are statements which support causal and other scientific explanations, that enable us to resolve coincidences, and it is this ability to resolve coincidences which gives laws their empirical character. I do not pretend that the notion of 'coincidence' itself can be analysed without reliance on modal vocabulary, but we can at least distinguish natural laws from other modal generalisations by reference to their empirical character. So both 'cause' and 'law' can be elucidated in other terms.

## EMPIRICAL CONTENT

In chapter 2 (pages 35–6), I observed that the language of science was full of dispositional notions. Terms for physical quantities, such as mass or electricity, are to be understood by reference to the usual behaviour of those quantities and substances in various circumstances. Indeed, it is hard to see how we could form a conception of the physical phenomena which enter into scientific laws other than in nomological terms; there simply is no other way we can think of them.[1] Given this, the following question arises: if scientific laws help to fix the meaning of scientific generalisations, at least some of those laws must be *a priori* truths, but if they are

---

[1] Several philosophers have argued that any conception we can form of a physical quantity or substance must be dispositional. See Ducasse, 1951: chapter 10, Holt, 1976:20–9, Robinson, 1982: chapter 7, and Blackburn, 1990:62–5.

*a priori* truths, what exactly is the difference between an empirical theory and a mathematical or logical theory, whose validity can be determined without experimentation. In what sense is science *a posteriori*?

I will tackle this question by means of a geometrical example. Suppose the following two generalisations are each used to specify what a triangle is:

L(1) A triangle is a figure bounded by three straight lines.
L(2) A triangle is a figure with interior angles of 180°.

A 'straight line' here is the shortest line between two points. Now it was thought, by philosophers like Kant, that L(1) and L(2) were generalisations devoid of empirical content. Not only were they each *a priori* truths, but it was an *a priori* truth that any figure which satisfied L(1)'s definition of a triangle would also satisfy L(2)'s. Of course, measurement and observation were required to determine whether the surface of a given physical object had a triangular shape, but it was not necessary to check both sides and angles in order to do this, for we knew *a priori* that there could be no physical object which both satisfied L(1) and falsified L(2).

However, it was also widely known that the fact that a figure satisfied L(1) did not, by itself, entail that it would also satisfy L(2) and *vice versa*. L(1) and L(2) are interderivable only given Euclid's axiom of parallels which, together with the other axioms, implies that through a point outside a given straight line, one, and only one, straight line can be drawn which fails to intersect the given line, no matter how far extended. In the nineteenth century, mathematicians formulated logically consistent geometries which denied this Euclidean axiom. Lobachevsky postulated that, through any given point, an infinitude of non-intersecting straight lines may be drawn, and derived the result that the sum of the interior angles of any triangle is less than 180°, while Riemann hypothesised that no non-intersecting lines could be drawn through a point outside a given line, and concluded that the interior angles of any triangle sum to more than 180°.

Earlier in our own century, Einstein described, in his Theory of General Relativity, a physical space-time which actually had a Riemannian structure, and his theory came to be widely accepted on the basis of measurement and experimentation. So the assertion that a figure which satisfies L(1) must satisfy L(2), far from being *a priori* true, had been shown to be false. This was not just the discovery that our world happens to contain no triangles, no figures which satisfy both L(1) and L(2), rather it was a demonstration that there could be no figures which satisfied both L(1) and L(2) and thus that Euclidean geometry provided an empirically inadequate model of the physical world. With this, the geometry of physical space and time had become a branch of physics.

Here we have an example in which a theory which was thought not to be an empirical theory acquired the status of an empirical theory. What changed exactly? One might think that what changed was the status of L(2): before the nineteenth century it was regarded as part of the definition of a triangle and thus as an *a priori* truth, after Einstein L(1) alone defined triangularity, and L(2) was a (false) empirical generalisation about triangles. This account has the slightly strange consequence that the meaning of 'triangle' must have changed during the nineteenth century, in order to allow an *a priori* truth to become an empirical falsehood. More importantly, it does not explain why physical geometry *as a whole* should have changed its epistemic status, rather than just individual geometric claims.

I shall say that, all along, the meaning of 'triangle' was fixed by a cluster of generalisations about triangles, but not until the nineteenth century did mathematicians realise that these generalisations determined criteria for the application of 'triangle' which were *logically independent* of one another (because the axiom of parallels could be replaced). When this was discovered, physics acquired a new job: to find out whether all those figures bounded by three straight sides had interior angles of 180°. Hence, the geometry of physical space *tout court* became a matter for empirical investigation. Physical geometry became a science not because some one generalisation somehow changed its epistemic status, but rather because it was discovered that its generalisations, taken together, made claims about the world which ran the risk of being false. When physicists established that these claims were false, they were faced with the choice of abandoning either L(1) or L(2). Considerations of theoretical simplicity etc. caused them to abandon L(2) rather than L(1). Since L(1) was still in place, this can be represented as the discovery that physical triangles have interior angles of more than 180°, rather than as the discovery that there are no physical triangles.[2]

What this example suggests is that a term like 'triangle' can play a role

---

[2] There is some overlap between this line of thought and that outlined in Putnam, 1975:42–54.

in a truly empirical theory provided the generalisations which give it meaning also ensure there are logically independent tests for whether something is a triangle or not. So long as it was thought that there were no such independent tests for triangularity, someone who believed Euclidean geometry to be true of the physical world felt he was taking no epistemic risks. He had to decide, by measurement, whether the theorems of his theory were relevant to a particular figure and he might be wrong about that, but there was no question of his measurements undermining the geometrical theory by showing that figures which satisfied some of his geometrical theorems did not satisfy others. Either the theory did apply or it did not, it could not apply and yet be falsified.

I should note that this example has a feature which does not generalise. It was discovered that the constraints placed on physical shapes by Euclidean geometry were physically inconsistent with one another – no triangle could satisfy both constraints – and so space was shown to be non-Euclidean. But a theory can equally well be refuted by demonstrating that it lays down two criteria for the application of a theoretical term, criteria which are physically independent of one another: some things satisfy both criteria, some neither, but others (the falsifiers) satisfy just one. And, of course, there are unrefuted physical theories whose terms have logically independent criteria of application, but which have been so successful that we may safely conclude it is no coincidence when these criteria are jointly satisfied.

Mellor gives us a fictional example of a theory which is open to refutation in a way different from our geometrical theory (Mellor, 1971:110–14). Say that the term 'tributary' is embedded in the following generalisations:

L(3) A tributary is the shorter of two river branches.
L(4) A tributary has the smaller volume flow of two river branches.

These are each statements of equivalence – each provide necessary and sufficient conditions for a river branch to be a tributary. They are manifestly logically independent and so the theory of tributaries is a theory with empirical content. Now we would not expect to discover that no river branch could satisfy both L(3) and L(4), but we might well observe branches which satisfied one but not the other. For example, it might be that the shorter of two river branches is sometimes also the one with a softer and more easily eroded bed. Thus the shorter branch burrows deeper than the main river, and its volume of flow comes to exceed it. If this could happen, we would be faced with a choice between qualifying or dropping either L(3) or L(4). In order to make that choice, we should have to look at the other law-like generalisations in which 'tributary' occurred, and how they would be affected, but, since this would involve more fiction, I shall not pursue the matter.

'Mass' is another instance of a theoretical term embedded in generalisations which give it logically independent application criteria. By considering Newton's second law (Force = Mass × Acceleration) we can see that a single generalisation may furnish us with logically independent tests for the application of the terms it employs; a single generalisation may have empirical content all by itself, provided it entails that the objects which instantiate it are disposed to engage in logically independent pieces of behaviour under various conditions. Newton's law, like many other physical laws, is a functional law; it states that certain physical quantities, which may assume many different values, will always satisfy a certain formula. And whether these quantities satisfy the formula when they assume one set of values is logically independent of whether they do so when they assume another.

If a ball has a mass of 3 grams, Newton's second law tells us it will accelerate at different rates upon the application of different forces. Now whether it accelerates at 5 meters per second per second upon the application of a force of 10 newtons is logically quite independent of whether it accelerates at 10 meters per second per second upon the application of a force of 20 newtons. Yet the second law predicts that, *ceteris paribus*, it will do both. Thus, this law is open to empirical testing on just this point. An inductive leap is needed to get from the fact that the ball's acceleration is 5 meters per second per second in the one case to its being 10 meters per second per second in the other. So the law gives 'mass of 3 grams' logically independent criteria of application.

When I speak of logical independence, I do not mean that it is merely a contingent fact that an object with a mass of three grams accelerates *both* at one rate under one force *and* at a different rate under another. Chapter 2 concluded that we cannot assume the contingency of natural laws. And if the causal laws which actually govern the behaviour of mass, force and acceleration were necessary truths, and Newton's laws were those laws, it would be a necessary truth that an object with a mass of 3 grams accelerates at these different rates under these different forces. What I mean by 'logically independent' is that *a priori* reasoning alone cannot enable us to infer that the object will behave in one way, given that it behaves in the other. If there are necessary truths in this area, it requires empirical investigation to establish them.

But someone may still wonder why the sheer number of independent criteria of application should matter so much. Given a term T(1) with only one criterion of application or with several criteria which are not logically independent of one another, we still have to carry out an empirical investigation in order to determine whether a given object satisfies T(1). The difference between this and the rather more difficult task of determining whether our object satisfies a term T(2) with two mutually independent criteria of application seems one of degree rather than of kind. Why do we pass into the realm of empirical science just when we have to deal with T(2) rather than T(1)? My reply has been that empirical theories (a) lay down generalisations which govern the application of their terms, and (b) assert that either an object satisfies all of these generalisations or else it satisfies none of them. Where these generalisations are logically independent, such a claim can be shown to be false by a specific object, but where they are not, this cannot happen.

This reply leads me onto my next point. It is characteristic of science that it goes beyond mere classification and delivers explanation. To explain in the way that empirical theories explain is precisely to assert that the joint satisfaction of independent criteria of application for a theoretical term is no coincidence. So while T(1) may serve many classificatory purposes, only the introduction of terms like T(2) opens up the possibility of scientific explanation. One can explain, in this empirical fashion, without offering a causal explanation, and I shall consider some non-causal explanations later on in this chapter but, for now, let us ignore them and concentrate on the very many explanations offered by scientists which clearly are causal, and, in particular, on those involving dispositional terms.

## CAUSAL EXPLANATION

Several philosophers have claimed that a disposition must have independent displays if it is to explain them (Mellor, 1971:76–82 and 114–21; Mellor, 1974:174–7). This stipulation has been used to rule out vacuous dispositions, such as the dormitive virtue of sleeping pills, on the grounds that a genuine disposition, one which explains sleep, must have more than one type of effect. Intuitively, there must be more explanatory potential in the *explanans* than the fact that it explains the *explanandum*, otherwise the explanation is empty. The *explanandum* need not actually explain anything else, but it must have the ability to do so. To put the point in an epistemic key, it should be possible to run an independent check on the presence of the *explanans*, independent that is of the occurrence of the type of event it is currently explaining, and such an independent check will be possible only if the dormitive virtue does things besides put people to sleep.

However, we must be careful not to misconstrue this 'multiple-display' requirement. The fundamental problem with dormitive virtues is that the ascription of a dormitive virtue does not tell us under what circumstances the pill will put someone to sleep. Once it is said that sleep will result only when the pill is administered in conditions $C$, we have automatically satisfied the multiple display requirement, since we have implicitly committed ourselves to the hypothesis that under not-$C$ conditions (*ceteris paribus*) a different effect will occur, namely full consciousness. And this is something which cannot be logically deduced from what happens under $C$-conditions alone. In general, if object $x$ behaves in way $P$ in some circumstances but not others, we may ascribe to $x$ a genuine disposition to do $P$ in some circumstances $C(1)$ and not-$P$ under other conditions $C(2)$. The truly vacuous disposition is one which would display itself to all and sundry in every possible circumstance.[3]

Our concept of mass is a concept of a physical quantity with a complex causal role. I have argued that any such physical quantity must explain different outcomes in different circumstances. Shoemaker propounds the following thesis:

Conditional powers X and Y belong to the same property if and only if it is a consequence of causal laws that either (1) whatever has either of them has the other, or (2) there is some third conditional power such that whatever has it has both X and Y. (Shoemaker, 1984:224)

A conditional power is just a power displayed under certain conditions. Two conditional powers are distinct if they are logically independent, that is if an object's having the one power entails nothing about whether it will have the other. An object which produces logically independent effects $e(1)$ and $e(2)$ under conditions $C(1)$ and $C(2)$ has a couple of powers, but so too does an object which produces $e(1)$ under $C(1)$ and not-$e(1)$ under not-$C(1)$, provided these powers are logically independent.

[3] Reichenbach's principle that all universal forces should be set to zero is relevant here. See Reichenbach, 1958:24–8.

Shoemaker's point is that if a property is associated with more than one power it should be no coincidence that objects with this property have all of these powers. If the same (dispositional) property of a ball explains why it accelerates at 10 meters per second per second under a force of 5 newtons, and at 20 meters per second per second under a force of 10 newtons, it must be no coincidence that the ball behaves like this on these two different occasions, that it has these two conditional powers. As Shoemaker remarks, to associate different conditional powers with a single property, to discover which combinations of powers, and thus of effects, are no coincidence, we must engage in empirical inquiry (Shoemaker, 1984:222–5).

Mellor observes that 'we *could* construe a thing's inertial mass as a mere conjunction of two properties, one displayed in accelerations under forces up to (say) 1 newton, the other displayed in accelerations under greater forces' (Mellor, 1974:176). Why do we not? Well, if we did it would look like an amazing coincidence that the ball accelerated at certain rates under some forces and at other rates under different forces, for these facts would be owing to the ball's possession of two independent properties. But why acknowledge such a coincidence when there is a perfectly decent hypothesis, namely that the same mass explains both accelerations? As many philosophers have pointed out, the fact that the hypothesis eliminates such coincidences is, *ceteris paribus*, a good reason to believe it.[4]

Shoemaker claims that a property *just is* a set of causal powers with a certain causal unity. I do not wish to endorse this claim, but we can turn his remark around and formulate a thesis about causation: a causal explanation ascribes a property to a certain object, a property which is necessary and sufficient for the occurrence of one effect (under some circumstances) and necessary and sufficient for the occurrence of other logically independent effects (under different circumstances) and which would ensure that if these effects all occurred, their joint occurrence would be no coincidence. These different effects may occur either at different moments between which conditions around the object change, or simultaneously if the prevailing circumstances relevant to one are different from those relevant to the other. And the fact that these effects are logically independent of one another ensures that we cannot determine *a priori* whether their joint occurrence is a coincidence or not.

---

[4] This mode of inference is known as 'inference to the best explanation'. For one excellent discussion of its role in scientific inquiry, see Salmon, 1984:213–27.

This is my analysis of causal explanation in terms of the notion of a coincidence. Since I make no distinction between causation and causal explanation, it can also be treated as an analysis of causation.

## NON-CAUSAL EXPLANATION

Two tasks lie ahead. First, I must apply my account of the explanations which empirical science delivers to distinguish causal explanations from those non-causal explanations considered in chapter 3. Second, I must deal with those explanations delivered by empirical science which are non-causal explanations. This section is devoted to the former task and my final section to the latter.

We can cope with

(7) Gauss was surprised because of the convergence of series S.

without applying a metaphysical criterion to sort event-objects into the real and the unreal. Causal explanations are supported by generalisations with empirical content, and such generalisations have, as their instances, explanations made up of sentential components which admit of spatio-temporal qualification. On these grounds we may insist that the sentential components of a causal explanation must be qualifiable by spatio-temporal operators and the sentence 'series S converges' clearly fails this test. (7) only looks as if it might be supported by empirical generalisations because we confuse it with 'Gauss was surprised because he discovered that series S converges' where this last sentence is an explanation whose explanans does admit of spatio-temporal qualification.

What of

(8) I wrote my name, in part because I wrote 'D'.

The relevant question to ask is this: from which generalisation does the subjunctive 'if I had not written the letter "D", I would not have written my name' receive support? The salient generalisation states that to write the whole of a name you must write each part, the writing of each letter comprising a name is necessary for the writing of the whole name; in general, the existence of the whole requires the existence of each of its parts. Here several conditions must be fulfilled for my name to be written, but it would hardly be possible to discover that while one needed to write some parts of a name in order to write the whole name, one did not need to write certain other parts. Nor would it be possible to discover that a given letter, part of more than one name, was necessary for the writing of only some of the names of which it was a part. So the generalisation supporting (8) is not subject to independent tests and lacks the required empirical content.

It might help to introduce a slightly different example at this point.

> (14) My car was touching the pavement because its front wheel was touching the pavement.[5]

It is, I take it, perfectly clear that (14) does not constitute a causal explanation, despite the truth of the relevant conditionals. Advocates of event-objects will claim that this is because the event of my wheel's touching the pavement was part of the event of my car's touching the pavement. Alternatively, we should highlight the following generalisation as the one which ensures that my wheel's disposition is sufficient for my car's disposition: for all objects $x$ and $y$, if a part of $x$ touches a part of $y$ then $x$ touches $y$. Now, upon realising the truth of this generalisation for some pair $x$ and $y$ in respect of one of their parts, we need hardly confirm that it is so in respect of their other parts, or in respect of parts of other pairs of objects. Therefore, this generalisation lacks suitable empirical content and (14) is a non-causal explanation.

Our other examples

> (9) I broke the law because I parked on a double yellow line.
> (10) I became an uncle yesterday because Mary gave birth yesterday.

yield to the same treatment. The subjunctive 'if I had not parked on a double yellow line, I would not have broken the law' is supported by a law of the state rather than a law of nature. A law of state is not an empirical generalisation, it is not refuted by crime – hence the need for a police force. Further, it is an *a priori* truth that if my sister has a baby then I become an uncle. To say that I became an uncle because my sister had a baby is not to say something which might be falsified by observing the other 'effects' of my sister's having a baby. One could hardly remark: 'are you sure that's what went on? Let's not commit ourselves until we see what has happened to your other siblings.' It would make no sense to wait for confirmation that my brothers have become uncles and my sisters have become aunts before concluding that my transformation has been explained correctly. To put it another way, the generalisation

---

[5] The example comes from Jackson, 1977:18.

connecting my sister's having a baby with my assumption of unclehood does not provide for logically independent effects of the birth, and so it is without empirical content.

Much the same can be said of

(11) I built the second tree house because you built the first tree house.

A generalisation about numerical ordering in time will ensure that the removal of your tree house from the top of the list of tree houses would have consequences for the rank ordering of everyone else's tree house. But there would be no point in checking that the third tree house had become the second one at the moment when the second became the first. No inductive leap is needed to get from some one of these effects to the occurrence of the others. Therefore, this explanans-event lacks logically independent effects.

Perhaps I am not quite out of the woods yet. In order to put (8) and (10) into contact with non-empirical generalisations, I surreptitiously redescribed the objects implicated in these explanations. I substituted 'my sister' for 'Mary' and 'the first letter of my name' for 'the letter "D"'' and there is no analytical connection between the properties mentioned in either pair of descriptions. Might this process of redescription not equally well be used to put (8) and (10) into contact with empirical generalisations, thereby 'demonstrating' that they are causal explanations after all?

Kim places a limit on such redescription which would enable us to bring (8) and (10) under the relevant non-empirical generalisations while isolating them from other, empirical generalisations. He argues that explanatory contexts are referentially transparent, so when one says truly that the $R$ is $P$ because the $S$ is $Q$, one may substitute co-referring expressions for 'the $R$' and 'the $S$' without fear of rendering the sentence false.[6] Here what gets redescribed is not an event-object, the having of some property, which poses as the relatum of a causal relation, but rather the object which has the property. And mere redescription of the objects implicated in (8) and (10) could not ensure that these explanatory statements (when properly interpreted) were supported by generalisations with empirical content. For instance, in (8), what is up for explanation is my assumption of unclehood and the job is done by

---

[6] Kim, 1969:204–13. In this paper Kim also rebuts a couple of objections to the transparency thesis which I shall not discuss myself. The first objection is raised in Davidson, 1980a:152–3. The second is raised in Mellor, 1987:120–1.

referring to a women who is in fact my sister. I do not see how a different, empirically based explanation of this fact could be constructed just by redescribing my sister and I.

Several philosophers have contradicted Kim by arguing that explanatory contexts may not be referentially transparent (Anscombe, 1981b:175–6 and Mackie, 1974: chapter 10). For example, should I set out to explain to someone why I became an uncle yesterday, telling them that Mary gave birth will do no good at all unless they already know, or can infer from what I say that Mary is my sister. Nor will it be clear to them why I had to write 'D' in order to write my name unless they are already aware, or come to believe, that 'D' is part of my name. So it does seem to matter how the objects implicated in an explanation are described. The explanation leaves a lot to be desired if the objects involved are referred to in an inappropriate manner.

However, there is a great difference between producing an explanatory statement which is not very helpful and producing one which is literally false. (8) and (10) are, as they stand, perfectly true statements, though they may not be very useful to the ill-informed or dim-witted. Whether an explanation tells an audience what they need to know will be a function of what the audience already knows, but the truth value of an explanatory statement is not. As I said in chapter 1 (pages 9–10), the speaker's beliefs about his audience help to determine what explanatory question is being asked and answered, so the meaning of an explanatory statement does depend on its context of utterance. But once the explanatory question is fixed, the truth value of the statement which answers it may be determined independently of the audience's knowledge. Mary's giving birth explains why I became an uncle regardless of whether anyone knows that Mary is my sister.

I want to round off this section by considering two types of explanation which some philosophers have held to be non-causal. Consider first: 'I turned on the light because I flicked the switch' – this is clearly an explanation, but is it a causal explanation? Several philosophers have claimed that while my flicking the switch caused the light to go on, my flicking the switch did not cause my turning on of the light. For Davidson and Hornsby, these two actions, the flicking and the turning on, are causally unrelated because they are the very same event-object and nothing can bring itself about (Davidson, 1980c and Hornsby, 1980b). For Goldman and Kim, these two event-objects are not identical, rather they stand in some constitutive and *non-causal* relation (Goldman,

1970 and Kim, 1974:44–7). Since there is no causal relation in the offing, presumably we are meant to infer that our explanation of the light's coming on is a non-causal explanation.

If these philosophers are correct, my analysis of causal explanation must be deemed inadequate, for there is no non-empirical generalisation which says that my flicking the switch is either necessary or sufficient for my turning on the light. However, I am inclined to question orthodoxy on this point. There seems nothing wrong with the sentence 'His flicking the switch causally explains his turning on the light.' One engenders a difficulty only by first thinking of the relata of the causal relation as event-objects (actions) with definite locations and then wondering how these event-objects can be distinct when my turning on the light appears to occupy the same spatio-temporal slot as my flicking the switch.

I do not wish to prejudice the question as to whether actions are event-objects; my point is only that causal relations do not obtain between event-objects. So, for the sake of argument, let us suppose these actions are event-objects and that they are identical. In that case, why should the truth of 'His action was a flicking of the switch' not causally explain the truth of 'His action was a turning on of the light', as an object's having one property may causally explain why that very object acquires another property? These properties are not acquired by the action simultaneously, for the action becomes a turning on of the light at the moment when the light has come on, and that presumably occurs only after this action has become a flicking of the switch. The fact that the event-object in question occupies the same spatial zone throughout its existence is, in itself, no objection. There would be a problem here only if we thought that this event-object was present at both ends of a causal relation, bringing itself into existence.

Can we also allow some part of an event-object's having a certain property to cause the whole event-object to have some property? I do not see why not. Consider: 'The Second World War lasted for 5 years rather than 4 because of the Germans' determined resistance to the Soviet advance.' Presumably, 'the German's determined resistance to the Soviet advance' will be thought to denote an event-object which is part of the event-object denoted by 'the Second World War'. And I can see no objection to saying that the German resistance caused the war to be prolonged. Again, it is only if there is some causal relation which obtains between these event-objects themselves that we get the absurdity of an object bringing some part of itself into existence.

Jackson and Pettit give us our second example of an apparently non-causal explanation.

> Electrons A and B are acted on by independent forces F(A) and F(B) respectively, and electron A then accelerates at the same rate as electron B. The explanation of this fact is that the magnitude of the two forces is the same ... [Yet] this sameness does not make A move off more or less briskly; what determines the rate at which A accelerates is the magnitude of F(A), not that magnitude's relationship to another force altogether ... Or, in other words, the equality *per se* of the forces acting on the electrons does not do any causal work. The work is all done by the individual forces acting on the electrons. (And if the equality *per se* did do some work, how remarkable that it arranges to do exactly the right amount so as not to conflict with the result produced by the individual forces). (Jackson and Pettit, 1988:392–3)

Were this the correct description of the case, we would have on our hands a non-causal explanation which is supported by the *a posteriori* laws of mechanics. But I find it hard to dredge up from the passage any cogent argument for the causal inefficacy of the similarity between these electrons.[7]

One possible line of thought is this: similarities and differences cannot be causally efficacious because they are relational properties. But I do not find this very convincing. If two thing's having a certain relational property is constituted by their having certain intrinsic properties, and if these intrinsic properties are causally efficacious, why should this causal efficacy not be inherited by the relational features which they constitute, at least where the relational feature is not a simple conjunction or unnatural agglomeration of the intrinsic? Nor would this relational property be some kind of causal competitor to the intrinsic properties – they can hardly conflict when the possession of the relational property is nothing over and above the possession of the intrinsic.

Jackson and Pettit point out that electron A would accelerate as it did even if a quite different force were applied to B, so the similarity in the forces is irrelevant to A's acceleration. But this depends on what it is about A's acceleration we wish to have explained. Were B to experience a different force from A, something about A's acceleration certainly

---

[7] Jackson and Pettit themselves conclude that this is a causal explanation, but only because they reject the assumption that 'causal explanations that proceed by citing some feature must cite a causally efficacious or productive feature' (1988:392). I wish to retain this assumption, and so must argue that the explanation does cite a causally efficacious feature, namely a similarity. In Owens, 1989c, I arrived at the opposite conclusion about this example. See also chapter 1, pages 14–15.

would change, namely it would no longer be the same as B's. And why should this change be unamenable to causal explanation? The bracketed phrase suggests that A and B's acceleration would be overdetermined if we allowed the similarity in the forces applied to be causally efficacious but, since A and B's experiencing the same force is *constituted* by their experiencing the individual forces which they do, this simply does not follow. Jackson and Pettit have not given us an example of a non-causal explanation.

## CONSTITUTIVE EXPLANATION AND EVENT CONSTITUTION

Here is the story so far: causal explanations involve generalisations which support subjunctive conditionals, necessity and sufficiency conditionals, conditionals whose antecedents (the explaining events) can render the occurrence of logically independent effects no coincidence. Laws are precisely those generalisations which can play this role, and it is their ability to play this role which gives them empirical content. Causes and laws are simultaneously identified by their power to resolve coincidences.

This story implies that every explanation backed by empirical law is a causal explanation, and that every causal explanation is backed by an empirical law. However, it is not hard to produce examples of non-causal explanations supported by empirical laws and of causal explanations supported by no empirical law. Since some of these examples are perfectly genuine, I must complicate my account so as to accommodate them. But once this has been done, we are still left with the conclusion that 'cause' and 'natural law' are each to be analysed in terms of 'coincidence'.

Two examples already introduced raise the issue of causal explanations backed by no empirical law. Here are the causal explanatory counterparts of (12) and (13):

(12′) There was a defeat because of the circumstances which explain the defeat.
(13′) He died because of the fatal wound he received.

These statements are surely true and yet the relevant subjunctives rest on generalisations which lack any empirical content. We do not have to look to other effects of the defeat to check that they are caused by the defeat, and death from a fatal wound is *a priori* inevitable (unless another cause of death supervenes).

Here, we must acknowledge a principled exception to the requirement that causal subjunctives be supported by generalisations with empirical content. Some non-empirical generalisations are such that the objects instantiating them do so only in virtue of having properties distinct from those mentioned in the non-empirical generalisation itself, properties which are connected by some generalisation with empirical content. To say that the cause of the defeat caused the defeat is just to say that some object had some property, the having of which causally explained the defeat. To say that the fatal wound caused the death is just to say that there was some property of the wound the having of which causally explained the death. Each of these underlying causal explanations will rest on some suitable generalisation. So a causal explanation may be supported by a non-empirical generalisation provided this generalisation is instantiated only in virtue of the instantiation of some empirical generalisation.

I promised in chapter 1 to say more about event-constitution, a promise already redeemed to some extent by my discussion of (8) and (14). I propose to formulate an account of event-constitution in terms of the sentential connective, 'true in virtue of', rather than by using a relational predicate satisfied by concrete particulars. But what does this connective mean?

The obvious reply is to analyse 'true in virtue of' in terms of entailment: my car is touching the pavement in virtue of its front wheel's touching the pavement because the front wheel's touching the pavement entails that the car to which it is attached is also touching the pavement. Generalising: $p$ is true in virtue of $q$ if, and only if, there is some *non-empirical* generalisation which ensures that $q$ is a sufficient condition for $p$. This account neatly fits the case of the constituents of a coincidence. A non-empirical generalisation underwrites the entailment of 'We coincided at the station' by a combination of 'You were at the station at noon today' and 'I was at the station at noon today', so there can be no causal relation between this coincidence and its constituent events.[8]

The relation of event-constitution, so defined, will hold between states of affairs which might be regarded as involving quite distinct event-objects, for example your tree house being first and mine being second. Furthermore, it will not be asymmetric. But these differences between event and object constitution mean only that I may help myself to the

---

[8] Compare Jackson, 1977:15–9 and Owens, 1989c:52–6.

former relation with a clear conscience. Using this relation, we have an analogue of Hume's (3): causes cannot be constituents of their effects. And we can also formulate a more relaxed version of Hume's (2) by allowing that some *a priori* knowable generalisations may support a causal statement provided the causally related events fall under them in virtue of their instantiating some empirical generalisation.

But the relation of event-constitution just introduced cannot help us with empirical laws which do not support causal explanations. Are there not legions of non-causal laws, perfectly empirical but making no mention of causation? What exactly differentiates them from the causal laws which support causal explanations?

For a start, we must note that laws which make no mention of causation may nevertheless support causal explanations. As I indicated in chapter 2 (pages 25–6), generalisations such as the Boyle–Charles law lay down a functional relationship between several variables: temperature, pressure and volume. It does not stipulate that a change in temperature is the cause of any change in pressure or volume or *vice-versa* – the word 'cause' occurs nowhere in the law – but it does help to support assertions about the causal order of events in individual cases. For instance, I compress the gas in a certain container and the pressure rises as a result – here the pressure rose because the volume decreased. True, the law alone would not tell us that a reduction in volume was the cause, but the law, together with the pattern of coincidences engendered by the operation of this and other laws, entails that the volume changed the pressure and not *vice versa*.

In chapter 5, I shall describe how this pattern of coincidences gives direction to causation. Once that has been done, we can rule out one class of non-causal explanations – those explanations supported by empirical law which are non-causal because they fail to respect the direction of causation. I want to conclude this chapter by examining a rather different class of non-causal explanations, again supported by empirical law, which I shall call constitutive explanations.

Is (15) a causal explanation?

(15) The temperature of this gas is rising because the kinetic energy of its constituent molecules is increasing.

No-one could deny the truth of the subjunctive 'if the kinetic energy of the gas' constituent molecules had not increased, its temperature would not have risen'. Furthermore it was an empirical discovery that the temperature of a gas was associated with the kinetic energy of its molecules, no non-empirical generalisation connects heat with molecular motion. So must I not claim that (15) is a causal explanation? Yet the universal consensus is that (15) is non-causal because the rise in temperature *just is* the increase in kinetic energy. These are not separate phenomena, one of which might causally explain the other (Achinstein, 1983:235–7, Lewis, 1986c:223–4).

The 'in virtue of' relation and a notion of event-constitution formulated by means of it cannot help here. Rather, what we have is an empirically established property identity: temperature = mean kinetic energy. So the point must be this: '$y$ is $Q$ at $t(2)$ because $x$ is $P$ at $t(1)$' cannot be a causal explanation where $x = y$, $P = Q$ and $t(1) = t(2)$. Explanations like this are constitutive explanations and constitutive explanations cannot be causal. But what is it for two properties to be identical, for '$P = Q$' to be true?

Let us consider how scientists arrived at (15). 'Temperature' appears in certain laws about gases, for example the Boyle–Charles Law relating the temperature, pressure and volume of a certain gas. For instance, if we heat a certain quantity of gas in a container and want to keep the pressure exerted by the gas on the edges of the container constant, we must allow the container to expand; the rise in temperature is the cause of this expansion. So temperature is, among other things, that property of gases which causes their containers to expand under these conditions. Maxwell and Boltzmann demonstrated that this expansion was caused by an increase in the kinetic energy of the gas' constituent molecules. But they did not regard themselves as having discovered a cause of the expansion distinct from the rise in temperature, a cause which, together with the temperature, either jointly determined or overdetermined the expansion. Rather they thought they had disclosed what the cause of the expansion was, what it was for the gas to have that temperature.

So, the empirical work involved in establishing that temperature is kinetic energy has been completed once we have shown kinetic energy to be responsible for the expansion of gas containers under some conditions, and other effects under other conditions – no *further* empirical work is required for us to arrive at the conclusion that temperature in a gas is constituted by the kinesis of the gas's molecular energy, and thus that, when the gas' temperature rises, this is because the kinetic energy of its constituent molecules has increased, for 'temperature' gets its meaning from the generalisations which connect it with such causes and effects.

This suggests that statements like 'temperature = mean kinetic energy' are based on statements like 'the occupant of causal role C = the occupant of causal role D'. Shoemaker expresses a similar thought in the passage quoted earlier

> Conditional powers X and Y belong to the same property if and only if it is a consequence of causal laws that either (1) whatever has either of them has the other, or (2) there is some third conditional power such that whatever has it has both X and Y. (Shoemaker, 1984:224)

Previously, my discussion concentrated on Clause (2) but we should now note Clause (1)'s claim that if two properties have the same conditional powers associated with them, they are the same property. The implication here is that properties are to be individuated by their causal roles. In chapter 2, I declined to endorse Shoemaker's arguments for the view that properties have their causal roles essentially, but it may well be that such a view provides the best account of empirically established property identities.

Whatever view one takes of property identity, one must allow for *a posteriori* property identities, and these identities can be used to explain why statements like (15) are non-causal. The fact that the gas molecules have a certain mean kinetic energy certainly explains the fact that the gas has a certain temperature. Nevertheless, since to have a certain mean kinetic energy just is to have a certain temperature, this explanation is non-causal. Much the same should be said about the statements 'this figure has three sides because it is a triangle' or 'this figure has three sides because it has interior angles of $x°$'. To have any of these three geometrical properties *just is* to have the other – these properties could not play different causal roles – so explanatory statements linking them are empirical but non-causal explanations.

# 5

# *The direction of causal explanation*

While causes explain their effects, effects do not explain their causes – this fact is constitutive of the causal relation. If the striking of the match caused it to light, then the match's lighting cannot have been a cause of its striking. If we can explain why the match lit by mentioning the striking, we cannot also explain why the striking took place by referring to the lighting.[1] So much is obvious, but analysts of causation have found the obvious hard to digest.

Take our causal claim: 'the match's being struck caused the house to burn'. What makes this assertion true? An obvious starting place is the thought that this causal statement is true because a struck match was either necessary or sufficient, or both necessary and sufficient, for the house to burn. To express this in terms of subjunctive conditionals: 'the house burnt because the match was struck' is true if, and only if, either 'if the match had not been struck then the house would not have burnt' is true, or 'the house would have burnt given that the match was struck' is true, or both are true. But this simple suggestion quickly comes to grief.

If there is a law of nature which ensures that the striking of a match is necessary and sufficient for a fire then it will equally be a law of nature that a fire is necessary and sufficient for a striking. If a striking is just sufficient for a fire, then a fire will be necessary for a striking and the absence of a fire will be sufficient for the absence of a striking. On the other hand, if a striking is necessary for a fire, then a fire will be sufficient for a striking and the absence of a fire will be necessary for the absence of a striking. Relations of nomological dependence are temporally reversible

[1] These formulations would have to be amended if causal loops were possible. Suppose that within a causal loop every event causes every other event. Nevertheless there is definite order in which events must be taken if each is to explain the occurrence of the next event. We cannot go round the loop in any direction we please. To accommodate causal loops, we should stipulate that the causal relation is temporally *oriented* rather than temporally asymmetric. For simplicity, I will ignore this qualification.

in a way that relations of causal dependence could not be. So '*x*'s having
*P* causes *y* to have *Q*' cannot mean anything like: *x* has *P* and *y* has *Q*,
and there is a law which ensures that *P*-events are either necessary or
sufficient for *Q*-events.[2]

It seems that regularity theories of causation are in deep trouble.
However, the reversibility of these relations of nomological dependence
can be expressed in terms of so-called 'back-tracking' conditionals, so the
difficulty which afflicts regularity analyses of causation arises for
subjunctive analyses also. We may suppose the match being struck caused
the house to burn because if the match had not been struck then the house
would not have burnt. But might it not be equally correct to say that if
the house had not burnt, the match would not have been struck? After
all, there is a law which ensures that any match struck in those
circumstances would have to cause burning. Furthermore another way
for the causal statement to be true is in virtue of the fact that the house
would have burnt given that the match was struck. But might it not be
equally correct to say that if the house burnt, the match would have to
have been struck. How else would the house have burnt?

Most often, it is quite certain that the fire in the house did not cause the
match to be struck. So the reversibility of nomological dependence
cannot mean the reversibility of causal dependence. Given that, we have
two alternatives. The first is to cling onto a subjunctive analysis of
causation while seeking to separate subjunctive from nomological
dependence. Lewis takes this route by maintaining that subjunctive
dependence does not inherit the reversibility of nomological dependence.
I shall examine his views later. The other option is to insist that causation
involves more than either nomological or subjunctive dependence – it
requires explanation.

There is a third escape route which should be mentioned: stipulate that
the direction of causation *is* the direction of time. As things are, causes
always precede their effects, so we could stipulate that the cause is the
earlier event and, since temporal priority is an asymmetric relation, this

---

[2] For a more sophisticated analysis of causation in terms of necessary and sufficient
conditions see Mackie, 1965. Mackie explicitly acknowledges the difficulty about the
direction of causation, but his eighteenth- and nineteenth-century predecessors did not.
Hume, 1978:75–6 and Mill, 1906:225 both analysed causation in terms of necessary and
sufficient conditions, but neither felt any need to explain why causes should precede their
effects. Indeed, philosophers still advance theories of causation while either declining to
address this issue or avoiding it by stipulation: two among many are Ducasse,
1951:105–6 and Eells, 1991: chapter 5.

will ensure the asymmetry of causation. The match's striking caused the fire to light and not *vice versa* because it occurred before the fire's lighting. I have two reasons for abjuring this stipulation. First, there is nothing incoherent about simultaneous or backwards causation; though such phenomena may not actually occur, I believe they are perfectly possible. But even if they were impossible, some subtle metaphysical argumentation is needed to rule them out and not just a gesture towards the meaning of the word 'cause'. Secondly, ensuring, by stipulation, that causation was temporally asymmetric would not help us with the explanatory asymmetry. It would still be an open question why earlier causes explained later effects and not *vice versa*. Much better to provide a theory of causal explanation which underwrites the explanatory asymmetry and, in the process, accounts for the apparent temporal asymmetry of causation also.

In my view, the source of the trouble lies in the weakness of the notion of causal explanation used by analysts of causation. We need only adopt the stronger notion delineated in chapter 1 for it to become obvious that causal explanation has a temporal direction. Causal explanation has a temporal direction because if we move through the causal nexus in the past-to-future direction, we find fewer coincidences than if we run through it in the opposite direction. And since coincidences are inexplicable, someone interested in causal explanation should minimise their number. If, as I urged in chapter 4, causation is causal explanation, we may identify the direction of causation with the direction of causal explanation and our problem is solved.


## CAUSAL FORKS

A common cause explains the co-occurrence of two effects while a common effect does not explain the co-occurrence of two causes. When the commander of the firing squad barks 'Fire' this accounts for the simultaneous firing of a bullet from two different guns, while the simultaneous firing of these bullets cannot be explained by reference to the fact that they each cause the death of the executed man. This looks like a special case of the general explanatory asymmetry between causes and effects but it has been suggested that this special case may account for the general asymmetry rather than *vice versa*.

## (a) Mackie

Say that a match's striking is followed by two events, a little light is shed on a room and the room's temperature goes up by a fraction. We may suppose that these events could have been predicted by laws which stipulate that, when such a match is surrounded by a medium that is both transparent and conducts heat (and various other conditions obtain), the match's striking will be followed by the heating and by the illumination of the room in which it is struck. Suppose further that these laws ensure that in those circumstances, if the room was both lighted and warmed, there must have been an earlier match striking. Here we have what I shall call a nomological fork.

In a nomological fork, three events are connected by laws of nature which ensure that each is necessary and sufficient for the other. *Ex hypothesi*, the striking is necessary and sufficient, in the circumstances, for both the heating and the lighting. Since 'is necessary and sufficient for' is a symmetrical relation, we may infer that the heating and the lighting are themselves necessary and sufficient for the striking. And since 'is necessary and sufficient for' is a transitive relation, we may infer that the heating and the lighting are necessary and sufficient for one another. So how are we to discern a causal asymmetry in this nomological fork when the nomological relations among its constituent events are reversible in time?

I shall approach this issue by raising a rather different and apparently unrelated question. The nomological fork just described has the feature that an earlier event, a striking, is both necessary and sufficient for two later events, the heating and the lighting. My question is: might some other fork have the opposite feature, might there not be two earlier events each necessary and sufficient for a common later event?

Mackie denies that such forks are possible. We can easily imagine cases of overdetermination: the striking of the match would have been overdetermined if it were preceded both by my hand movement and by a sudden extremely concentrated gust of wind blowing the match along the box. There is a law which ensures that each of these events is sufficient for the match to be struck. But, Mackie says, there definitely will not be a law of nature which ensures that such movements are always accompanied by gusts of wind, so there will be no nomological fork which includes the striking, the gust and the hand movement (Mackie, 1974:164–5).

Why will there be no such law? Why can we not derive such a law from generalisations which tell us that, in certain circumstances, both the movement and the gust are necessary for the striking to occur? Mackie does not say, but the point must be that the background conditions which would ensure that the gust of wind was necessary are inconsistent with those which would ensure that the hand movement was necessary. The conditions in which the gust would be required to effect the striking are precisely those in which no hand movement would occur and *vice versa*. Therefore, we cannot, by combining these background conditions, derive a law which says that, in the circumstances, both were necessary (Papineau, 1985:280).

Compare our overdetermination fork with a genuine nomological fork. The presence of a translucent medium (among other things) guarantees that the striking is sufficient for the illumination, and thus that the illumination is necessary for the striking. This is all quite consistent with the presence of a conducting medium which means that the striking is sufficient for the heating, and thus that the heating is necessary for the striking. Therefore, one can derive a law which says that when a medium with both properties is present, both events are necessary for the striking and thus each is necessary for the other.

Now let us return to the issue we started out with. Implicit in Mackie's discussion is an atemporal criterion for the temporal direction of causation. Whenever we come across a nomological fork, we can distinguish the root event from the tip events as follows: some of the laws linking the three events in the fork will be derived from other such laws, and the tips of the fork are those events which are linked by a law that is derived from the law linking both of those tips with the root event. This is a contextual definition of 'root event' and 'tip event', and it is one which makes no use of the terms 'earlier' and 'later'. In our example, the law saying that the heating and the lighting are each both necessary and sufficient for the other is derived from the law linking each of these events with the striking. So the striking is the root event. We can now state our criterion: take any natural process with a nomological fork in it, we can confidently identify the event at the root of the fork as the cause, and the events at the tips of the fork as the effects, and can do this without regard to the temporal order in which these events occur.

Have we succeeded in giving direction to causation? We have certainly fashioned a criterion which differentiates the overdetermination forks that we commonly recognise from forks with a common cause in them. Common cause forks form nomological forks, but the standard overdetermination fork does not. As we have seen, this is because overdetermining causes are generally each sufficient, but not necessary, for their effects, while common causes are both. Nevertheless, I would deny that we have disclosed any relevant asymmetry within the nomological forks themselves. For, if the striking of the match is necessary and sufficient for both heating and lighting, then, by the same token, the heating and lighting are each necessary and sufficient for the striking. Why is this not a case of the causation of an earlier event by two later events, later events which are nomologically necessary and sufficient for each other?

Of course, the atemporal criterion I offered to Mackie earlier on would rule out the possibility that our striking is caused by the heating and the lighting. For, according to it, the striking is the root event in this fork, and thus the cause event. Yet this criterion begins to look like a mere stipulation once we are brought to see that, but for it, the causal relations within nomological forks could run either way. There must be some rationale for this stipulation before we can credit ourselves with a theory of the direction of causation.[3]

Once we insist on reversing the direction of causation within nomological forks, there are two possible readings of the forks' causal structure open to us. On the one hand, we could construe a reversed fork as a new case of overdetermination, with the lighting and heating causally overdetermining the striking. The novelty would be that, in these circumstances, one could not have the one overdetermining cause without the other. On the other hand, we might construe a reversed fork as a case of two necessary conditions which are jointly sufficient for the outcome, so the lighting and heating would each be individually necessary and jointly sufficient for the striking. Here again, in the circumstances which prevail, we could not have had the one necessary condition without the other.

I think we must read the reversed nomological fork in the former fashion as a variety of overdetermination fork. We are forced to this conclusion by the way we construe the unreversed nomological fork. A nomological fork is standardly treated as containing a common cause

---

[3] Mackie himself regards the causal fork asymmetry as an indication that we have an atemporal concept of causal asymmetry, rather than as the fact which constitutes that asymmetry. He goes on to give an account of it in terms of the notion of 'fixity'. See Mackie, 1974: chapter 7.

sufficient for two effects. There are *two* effects precisely because some of the background conditions relevant to the production of one effect are distinct from some of those relevant to the production of the other. In our example the presence of a conducting medium, at any given point in the room, is nomologically independent of the presence of a translucent medium at that point – for example we could have a local vacuum through which light passed but not heat (except in the immediate area of the match where a combustion event is needed to get the whole thing going). It follows that the striking is sufficient for two separate effects: the lighting and heating of that point in the room. This is so notwithstanding the fact that, if the medium transmits both heat and light, we cannot have one effect without the other.

Reversing the nomological fork, we find some of the background conditions which ensure that the lighting is sufficient for the striking are also independent of those which ensure that the heating is sufficient for the striking. If we had a translucent medium which was not a conducting medium at some point around the match, then only the lighting (at that point) could be considered an operative sufficient condition for the striking. So the lighting is separately sufficient for the striking, notwithstanding the fact that, if the medium transmits both heat and light, the lighting cannot be operative without the striking. A similar story could be told about the heating. Since separately sufficient conditions of a common effect overdetermine that effect, we may conclude that a reversed common cause fork is an overdetermination fork.

I conclude that, though Mackie has given us a way of distinguishing common cause forks from the overdetermination forks which we normally recognise, he has done nothing to stop us reading the common cause forks as a novel type of overdetermination fork. And, if this is allowed, we have no account of why the direction of causation runs as we think it does within the nomological forks themselves. Since the idea was to fix the direction of causation by reference to what happens in the case of a nomological fork, this account is thoroughly undermined.

### (b) Lewis

Our task is to prevent the reversibility of nomological relations from infecting causal relations. Lewis suggests that we do this by loosening the tie between laws and subjunctives, and then explaining causation in terms of subjunctive, rather than nomological, dependence. If we can do so, the reversibility of nomological dependence need not make causation reversible. Lewis bases the temporal asymmetry of subjunctive dependence on the following fact about the world: any event will be nomologically necessary for more later events than earlier events. I will first describe this asymmetry, and then say how it is meant to underwrite the irreversibility of subjunctives (Lewis, 1986d).

A first, crude stab at formulating the asymmetry might put it like this: an event is nomologically connected with more events at any given time in the future than with events at any given time in the past. To return to our example once more, the striking of the match will be nomologically relevant to many different events occurring half a second later: the lighting, the heating, the noise of the striking etc. But there will normally be only a single event occurring half a second earlier which is nomologically relevant to the striking itself, namely the hand movement. The qualification 'at any given time' is necessary to avoid falling foul of the fact that if we took all past and future events together there might well be an infinite number of both past and future events nomologically connected with the striking.

However, this statement is too crude, for it fails to discriminate between two different ways in which one event can be nomologically relevant to another: it may be either nomologically necessary or nomologically sufficient, and these relations give rise to two quite distinct asymmetries. One of them may be formulated as follows:

[1a] For any event, the number of events at any given point in the future for which it is necessary is greater than the number of events at any given point in the past for which it is necessary.

or, equivalently as

[1b] For any event, the number of events at any given point in the future which are sufficient for it will be greater than the number of events at any given point in the past which are sufficient for it.

I take it this is the asymmetry which Lewis intends. It seems clear that the match's striking will be nomologically necessary for more than one succeeding event: the lighting, the heating, the noise of the striking, and thus there will be more than one immediately later event which is nomologically sufficient for it. By contrast, there will normally be only a single preceding event which is nomologically sufficient for the striking, namely the hand movement, and thus only a single immediately earlier event for which the striking is nomologically necessary. To put it another way, strikings will rarely be nomologically overdetermined by past events while they usually are nomologically overdetermined by future events.

The second asymmetry goes as follows:

[2a] For any event, the number of events at any given point in the future for which it is necessary is greater than the number of events at any given point in the past which are necessary for it.

or, equivalently,

[2b] For any event, the number of events at any given point in the future which are sufficient for it is greater than the number of events at any given point in the past for which it is sufficient.

It is, at the very least, an open question whether this asymmetry exists at all, and I do not think Lewis ought to put any weight on it. We may undermine both [2a] and [2b] simply by observing that there are a multitude of negative conditions which must be satisfied by an event's immediate past if that event is to occur. All manner of preventative and disruptive factors must be absent if a causal process is to come to fruition. [1a] and [1b] are unaffected by this, since the conjunction of these and other necessary conditions will usually form a single condition immediately sufficient for the event in question.

Even if we refrain from introducing negative background conditions, [2a] and [2b] are dubious. As we have seen, the match's striking will be nomologically necessary for more than one (proximal) later event, but it will also be the case that more than one (proximal) earlier event is nomologically necessary for the match to be struck. For the hand movement to be followed by a striking, the match must be in contact with the box, the hand must be steady and sufficiently strong etc. Who is to say that there will be fewer such cause events than there are effects of the striking? We need a complex set of background conditions to ensure that this movement leads to a striking, and thus to ensure that the movement cannot happen without the striking. What matters for Lewis' purposes is not this, but the (usual) absence of any independent occurrence (such as a gust of wind) which, helped on by a different set of background conditions, is also nomologically sufficient for a striking – the striking will not normally be overdetermined.

The contingent feature of the world registered in [1a] produces a continuous branching structure of events. Each event is at the node of some fork which opens towards the future, for each event is nomologically necessary for more than one occurrence in the immediate future, and these future occurrences constitute the tips of the fork. Occasionally, an event may also appear at the tips of two different forks, when nomologically overdetermined by two events in the immediate past, placing it at the node of a fork which opens towards the past. But any such event will be at the node of more forks open to the future than forks open to the past.

Here, one must guard against a misapprehension. The existence of this branching structure does not require that the number of events be increasing over time or that the universe be always expanding or any such thing; Lewis' asymmetry does not beg these cosmological questions. The branching structure specified by [1a] and [1b] exists where a given event bears certain specific nomological relations to more events at a given point in the future than it does to events at a given point in the past. This entails nothing about the relative quantity of past and future events to which our event bears other nomological relations. Only someone who asserted both of the nomological asymmetries outlined above would be committed to these cosmological hypotheses.[4]

How exactly does this contingent fact about our world give causation a past-to-future direction? Lewis equates a cause with a causally necessary condition and analyses causal necessity in terms of a subjunctive conditional: $x$'s being $P$ causes $y$ to be $Q$ if, and only if, if $x$ had not been $P$ then $y$ would not have been $Q$.[5] He claims that while, within each of the forks which together constitute the branching structure, the event at the root of the fork will be subjunctively, and thus causally, necessary for the events at its tips, this root event will not exhibit a similar subjunctive dependence on the occurrence of the tip events. And this is so

---

[4] In substance, this paragraph is due to Michael Martin.

[5] Lewis, 1986a:159–72. As anyone who has read chapter 3 will observe, this formulation misrepresents Lewis' analysis in two ways. First, Lewis thinks of causation as a relation between concrete particulars, a view which I rejected. Since his doctrine of the direction of causation seems to me to be independent of his views about the logical form of causal statements, I have taken the liberty of translating his analysis into my terms. Second, Lewis distinguishes causation from causal dependence and it is causal dependence which he defines in terms of subjunctives. The relation of causation is the ancestral of the relation of causal dependence, so for him, causation is transitive while causal dependence is not. Since this complication is not relevant for my purposes, I have ignored it.

notwithstanding the fact that, if the root event is nomologically sufficient as well as necessary for the occurrence of the tip events, these tip events will be nomologically necessary for the occurrence of this root event.

For example, the illumination of the room is nomologically necessary for the striking of the match, since the striking of the match is nomologically sufficient for it. But, according to Lewis, the illumination of the room is not causally necessary for, and thus is not a cause of, the striking of the match. This is a consequence of the falsity of the backtracking subjunctive 'if the room had not been illuminated then the match wouldn't have been struck'. Lewis assumes that such a subjunctive conditional is true if, and only if, the most similar world in which its antecedent is true is one in which its consequent is true also (Lewis, 1973: chapter 1). So our backtracking subjunctive will be true if, and only if, the most similar world in which the room is not illuminated is one in which the match is not struck either. And Lewis urges that this truth condition is not satisfied.

It is the branching structure which ensures that all such backtracking conditionals are false. The striking of the match will be nomologically necessary for a large number of later events. Given this, if the non-occurrence of the room's illumination were to be accompanied by the non-occurrence of its cause, the match's striking, the world in which the room was not illuminated would be very different from our own. It would be a world not only without the illumination and the striking, but also devoid of the other effects of the striking – the heating, the scraping noise etc.

Lewis asserts that the most similar world to our own without the room's illumination is one in which the match is nevertheless struck, is followed by noise and heating in the usual way but is not conjoined with the room's illumination. This will involve a breach in the law of nature which says that the striking is sufficient for the illumination, and the illumination is necessary for the striking. But, according to Lewis, such a miracle involves less of a departure from actuality than the loss of all the other accompaniments of the striking. Thus 'if the room had not been illuminated, the match would not have been struck' is false, since the most similar world in which the room is not illuminated is one in which the match is nevertheless struck (Lewis, 1986d:49–51).

Lewis provides us with an atemporal criterion of the temporal direction of causation. As he says, the asymmetry of subjunctive dependence derives from an asymmetry of nomological overdetermination: events are more overdetermined by later occurrences than by earlier ones, therefore they are necessary for more later events than earlier events. But there is no *a priori* reason why the converse should not be true and, if it were, causation would run from future to past.

Lewis' assertion that back-tracking necessity subjunctives are false is disputable (Horwich, 1987:161–3). It appears very natural to say that if the room had not been illuminated, then the match could not have been struck. But, even if we concede Lewis' point, the existence of the asymmetry of overdetermination seems quite consistent with the supposition that each of the 'effects' of the striking is, in fact, a cause of the striking in virtue of being causally sufficient for the striking. We are supposing that the illumination is nomologically both necessary and sufficient for the striking. And, even if we should not infer that such 'effects' are causally necessary for the striking, Lewis has given us no reason to deny that they are each causally sufficient for the striking. He has not attempted to falsify sufficiency subjunctives like 'if the room were illuminated then the match would have to have been struck'.

Lewis himself would not be worried by this observation for he defines causation in terms of causal necessity, leaving causal sufficiency out of account. But this is surely a gap in his theory. How is he to deal with cases where more than one nomologically sufficient condition for a given effect is present, and thus neither of the potential causes are nomologically necessary for the effect in question? The two bullets fired by different members of the firing squad were each sufficient for the death of their victim, but neither was necessary because the other bullet would have done the job alone. Yet at least one (and possibly both) of the bullets caused the death.[6]

Because Lewis equates causation with causal necessity he must deny that these overdetermining conditions are causes at all. Further, he is able to ignore the possibility that future events causally overdetermine past events. Lewis agrees that any given event is more nomologically overdetermined by future events than by past events and only through assuming (in effect) that causal overdetermination is impossible does he avoid the conclusion that future events causally overdetermine past

[6] Lewis struggles heroically with the problem posed by causes that are not causally necessary for their effects on pages 193–212 of Lewis, 1986a. He regards all the realistic examples of overdetermination as cases in which one cause pre-empts another, and he then attempts to deal with pre-emption by relying on the intransitivity of causal dependence. However, his way of dealing with what he calls 'later pre-emption' is clearly unsatisfactory and he confesses as much on pages 206–7.

events. The causal overdetermination of the past by the future is an hypothesis which neither Mackie nor Lewis manages to rule out.

I believe that Lewis' asymmetry of overdetermination can be used to fix the direction of causation. However, I do not intend to do this by asserting that some subjunctives would remain true despite the falsification of the laws which actually support them. Rather, I uphold the constitutive connection between laws and subjunctives and instead maintain that the truth of necessity and/or sufficiency subjunctives is not enough for causation. The cause must ensure that its effects are no coincidence.

In chapter 1, I argued that a coincidence cannot be explained. By citing conditions each necessary and sufficient for the events which constitute the coincidence, we can explain why each component of it occurred. But we can go no way towards explaining why they all occurred together. Since I tie causation to explanation, I infer that coincidences have no causes. I am not saying that coincidences cannot be causes. Overdetermining causes cause their common effect because each cause is sufficient for the *whole* of the effect: the overdetermined effect is explained by each of its overdetermining causes. But, where the overdetermining causes are independent of one another, their co-occurrence can be neither explained nor caused. It is a coincidence and it has no cause.

For instance, it is a coincidence that both my hand movement and the gust of air were present to propel the match along the match box. Such coincidences rarely occur since later events are rarely overdetermined by earlier events, but the converse kind of coincidence is extremely common. The striking of a match will regularly be 'overdetermined' by the illumination of a room, the heating of the surrounding air, the noise in that room etc. And we can use this asymmetry of coincidence to fix the direction of causation.

Where the world has the branching structure illustrated in *Figure* 1, the number of coincidences we find in that world will depend on the direction in which we run through the structure. If we move from earlier to later events, we will come across relatively few coincidences, events whose joint occurrence cannot be explained by reference to a common root. But if we run through the branching structure in the opposite direction towards the past, we shall find many more such coincidences.

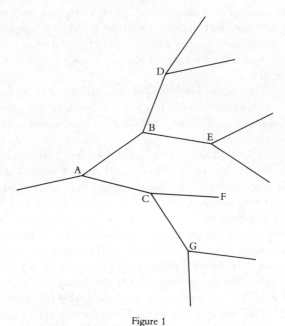

Figure 1

Consider the *Figure*. We may explain the occurrence of the event pair BC by reference to their common necessary condition A, but were we to move on B and C from the opposite direction, we would be unable to find a common necessary condition for B and C. B and C are not independent occurrences relative to A, but they are independent occurrences relative to D, E, F and G. D, E, F and G can be broken down into two discrete subsets which are separately sufficient for B and C (namely {D,E} and {F,G}). Since the co-occurrence of these subsets is a coincidence, if they alone necessitated B and C, the co-occurrence of B and C would also be a coincidence. Therefore D, E, F and G cannot be combined to explain the joint occurrence of B and C.

No such thing is true of A. We can explain why both B and C occurred by referring to their common necessary and sufficient condition A. Of course, A will be necessary and sufficient for B only given certain mutually independent background conditions – similarly for C. And the joint obtaining of these background conditions will itself be a co-incidence. But, though the coincidence of these individually necessary and jointly sufficient conditions is inexplicable, this coincidence will explain the occurrence of both B and C provided these conditions are not separately relevant to B and to C. And the fact that A is necessary for both B and C by itself ensures that we cannot find discrete sets of earlier conditions separately relevant to the occurrence of B and to the occurrence of C.

To regard bunches of later events as causally sufficient for individual earlier events would be to create a mass of coincidences, coincidences which would not exist if these individual earlier events were instead causally necessary for bunches of later events. Such amazing conjunctions of overdetermining causes can be avoided if we deny that later events are causally sufficient for earlier events, and instead account for these conjunctions of later events by supposing that their constituents share a common causally necessary condition in some earlier event. Thus, to explain the passing scene by postulating causal connections, we must suppose that later events are not causally sufficient for earlier events and that earlier events are causally necessary for later events.

I have now introduced a causal asymmetry, not by stipulation but through demanding explanation. But is this enough to establish that causation, as such, has a direction? Even granting that later events cannot be causally sufficient for earlier events, it remains possible for later events to be causally necessary for earlier events – after all, earlier events are nomologically sufficient for later events so later events must be at least nomologically necessary for their predecessors. I reject this possibility on the grounds that no explanatory purpose would be served by supposing that later events were causally necessary for earlier events, once it is conceded that later events are not causally sufficient for earlier events.

Given causal necessity runs from past to future, we may infer that causal sufficiency runs in that forward direction at least: what is a causally necessary condition other than a condition necessary for the production of an effect ie. a condition necessary for the presence of something which is causally sufficient for the effect? But on the same grounds we can infer from the absence of any relations of causal sufficiency running from future to past to the absence of any relations of causal necessity running in that direction. What explanatory role could such relations of causal necessity play?[7]

---

[7] Here I am, as throughout the book, assuming determinism, but the point can also be stated in a probabilistic mode: if a cause is something whose absence lowers the probability of an effect, that is precisely because it is something whose presence raises the probability of its effect. If later events never bring about an increase in the probability

Note that we can't infer from the absence of relations of causal necessity in a given direction to the absence of relations of causal sufficiency in that direction. This is because of the possibility of massive overdetermination – a situation in which there are many events causally sufficient but causally unnecessary for their effects. This is precisely the possibility which undermined Lewis' account, and Lewis cannot use what I have said here to move from his asymmetry of causal necessity to a full blown causal asymmetry.

Having established the direction of causation, we are now in a position to distinguish causally related events from events with a common cause. Let us say that I have a genetic condition which causes me to both smoke and have a sallow complexion. The genetic condition is both necessary and sufficient for smoking, and necessary and sufficient for a sallow complexion. From this, we can infer that smoking is necessary and sufficient for a sallow complexion. Further, given that I smoke, it is no coincidence that I have a sallow complexion. But it would obviously be a mistake to conclude that my smoking causes me to have a sallow complexion.

My genetic condition renders the joint occurrence of the smoking and the sallow complexion non-coincidental, but not *vice versa*, so given my account of the direction of causation, we can infer that it causes both the smoking and the sallow complexion, and they do not cause it. But the route by which my smoking is supposed to cause my sallow complexion is via their nomological connection with my genes; since we have just ruled out the hypothesis that my smoking causes my genetic condition, this route is blocked, so my smoking does not cause my sallow complexion.

I have described the branching structure as the product of an asymmetry of overdetermination, so it is important to be clear just what I mean by 'overdetermination'. Several philosophers have distinguished between overdetermination and what one might call pre-emption (Mackie, 1974:43–7). Our firing squad may be organised in two rather different ways. On the one hand it may contain two soldiers who fire simultaneously. Here, one supposes, their bullets overdetermine the death provided they both hit a vital organ simultaneously. On the other hand, it may contain two soldiers, one of whom is meant to fire first

of earlier events, that is good reason to hold that their absence does not bring about a reduction in probability either.

while the other acts as a fail-safe mechanism, firing a little later just in case another bullet is needed to finish the victim off. If the victim dies before the second shot is fired, the first soldier's bullet is the sole cause of the death even though, in the circumstances, it is not nomologically necessary for the death. The first bullet pre-empts the causal action of the second.

Now it has been argued by Bunzl that there are no realistic examples of overdetermination (Bunzl, 1979). All purported instances turn out, when we inspect the mechanism in detail, to be either examples of pre-emption or else cases in which two events are each nomologically necessary for the effect, and are jointly (but not individually) sufficient. For example, when seeking the cause of the executed man's death we shall find that either one bullet got in first and prevented the other from having any effect, or else the death was owing in part to (some of) the impact of one bullet and in part to (some of) the impact of the other bullet. Will Bunzl's thesis deprive me of the asymmetry which I need to establish the direction of causation?

No. Even if we follow Bunzl and decline to describe these cases as instances of overdetermination, there will be quite enough coincidence in them to be going on with. Suppose one bullet pre-empted the other, so only one of the bullets actually caused the death. Nevertheless, it was a great coincidence that an independent bullet was fired which would have been sufficient for the death had it been given the chance. Suppose that the bullets jointly caused the death, both were active but neither was given the chance to be sufficient by itself for the death. Here again, it is a great coincidence that there are two causes which *would have been* individually sufficient for the death had the other not been present. These coincidences are the ones on which I wish to focus, and they are present however we describe the actual causal structure of the 'overdetermination' situation. The distinction between cases of overdetermination, pre-emption and joint causation by causal factors which would have been independently sufficient for the outcome is important for some purposes, but not for mine, so I shall call them all cases of over-determination.

## DUMMETT'S APPLE

Do the events in our world arrange themselves in the branching structure characterised by [1a] and [1b]? In this section, I shall describe a typical causal process noted by Dummett, and the way he reverses it, thus

illustrating the branching structure. His example also serves to demonstrate that I have provided a truly atemporal criterion of the temporal
direction of causation, since it shows how the direction of causation
might diverge from the direction of time.

According to Dummett we can imagine observing a world in which
earlier events are to be causally explained by reference to later events:

The sapling grows gradually smaller, finally reducing itself to an apple pip; then
an apple is gradually constituted around the pip from ingredients found in the
soil; at a certain moment the apple rolls along the ground, gradually gaining
momentum, bounces a few times, and then suddenly takes off vertically and
attaches itself with a snap to the bough of an apple tree. Viewed from the
standpoint of gross observation, this process contains many totally unpredictable
elements: we cannot, for example, explain, by reference to the conditions
obtaining at the moment, when the apple started rolling, why it started rolling
at that moment or in that direction. Rather we should have to substitute a system
of explanations of events in terms of the processes that led back to them from
some subsequent moment. If through some extraordinary chance we, in this
world, could consider events from the standpoint of the microscopic, the
unpredictability would disappear theoretically ('in principle') although not in
practice, but we should be left – so long as we continued to try to give causal
explanations on the basis of what leads up to an event – with inexplicable
coincidences. 'In principle' we could, by observing the movements of molecules
of the soil, predict that at a certain moment they were going to move in such a
way as to combine to give a slight impetus to the apple, and that this impetus
would be progressively reinforced by other molecules along a certain path, so as
to cause the apple to accelerate in such a way that it would end up attached to the
apple tree. But not only could we not make such predictions in practice: the fact
that the 'random' movements of the molecules should happen to work out in
such a way that all along the path the molecules always happened to be moving
in the same direction at just the moment that the apple reached that point, and,
above all, that these movements always worked in such a way as to leave the
apple attached to an *apple* tree and not to any other tree or any other object –
these facts would cry out for explanation and we should be unable to provide it.
(Dummett, 1964:339–40)

Here, according to Dummett, we are observing a world in which the
direction of causal explanation runs from future to past, rather than *vice
versa*. The direction of causal explanation is that direction in which we
must move in order to minimise the number of coincidences. And, if the
situation Dummett has described is really possible, then the direction of
causal explanation may be opposed to the direction of time.

One may doubt whether it is so easy to observe a time-reversed causal
process, and in the next section I shall confirm this suspicion – I shall urge
that, though it may be possible to see a causal process which is in fact

time-reversed, it is impossible to see it *as* a time-reversed causal process. But the presence of an observer is inessential to the use I wish to make of the example. What I mean the example to show is this: to conceive of a situation in which the temporal order of the elements in a typical causal process have been reversed is to conceive of a situation in which the direction of causal explanation has been reversed also. And to conceive of a situation is not to imagine perceiving it.

But how exactly does Dummett's example illustrate the asymmetry introduced in the last section? In answering this question, we must carefully distinguish the asymmetries described by the [1]s and the [2]s respectively. Dummett's example could be regarded as an instance of either, but I only wish to make this claim for the [1]s. Dummett himself does not separate the two.

The events surrounding the impact of the apple on the ground illustrate our asymmetry of overdetermination. Going from past to future, there is a single condition sufficient for the displacement of the molecules of earth, namely the apple's impact but going from future to past, the apple's impact will be overdetermined by each of the molecular movements it gives rise to – since such an impact is necessary for each of those molecules to move in that fashion, each of those movements is sufficient for the impact to have taken place.[8]

Furthermore, in the time-reversed world, the apple tree's status as an apple tree is hugely overdetermined by earlier events. I take it that one apple is sufficient to make our tree an apple tree. In fact, many apples arrive on the apple tree, apparently quite independently. The processes seemingly involved in projecting one apple onto our tree appear quite independent of those involved in the arrival of other apples. So the many discrete earth movements involved in getting different apples onto the tree overdetermine that tree's status as an apple tree and this over-determination is an inexplicable coincidence.

By contrast, as things actually are, it is no coincidence that our tree produces many apples. There is a common cause of the production of each of the fruits on the tree, a feature of the tree (of its DNA) that is necessary and sufficient, in normal circumstances, for each of its fruits to be an apple. These normal conditions may be rather complex but they will not operate independently of one another and on different apples,

---

[8] Similar points could be made with Karl Popper's example of the concentric wave pattern produced by a stone thrown into the middle of a pond. See Popper, 1956:538 and Lewis, 1986:50–1.

they will not work separately to ensure that the different fruits on a given tree are apples; rather they will combine to explain why each fruit is an apple.

Given the above facts, Dummett's example is an illustration of the asymmetry of overdetermination described by the [1]s. However, as Dummett notes, it is no less of a coincidence that all the apples end up on the same tree rather than on different trees. Suppose that our apple tree was located in an orchard adjacent to a pear tree and a plum tree. In the normal course of events there is some overlap between the areas in which these trees shed their fruit. But if we imagine the course of events to be reversed, it becomes hard to see why apples are not projected onto the pear tree and plums onto the apple tree etc.

But this coincidence is not germane to the [1]s. Here, what is to be explained is not why our tree is an apple tree, that is why it has at least one apple, but, rather, why it is only an apple tree, why it has only apples on it. And a necessary condition for this outcome is the independent non-arrival of each of the pears and the plums. So the coincidence here is not that the apple tree's status is overdetermined, but, rather, that there is a coincidental combination of conditions individually necessary and jointly sufficient for it to be solely an apple tree.

Now there is no question that this is a genuine coincidence. The only issue is whether it is any more of a coincidence than the fact that the tree does not have the kind of DNA which would enable it to produce pears and plums as well as apples. For, if the absence of pear and plum DNA in our world is just as much of a coincidence as the fact that pears and plums are not projected onto the tree in the time-reversed world, explaining why only apples appear on the tree by reference to earlier conditions would involve postulating no less of a coincidence than would explaining this fact by reference to later conditions.

I should conclude this section by hedging my bets a little. Several philosophers have put forward the view that it is the direction of causation which determines the direction of time (Reichenbach, 1956, Grunbaum, 1973 and Mellor, 1981). According to them, it is not really possible for effects to precede their causes, since it is precisely the direction of causation which fixes the direction of time. In this section, I have proceeded as if such a temporal switch in the direction of causation were possible in order to illustrate my own theory of the direction of causation but, as far as I can see, my view does not commit me to this possibility. If it turns out that temporal precedence derives from causal precedence, my account of the direction of causation may still stand, it is just that I could not draw attention to the branching structure and its consequences for explanation by setting it against the grain of time.

## EXPERIENCE AND CAUSATION

I have treated Dummett's apple example as an illustration of how the direction of explanation and the direction of time may diverge. However, it also demonstrates something about the experience of causation, namely that the apparent direction of explanation may differ from the experienced direction of causation. If someone were shown a film of apples falling from a tree in reverse, he would report that it looked as if events which appear earlier in the film caused those events which appear later in the film: the ground seems to project the apple onto the tree and the arrival of the apple seems to cause the snap etc. And he would report this while admitting that the events filmed are better explained on the assumption that those which occur later cause those which precede them. Does this show that the direction of causation may diverge from the direction of explanation and thus that we should distinguish causation from causal explanation? In order to answer this question we should first enquire why it is that the earlier events appear to cause the later events and not *vice versa*.

The answer is that the experienced direction of causation is inextricably bound up with the apparent direction of time: if event $e$ seems to occur before event $e^\circ$ and there appears to be a causal connection between $e$ and $e^\circ$ then $e$ must appear to cause $e^\circ$, not *vice versa*.[9] But this concession poses no threat to my position, provided one distinguishes the actual direction of causation from the experienced direction of causation. I concede that an event which is experienced as causing another event must be experienced as preceding that other event, but I shall urge that this is owing to facts about the experience of causation which have nothing to do with the connection which that experience is an experience of. Therefore, we need not conclude that causation and causal explanation are distinct, because the direction of causation is fixed by apparent orientation of the arrow of time, while that of explanation is not.

---

[9] I have not seen any psychological work on this specific point, but, throughout the classic psychological work on the subject of human experience of causation, namely Michotte, 1963, it is simply presupposed that a cause must appear to occur earlier than its effect.

Let us begin with the perception of temporal precedence and then move onto the perception of causation. Mellor suggests that *e* appears to precede event *e*° if, and only if, I see *e* before I see *e*°, and my experience of *e* causally influences my experience of *e*° in the right kind of way. To see a button's being pushed precede a flash of a light is just to see the pushing of the button and then to see the flashing of the light while retaining some memory of the push when I see the flash. Obviously, I will not see the push precede the flash if I have forgotten all about the push when the flash occurs – but I need not perceive anything over and above the push and the flash (Mellor, 1981:143–5).

I am convinced that the perception of *e* must actually cause the perception of *e*° if it is to appear to precede it. Perception of precedence requires memory of the seemingly earlier event and (as will be shown in chapter 7) memory requires causation of the remembering event by the remembered event. But I am not so sure that if *e* appears to occur earlier than *e*°, the subject's perception of *e* must actually occur earlier than his perception of *e*°. Since this part of Mellor's claim is not germane to my discussion, I shall leave it on one side.

What does concern me is an analogous claim about causation, namely the claim that we cannot see *e* cause *e*° unless our experience of *e* causes our experience of *e*°. Could one see billiard ball A hit billiard ball B and apparently cause its movement even though it was one's perception of B's movement which causally influenced one's perception of A's and not *vice versa*? Surely not. Could one see A's movement cause B's, even though one's perception of A's movement had no causal influence at all on one's perception of B's? Again, surely not. One must at least remember A's movement when one sees B's, if one is to see A's movement cause B's.

I have stated this claim about causal experience as a claim about the perception of causation, but it applies equally to hallucinations. If one hallucinates the movement of one billiard ball, how can one seem to see that ball as causing the movement of a second hallucinatory ball unless there is a suitable causal relationship between these hallucinatory experiences? How could one seem to see a causal connection between the two hallucinatory movements if one did not recall the first hallucination when experiencing the second? It is this memory requirement which ties the perception of precedence and the perception of causation together.

By combining my thesis about the experience of causation with Mellor's causal condition on the experience of temporal precedence we may explain why, given that $e$ seems to occur before $e^\circ$ and there seems to be a causal connection between them, $e$ must appear to cause $e^\circ$ and not *vice versa*. For $e$ to appear to precede $e^\circ$, the subject's experience of $e$ must causally influence his experience of $e^\circ$. So, given the asymmetry of causation, his experience of $e^\circ$ cannot causally influence his experience of $e$. So it follows, by my own hypothesis, that $e^\circ$ cannot appear to cause $e$.

A subject can certainly come to believe that $e$ is, in fact, an effect of $e^\circ$, even when his experience of $e$ precedes and causally influences his experience of $e^\circ$. But, where this happens, it will still look to the subject as if $e$ causes $e^\circ$, it is just that the subject would not, in this instance, believe his eyes. For instance, it is known that Clare never greets anyone spontaneously, but always responds to a welcoming shout with a hand wave. On a particular occasion, I see her waving her hand before I hear the shout and the relation between my experiences is such that it looks as if Clare's hand wave causes the shout. Nevertheless, I know this cannot be right and I will not believe my senses on this occasion.

As this last example shows, I am not supposing that all experiences of causation are veridical – only that the experience of causation requires a corresponding causal relation *among experiences*. Nor am I supposing that any two causally related experiences are experiences of a causal relation. If, while looking at a tree, I recall the image of a Union Jack which I once saw, this may induce me to discern a certain pattern in the bark of a tree without its looking to me as though that pattern was caused by a Union Jack. A suitable causal relation among experiences is necessary, but not sufficient, for an experience of causation.

The importance of this little theory is that it shows why causes must appear to occur earlier than their effects without forcing us to assume that causes must actually occur earlier than their effects. It provides a convincing explanation of the illusion suffered by the subject who reports that the apple appears to be projected onto the tree on being shown the film of the apple in reverse. The subject just cannot see an apparently earlier event, such as the presence of the apple on the ground as the product of an apparently later event, such as the snap of the bough. This tells us something about the way he perceives causation, but nothing about causation itself.

In this section, I have spoken of the experiences which would be produced by a film shown backwards. Obviously, a film shown in reverse is not an instance of backwards causation in anyone's book. The images on the screen do not interact with one another causally, rather they have a common cause in the projection mechanism, and within that projection mechanism earlier events cause later events and not *vice versa*. But a film projection mechanism is an excellent device for inducing illusions of causal interaction, and by asking how these illusions are produced we may show that certain experiences are impossible.

What fixes the direction of the causal relations which obtain between the subject's experiences? My answer is a straightforward application of the theory of causation outlined above. We will find that the experience of the apparent cause has many different effects (both psychological and physical), among which is the experience of its apparent effect. In order to explain the joint occurrence of all these events, we must suppose that the experience of the apparent cause brings them all about and not *vice versa*. In the absence of this type of structure, one experience could not cause another, and thus there could be no experience of causation.

## SOME OBJECTIONS

A sympathetic critic, having followed the argument thus far, might comment: 'you have established that the branching structure of events is an indication of the direction of causation. But might there not be a causal direction where this evidence is not available to us? Might the causal relation be present even when events do not arrange themselves in a branching structure?' There are two ways in which this may be thought to happen.

First, suppose the system in question has some processes like that involving Dummett's apple (hereafter called 'Dummett Processes') but also contains sequences of events which do not exhibit the required asymmetries. Surely the earlier parts of these symmetrical processes bring about the later parts (or *vice versa*)? Second, the system might be completely devoid of processes which exhibit the required asymmetries. Would this really be a natural system without causation (Tooley, 1987:224–8; Lewis, 1986:49)?

I shall first consider a symmetrical process, schematised in *Figure 2*, which is not cut off from every Dummett process. Events in this process are presumably ordered in time, so every event will be either earlier than, or later than, or simultaneous with, every other event. We suppose that the symmetrical process is nomologically linked to the Dummett process at $D(1)$. I claim that it follows from these two assumptions that the events

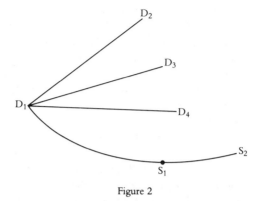

Figure 2

in this symmetrical process occurring later than D(1) are each caused by events in the Dummett process.

The Ds are events in the Dummett process and the Ss are events in the symmetrical process. The two processes connect at D(1). D(1) must cause S(1) and not *vice versa* because D(1) is nomologically connected to D(2), D(3) and D(4) and the co-occurrence of these events with S(1) can be explained only on the assumption that D(1) is their common cause. But this reasoning will also get us the conclusion that D(1) is the cause of any event linked to S(1) by a nomological chain. Take some such event S(2). The co-occurrence of S(2) and D(2), D(3) and D(4) will be inexplicable unless D(1) is regarded as their common cause.

We now know that both S(1) and S(2) are effects of D(1). What does this entail about the causal relationship between S(1) and S(2)? Nothing, so far as I can see; while S(1) and S(2) are causally ordered relative to the Dummett process, there is nothing to determine that D(1) causes S(2) via S(1), rather than D(1) causing S(1) via S(2), or D(1) causing both S(1) and S(2) without causing either of them via the other. S(1) and S(2) are causally ordered only relative to events in the Dummett process.

One way out of this difficulty would be to tie causal order to temporal order in the way advocated by Reichenbach and others (Reichenbach, 1956:32–6) For, if we can assume that causal order marches in step with temporal order then we can rule out the possibility that the later S(2) caused the earlier S(1), through they may have only a common cause in D(1). However, there is a problem with this strategy. Reichenbach (in the spirit of the Special Theory of Relativity) wishes to effect an analysis of temporal order in causal terms; he cannot simply use the temporal

106

order of the Ds and the Ss to determine their causal order, rather it must be the other way round. So, what he does is to assert that certain local spatio-temporal relations (and thus causal relations) are simply observable and then reconstruct the other causal and spatio-temporal relations from these. For my more limited purposes, I need not endorse the causal analysis of temporal order – Reichenbach's two assumptions about what is simply observable will suffice.

Reichenbach assumes that we can simply observe when the events involved in two causal processes with different histories coincide spatio-temporally for a while. For we can observe (a) when two events coincide spatio-temporally and (b) when two events are parts of the same natural process (say the transmission of a single light ray). Thus, we can see that the causal processes connecting $D(1)$ with $S(1)$ and $D(1)$ with $S(2)$ overlap and are not separate from one another in the way that would be required if $D(1)$ were to cause first $S(1)$ and then $S(2)$ quite independently of one another. Further, we can simply see that the very process which arrives at $S(2)$ had to pass through $S(1)$ – that its first segment coincided with a causal process terminating at $S(1)$ and therefore $D(1)$ cannot have caused $S(1)$ via $S(2)$. Given that $D(1)$ causes both $S(1)$ and $S(2)$, the only conclusion open to us is that it caused $S(2)$ by causing $S(1)$.

Is there any justification for assumptions (a) and (b)? The main point in their favour is that they are assumptions made by our most successful scientific theory of spacetime. Special Relativity assumes that we can simply observe spatio-temporal coincidence, and that we can see whether the light ray emitted at this point is the light ray received at some other point. These assumptions are essential to the techniques of measurement underlying the theory. I am content to accept them on that basis (Sklar, 1974: chapter 4). With the help of these assumptions we can also deal with the case in which the symmetric process does not proceed from the Dummett process, as in *Figure* 2, but merges into it, having originated elsewhere.

Can this account be extended to natural systems in which the asymmetry to which Dummett draws our attention is entirely lacking and which are isolated from any Dummett process? I cannot see how to do this, but I also fail see why we should wish to introduce causation into such a process. Were we confronted by a universe which consists only of a small ball orbiting a larger ball we should ask: what is the point of supposing that the parts of this process are connected by a temporally asymmetric causal relation? What explanatory function would be served by this supposition? There might be an answer to this question – various aspects of the smaller ball's orbit might have a common origin in the gravitational field created by the mass of the larger ball. But, if there really is no answer, it would be pointless to suppose that the mass of the larger ball brings about the orbit of the smaller. Here we should be content with the functional laws which enable us to infer the behaviour of the one ball from the behaviour of the other and *vice versa*.

Some have insisted that a world without my asymmetry of over-determination is no mere possibility – the asymmetry present in our world is essentially a macrophysical fact, a product of statistical facts which one can discern only when one takes particles *en masse*; at the level of the individual particle and its behaviour, the asymmetry simply does not exist. They conclude from this that any view which bases causal asymmetry on the asymmetry of overdetermination must claim that there is no causal asymmetry at the level of individual microscopic particles.[10]

I reply that this conclusion follows only if one makes a certain assumption about causation, namely that it is an intrinsic relation. A relation is intrinsic if, and only if, the relation holds between A and B in virtue solely of facts about A and B themselves. But anyone who, like myself, bases causal asymmetry on the asymmetry of overdetermination will reject this assumption: we say that, at the macro-level, it is the presence of a suitable branching structure which gives rise to causation and not the features of any individual branch formed by two causally related events, so we can hardly agree that causation is an intrinsic relation. And, once this is acknowledged, we are free to infer the direction of causation among individual particles from facts about how particles behave *en masse*.

It has been suggested that our understanding of the causal relation depends more than I have acknowledged on the role of causation in action. As Dummett points out, one of the major connotations of causation is that it is always rational to bring about a cause in order to get its effect (Dummett, 1978:333). Since to bring something about is *ipso facto* to ensure that it is no coincidence, this thought poses no problems for me. But some philosophers wish to go further – they claim that what it is for $x$'s being $P$ to cause $y$ to be $Q$ is for it to be the case that an agent

---

[10] For example, H. Price in an unpublished manuscript entitled 'Agency and Causal Asymmetry'.

can make $y$ a $Q$ by making $x$ a $P$, but cannot make $x$ a $P$ by making $y$ a $Q$. On their view, the causal order of a causally inter-related set of events is that order in which they would appear in a rational agent's plan of action (Von Wright, 1971:70–81).

Now I do not deny that a rational agent must take account of causal relations. Indeed, as I shall argue in chapter 8, causation is needed to analyse the very notion of an intentional action. But it is something else to suppose that causation may itself be analysed in teleological terms. Only on a magical view of human action could such an analysis avoid circularity. To see how this move might tempt us, let us return to the isolated symmetrical processes considered above.

It is natural, when confronted with a symmetrical process, to try to determine the causal order of its constituent events by asking of any given event in the process what we would have to bring about in order to bring about that event. It is equally tempting to suppose that, even in a symmetrical process, there must be an answer to this question. In order to answer it, we imagine acting so as to make $x$ a $P$, say, and then just waiting to see what will occur. Either $y$ will become a $Q$ or it will not – if it does then $x$'s being $P$ is its cause, if not then its cause is elsewhere.

But when concocting this thought experiment we forget to ask ourselves the following question: in virtue of what are we bringing it about that $x$ is a $P$ and then allowing that event to do its work, rather than bringing it about that $y$ is a $Q$ and then allowing that event to do its work? The magical answer is that we are making $x$ a $P$ because that is what we intend to do, and only by doing so do we intend to make $y$ a $Q$. But our intentions alone cannot determine the causal order of events. For instance, I may intend to flex my arm muscles in a certain way, and perhaps I can do this only by clenching my fist. Here, the muscle movement is the end and the clenching is the means. But the flexing of my muscles is the cause and not the effect of my clenching. The causal order of these events is up to nature and not up to me (Mackie, 1974:171–3).

Action requires a causal mechanism and nature determines the causal order of the events which are the working of that mechanism. But how does nature determine this order? As things are, action mechanisms involve Dummett processes. The fact that my intentions are a common cause of many things (other psychological phenomena, bodily movements etc.) but are not usually overdetermined, ensures that it is my intentions that cause the bodily movements which enforce my will, and not *vice versa*. In a world without asymmetries, there is nothing about me that will determine $x$'s being $P$ as the event that I brought about directly, and nothing that will determine that $x$'s being $P$ brought about $y$'s being $Q$ rather than *vice versa* (Reichenbach, 1956:43–7).

Acting on a symmetrical process entails bringing it into contact with a Dummett process. As we saw above, the events in any process which comes into contact with a Dummett process will be causally ordered by contact with events in the Dummett process. So we can legitimately infer that, were someone to intervene in a symmetrical process, certain events would be the effects of his action. But this does not mean that these events occur in any particular causal order when considered apart from the intervention.

### KNOWLEDGE AND TIME

It is often said that our knowledge of the past is far more extensive than our knowledge of the future. When investigating the past, we have access to our own memories, to the testimony of others, to historical and pictorial records etc. But when facing the future, we have only the content of our present intentions to go on, together with some laws of nature which may enable us to predict the future workings of fairly simple and isolated physical systems, like the fridge in the kitchen or the sun in the solar system. As a result, we can say with confidence who the last ten Prime Ministers of Great Britain were, but we cannot even make a stab at identifying the next ten Prime Ministers.

Horwich suggests the following explanation for this knowledge asymmetry: we have a large number of recording devices including human memory, photographs, tape recordings, footprints, fossils and paintings, devices which give us information about the past yet cannot store information about the future. But why are these devices incapable of registering the future? What Horwich says about them suggests the following account to me.[11]

A recording device has a neutral state (type) $S(0)$ and a number of other state (types) $S(1)$, $S(2)$, $S(3)$ etc. There exist a range of mutually exclusive external conditions $C(1)$, $C(2)$, $C(3)$ which, when they obtain, move the

---

[11] Horwich, 1987:84–9. Although my account was inspired by Horwich's at this point, I am unsure how closely they correspond. On pages 81–2, he explicitly denies that the asymmetry of overdetermination can be put to work in this context, but does not consider the best way of so using it.

machine from S(0), to S(1), S(2), or S(3) respectively. Further, it must be the case that, if C(1) had not obtained, the machine would not have moved into S(1) etc. So C(1) is both necessary and sufficient, in the circumstances which are normal for the machine's operation, for state S(1). We also assume that, once the machine is in one of these other states, it remains in that state with some tenacity.

Given these features, one can see how the machine can record the presence of external condition C(1) by moving into state S(1). S(1) is a state that can be brought about by C(1) alone (of the other C-conditions) and which could not be brought about unless C(1) obtained. Therefore, S(1) specifically registers the presence of C(1). And in view of the durability of S(1), this state can constitute a record of C(1). This is how a camera records the scene before it. The scene is registered on a photographic plate when the interaction of light with certain chemicals puts the plate into a specific state in which it remains after the scene has disappeared. Further, the camera would have put the plate into some other state had the external scene been different in some way consistent with its normal operating conditions.[12]

There is a final requirement which any recording device must satisfy. If it is to be at all useful, it must operate successfully in a variety of circumstances. Suppose that my camera delivers reliable pictures only in twilight and when pointing at a scene empty except for not more than one large object. This would seriously restrict the information it could store. But, more to the point, it entails that someone who relies on that photograph for information about what was in front of the camera must already possess a great deal of knowledge about that scene. They must (justifiably) assume that the light was right and that the scene was suitable. And a device which yields information on a given subject only to those who already possess a lot of information about that subject is not a serviceable recording device.

According to my account, a recording device will store information only on the assumption that, for any given state of the device, S(1), there is some specific external condition, C(1), which is both necessary and sufficient for it, at least in the conditions in which the device is likely to be used. If several quite different external conditions, C(1), C(2) and C(3) were each individually sufficient for the device to go into S(1), then the fact that it was in S(1) would give us far less information about the

---

[12] Various further complications arising from the existence of deviant causal chains will be discussed in chapters 7 and 8.

external conditions at the time in question – it would not tell us which of these alternative conditions obtained, only that some one of them obtained.[13]

But what if they all obtained together, what if S(1) were over-determined – would we know that the conjunction of C(1), C(2) and C(3) obtained, a piece of information as precise as the verdict that only one of them obtains? I demanded above that C(1) be necessary, as well as sufficient, for S(1) and where C(1), C(2) and C(3) are each individually sufficient for S(1); it might well be that none of them is necessary. In this situation, S(1) would be no different if C(1) were absent. Therefore, S(1) would not record the presence of C(1) and *a fortiori* would not record the presence of any conjunction of which C(1) is part.

But will C(1) always fail to be necessary for S(1) where S(1) is overdetermined by C(1), C(2) and C(3)? Not necessarily, as I pointed out on page 86; circumstances may be such that one overdetermining cause could not occur without the other. However, as we have seen, a recording device has to be capable of operating in a variety of circumstances – normal circumstances for that device must not be too narrowly circumscribed. S(1) must specifically indicate the presence of C(1) in fairly diverse background conditions. And thus, if C(1) is to be necessary for S(1), in the sense relevant to knowledge, it must be necessary for S(1) in all those conditions which are normal conditions for the operation of the device.

Now while, in the precise circumstances that obtain, the over-determining causes C(1), C(2) and C(3) may each be necessary as well as individually sufficient for S(1), it will be obvious that C(1), C(2), and C(3) need not occur together. It only requires a slight change in the circumstances for C(2) or C(3) to occur without C(1). So, C(1) will not (in the relevant range of circumstances) be necessary for S(1) when S(1) is overdetermined. Where C(1), C(2) and C(3) are each sufficient for S(1) and they can (in normal conditions for the instrument) occur apart, S(1) will record the alternation and not the conjunction of these states.

For example, suppose that at the moment when light impinged on the photographic plate, another cause within the camera was in the process of producing exactly the same chemical reactions. Here, one could not claim that the photograph recorded the conjunction of these causes, for it

---

[13] This characterisation of recording devices is a result of applying to machines some familiar requirements on empirical knowledge. See, for example, Armstrong, 1973: chapter 12.

was a fluke that both causes were present together, a fluke that would cease to obtain in very similar circumstances. Under slightly different conditions, an exactly similar photograph would be produced without the help of one or other of these causes, therefore these causes are not each necessary (in the relevant sense) for the production of the photograph.

We can now use the asymmetry of overdetermination to explain why there are devices which record the past but none which record the future. Earlier events are heavily overdetermined by later events. For any given earlier event, there will be a whole set of later events which are individually sufficient for it. Thus, the earlier event could hardly constitute a record of the occurrence of just one of these later events. And, since the recording device is not sensitive to changes in the set of overdetermining future causes registered, it does not register the conjunction of these future events either. At most, the earlier event is a record of the fact that some one of these later events will occur.

By contrast, there will usually be only a single type of earlier event which is sufficient for the occurrence of a given type of later event, and earlier events of that type will be both necessary and sufficient for later events of that type in those conditions in which the device is meant to operate. Thus such a later event constitutes a record of such an earlier event. And if that earlier event is composed of the conjunction of a number of necessary conditions, the later event will record the fact that this conjunction was present.

# 6

## *Levels of causation*

Having constructed a theory of causation, it is time to apply it. In the next three chapters, I shall focus on various areas where matters can be advanced by adopting some of the theses and making some of the distinctions already introduced. In this chapter, it is the relationship between the different sciences which concerns me, in chapter 7 the problem of deviant causal chains and in chapter 8 the explanation of human action. Each of these issues may be made more tractable by bringing my apparatus to bear on it.

One of the most obvious facts about contemporary science is that it is partitioned into different disciplines. Physicists, biologists, psychologists and economists each have a distinctive vocabulary in which they formulate laws and explain the events which interest them. In the heyday of positivism, philosophers sought to provide these scientists with a translation manual – a manual which would enable the physicist to restate in his own terms what the economist was saying when he offered an economic explanation for an increase in unemployment (Carnap, 1949). But such a manual could not be produced and philosophers of science were forced to acknowledge a plurality of scientific theories.

If we have more than one science on our hands, then we must provide some account of the relationship between them. An important part of this task is to effect a reconciliation between two widely shared opinions. On the one hand, there is the conviction that physics is the fundamental science. On the other hand, there is the insistence that special sciences such as biology, psychology and economics are autonomous disciplines whose lawlike statements and explanatory claims stand in no need of support from physics.

Under these conflicting pressures, the levels metaphor naturally suggests itself as a way of visualising the structure of science. According to this picture, there is a hierarchy made up of different levels of explanation. Physics is at the base of this hierarchy and the rest of the structure depends upon it. But the higher reaches of the scientific edifice have explanatory features which could not be discerned by someone who confined himself to exploring the ground floor. Of course, this metaphor is crucially vague until we say how exactly these higher level features can depend on those of the foundations when there are explanations which cannot be discovered at the base.

In the first section of this chapter, I try to formulate the claim that physics is the fundamental science. My formulation gives physics a certain ontological primacy, but it does not grant any special status to physical explanations. The second and third sections describe some popular accounts of the relationship between the different sciences, all of which hold that non-physical explanations are underwritten by physical explanations. In the last two sections, I urge that these models are acceptable only if we can employ certain patterns of inference in order to derive complex physical explanations from relatively simple physical explanations, principles of inference which were rejected in chapter 1. I conclude that the non-physical sciences provide explanations which have no physical counterpart – the primacy of physics does not entail the hegemony of physical explanation.

## THE PRIMACY OF PHYSICS

One very popular physicalist claim is this:

*Supervenience*: If two possible worlds are exactly similar in every physical respect, they are exactly similar in every respect.[1]

*Supervenience* assures us that there can be no difference in the non-physical state of two possible worlds without there being some difference in their physical state. If the non-physical facts supervene on the physical facts, then all God has to do in order to fix the non-physical facts about a world is to fix the physical facts about that world. Once the physical features of a world are determined, its non-physical features are determined also. *Supervenience* describes a relationship between all the physical facts and all the non-physical facts. However, the supervenience relation can also hold between a subset of the non-physical facts and a subset of the physical facts. By comparing different possible worlds we can find out which of the physical facts are specifically relevant to certain

---

[1] Kim, 1984a distinguishes several supervenience relations. *Supervenience* is closest to what he calls 'global supervenience'.

non-physical facts. And where certain physical facts fix certain non-physical facts, I shall say that these non-physical facts supervene on the subvenient physical facts.

'Supervenes' is not an asymmetric relation. The fact that non-physical facts supervene on physical facts does not prevent the physical supervening on the non-physical. *Supervenience* is quite consistent with the hypothesis that worlds similar in all non-physical respects also match in every physical respect. But this hypothesis is unlikely to be true. For instance, human pain, animal pain, extraterrestrial pain occur in creatures of quite diverse physical constitution; the states which subvene pain in these various creatures are liable to be physically heterogeneous; these creatures are psychologically similar, but physically different. Given this, it is not hard to imagine two worlds which match in respect of the distribution of pain within them, yet differ in their physical character. To put it another way, *Supervenience* does not enable God to fix some aspect of a subject's physical state just by fixing this sensational aspect of his psychological state.

Given that the physical does not supervene on the non-physical while the non-physical does supervene on the physical, physics is entitled to occupy the ground floor in an ontological hierarchy. But how is a claim so general as *Supervenience* to be established. How can we arrive at the conclusion that *all* the physical facts fix *all* the non-physical facts? By checking some of the consequences of *Supervenience* and then making an inductive leap to the truth of *Supervenience* itself.

I take it that if *Supervenience* is true, there are necessarily true generalisations which tell us that certain physical states of the world are sufficient conditions for certain non-physical states (Kim, 1984a:167–71). For instance, it is often said that facts about a person's sensations supervene on facts about the state of his brain – all the worlds which are similar in respect of brain-state facts are also similar in respect of pain facts. It follows that there is a true generalisation which says that when certain neural states obtain, certain pain states obtain, a generalisation which holds in every possible world, so this statement is a necessarily true generalisation. It is by confirming such generalisations that *Supervenience* itself is confirmed.

Is this necessarily true generalisation a causal generalisation? In chapter 2, we concluded that necessary truths may yet be causal generalisations but in chapter 4 (pages 79–81), I sought to distinguish causal generalisations from constitutive generalisations and I put statements like 'Heat

116

is molecular motion' firmly into the latter box. I also suggested that constitutive generalisations were to be established, either by discovering some non-empirical generalisation connecting the properties in question, or by identifying the causal roles of the properties in question. Do these thoughts apply to the case of pain?

It has been argued that pain is the state (whatever it is) necessary and sufficient for aversion behaviour given harmful stimuli.[2] Empirical inquiry may reveal that in certain circumstances a neurological state, C-fibre stimulation, will mediate between stimuli and aversion behaviour, and will be necessary and sufficient for the one given the other. On this account of pain, such empirical inquiry is enough to establish that the presence of C-fibre stimulation *just is* the presence of pain.

In my view, if *Supervenience* is to count as an adequate formulation of physicalism, we must insist that the psycho-physical generalisations which it entails are constitutive non-causal generalisations. Were these generalisations causal, mental phenomena would be something over and above the physical phenomena with which they are associated by law, something ontologically independent of them, but such a possibility is surely incompatible with physicalism. And this is so even if the causal generalisations connecting psychological with physical phenomena are necessary truths.

Lewis rejects *Supervenience* as a formulation of physicalism on the grounds that it is too strong.

Materialism is meant to be a contingent thesis, a merit of our world that not all other worlds share. Two worlds could indeed differ without differing physically, if at least one of them is a world in which materialism is false. For instance, our materialistic world differs from a non-materialistic world that is physically just like ours but that also contains physically epiphenomenal spirits. (Lewis, 1983b:362)

Since my main purpose in this chapter is to demonstrate that the ontological primacy of physics does not have the implications for explanation it is normally thought to have, it would not upset my dialectic if *Supervenience* turned out to be too strong as a formulation of physicalism. Nevertheless, I suspect Lewis' assured statement of the intentions of the physicalist rests on the assumption, queried in chapter 2, that laws of nature, including here those generalisations linking physical

---

[2] Lewis, 1983a emphasises the *causal* role of pain. As I make clear below, supervenience is not established by matching the causal relations of the supervenient and subvenient states but rather their nomological relations.

and psychological phenomena, are only contingently true. If we can infer from the existence of a whole set of generalisations connecting each non-physical with some physical phenomena that there will always be such a generalisation wherever there is a non-physical phenomenon, and we assume that these generalisations are necessary truths, then it seems reasonable to regard the assertion that there will always be such a generalisation as itself a necessary truth. So the materialist should not allow the possibility of immaterial phenomena.

*Supervenience* mentions neither causation nor explanation. But it is widely believed to entail the following thesis:

*Causal Pervasion*: If $x$'s having non-physical property $S(1)$ causally explains $y$'s having non-physical property $S(2)$ then there are subvenient physical properties of $x$ and $y$, namely $P(1 \ldots n)$ and $Q(1 \ldots n)$ such that $x$'s having $P(1 \ldots n)$ causally explains $y$'s having $Q(1 \ldots n)$.[3]

Say that my being in pain causes me to move my arm – so my pain is, in the circumstances, necessary and sufficient for this movement. According to *Supervenience*, I am in pain in virtue of being in a certain physical state, perhaps a neural state. Since my being in this neural state constitutes my being in pain, surely my being in this neural state is also necessary and sufficient for this movement? If I had not been in this neural state, I would not have moved my arm and, given that I am in this state, I will move my arm. So does not my neural state cause me to move my arm? Indeed, it is hard to see how the causal relations of the pain and the subvenient neural state could come apart.[4] Note that my arm's movement is not overdetermined by the pain and the neural state – this would be true only if the pain and the neural state were *independent* causes.

(This argument should be carefully distinguished from the following line of reasoning: 'my smoking is the cause of my heart condition and my smoking also causes my wife's heart condition, therefore my heart

[3] There is a close similarity between *Causal Pervasion* and physicalist claims made by several philosophers, for example, Fodor, 1981:139. Davidson's Principle of the Nomological Character of Causality, when combined with his view that physical laws are the only strict causal laws, has much the same import – see Davidson, 1980d:223–5. The most similar physicalist claim I can find is Peacocke's Principle of Physical Embedding: Peacocke, 1979:123–4. These philosophers all presuppose that every non-physical event is identical to some physical event. I have replaced this token-identity claim with a supervenience claim in my formulation.

[4] Something like this argument appears in Kim, 1984a. I used the argument myself in Owens, 1989b:61. I now reject the distinction between causal relevance and causal explanation made in that article.

condition is a cause of my wife's heart condition'. Opinions differ over whether the fact that our heart conditions have a common cause entails that if I had not had a heart attack, my wife would not have had one either. But it is agreed on all sides that my wife's heart condition is not an effect of my own (chapter 3, page 51 and chapter 5, page 97).

But what the argument shows is not that *Supervenience* entails *Causal Pervasion*, but rather that *Supervenience* entails the following thesis:

*Completeness*: If $x$'s having non-physical property $S(1)$ causally explains $y$'s having non-physical property $S(2)$ then there are subvenient physical properties of $x$ and $y$, namely $P(1 \ldots n)$ and $Q(1 \ldots n)$ such that $x$'s having $P(1 \ldots n)$ is necessary and sufficient for $y$ to have $Q(1 \ldots n)$.

As we learnt in chapters 4 and 5, there is more to being a cause than being a necessary and sufficient condition: causes must explain their effects, must ensure that they are no coincidence. But there is nothing in *Supervenience* to ensure that $y$'s possession of all the properties on which $S(2)$ supervenes, namely $Q(1 \ldots n)$ is no coincidence relative to $x$'s possession of the properties on which $S(1)$ supervenes, namely $P(1 \ldots n)$. In particular, as I shall demonstrate, we cannot infer that $x$'s having $P(1 \ldots n)$ causes $y$ to have $Q(1 \ldots n)$ from the fact that these events subvene $x$'s having $S(1)$ and $y$'s having $S(2)$ respectively together with the fact that $x$'s having $S(1)$ causes $y$ to have $S(2)$.

Supervenience does not entail *Causal Pervasion*. I shall argue that *Causal Pervasion* is false and should not be included among the tenets of a physicalist. There is a further thesis, often upheld by physicalists and entailed by *Causal Pervasion* which I also reject:

*Causal Closure*: For all physical properties $P$ and for all objects $x$, if $x$ has $P$ and there is a causal explanation of $x$'s having $P$ then there is a purely physical causal explanation of $x$'s having $P$.

Supervenience does not entail *Causal Closure* because while $y$'s having $Q(1 \ldots n)$ may be no coincidence given that $x$ has $S(1)$, it may nevertheless be a coincidence relative to its having $P(1 \ldots n)$. Again, I will illustrate this possibility below. Nevertheless, Supervenience does constrain the causal claims of the non-physical sciences in virtue of entailing *Completeness*.

It is widely supposed that evidence which supports economic or psychological explanations of human behaviour poses no threat to the physical sciences. The physiologist, the chemist and the physicist react with equanimity to the success of these special sciences in explaining the behaviour of physical entities such as human bodies. However, a physical scientist would be far more disturbed by data which purports to support the claims of astrology or telepathy. Most likely he would either query the evidence presented or deny that it supports these theories, but, if he were convinced by the evidence, he would feel the need to revise his physical theory in the light of it by acknowledging types of physical mechanism which he had not previously countenanced. But what is the reason for this difference, why should the physical scientist think of himself as in competition with some non-physical sciences but not others?

Compare telepathy with ordinary perception by sight. In perception by sight there is a physical organ, the human eye, which ensures a correlation between features of the environment and features of the subject's experience by means of a physical medium, namely light. Whenever a person has a visual experience of the tree in front of him, we can say in virtue of which neural state he has that experience, and then we can formulate a set of purely physical necessary and sufficient conditions under which the presence of such a tree in his environment will lead him to be in that neural state. Thus *Completeness* is not threatened. However, it is not at all clear what physiological system would underlie telepathic interactions, or what the physical medium of those interactions would be. If someone consistently acquired true beliefs about the mind of another in a way which did not involve his sensory organs, we would be faced with three alternatives: (a) we could regard his successes as a mere coincidence, though this position would become untenable once the evidence mounted (b) we could postulate a hitherto unacknowledged medium of perception and a hitherto unnoticed sensory organ which was sensitive to it (c) we could dispense with the medium and claim that one person's state of mind directly influenced the other.

(c) is clearly incompatible with current physics which rules out such action at a distance. If we are to provide a causal explanation of the correlation between two spatially disconnected items, like the experience and its object, in a way consonant with physics, we must find something to mediate this correlation, something that will fill the spatial gap. Furthermore, this connection must obtain in virtue of recognised physical facts concerning microscopic mechanisms and processes. If we opt for (b), we have no guarantee that this condition is satisfied. Either way, *Completeness* is violated by instances of telepathy – there is no set of physical conditions which is both necessary and sufficient for the state of mind of one person to lead to a telepathically acquired belief in another; this is what puts us into the trilemma.

I have formulated physicalism in terms of *Supervenience*. *Supervenience* captures the thought that everything *is* a physical thing. It also, by entailing *Completeness*, places physics on the ground floor of a nomo-logical hierarchy; for there is no reason to believe the converse of *Completeness*, namely that there are non-physical necessary and sufficient conditions for every physical occurrence, if only because there are very many small things with physical properties but no biological, psycho-logical, or economic properties. But while *Supervenience* constrains the causal claims of the non-physical sciences it does not purport to replicate them at the physical level.

## REDUCTIONISM AND CAUSAL PERVASION

Many philosophers are inclined to think that the primacy of physical science entails the primacy of physical explanations, though there is disagreement over how this latter claim should be formulated. Since *Supervenience* fails to secure explanatory primacy, something more must be added. In this section, I examine two proposals about what that further physicalist claim should be, and in the following section I formulate a third.

Fisher's law states that the level of prices in an economy is a function of the quantity of money in that economy, given that the velocity of money and the amount of goods and services produced remain constant. If we ignore this qualification, we can rewrite the law as follows:

*Fisher's Law*: If there is an increase in the money supply this will cause a rise in the level of prices.

So the occurrence of a monetary expansion would explain a rise in the rate of inflation. How is this economic explanation related to physical explanations?

One positivist proposal which has been revived in recent discussion is this:

*Reductionism*: If the occurrence of an $S(1)$-event causally explains the occurrence of an $S(2)$-event then there are physical properties $P(1)$ and $P(2)$ such that (a) an $S(1)$-event occurs if and only if a $P(1)$-event occurs (b) an $S(2)$-event occurs if and only if a $P(2)$-event occurs and (c) the occurrence of a $P(1)$-event causally explains the occurrence of a $P(2)$-event. (Nagel, 1961:345–58)

*Reductionism* states that there are physical predicates $P(1)$ and $P(2)$ which are invariably instantiated alongside the economic predicates 'is an increase in the money supply' and 'is a rise in the price level' respectively. $P(1)$-events are nomologically necessary and sufficient for $P(2)$-events and thereby causally explain them. So, wherever there is an economic explanation which can be given by invoking *Fisher's Law*, there is also a physical explanation which can be given by invoking the physical law linking $P(1)$-events with $P(2)$-events.

*Reductionism* is sometimes expressed as the thesis that the laws of the non-physical sciences can be deduced from those of the physical sciences together with certain bridging generalisations; my formulation of it captures this thought. For example, *Fisher's Law* could be derived from the law linking $P(1)$-events and $P(2)$-events by invoking the bridge generalisations connecting the $P$-predicates with the $S$-predicates. Of course, it is equally true that this physical law could be derived from *Fisher's Law* together with the bridge generalisations. The asymmetry between economics and physics lies in the following fact: while all economic predicates are invariably instantiated along with some physical predicate, not all physical predicates are invariably instantiated alongside some economic predicate, so physics as a whole cannot be derived from economics, but the whole of economics can be derived from physics.

*Supervenience* does not entail *Reductionism*. If economic facts supervene on physical facts then, wherever there is a monetary expansion, there will be a set of physical conditions whose obtaining is sufficient for that expansion. But these physical conditions need not also be conditions necessary for any increase in the money supply to take place.[5] Different monetary expansions may supervene on different physical facts and thus the truth of *Supervenience* is quite compatible with the falsity of clauses (a) and (b) in *Reductionism*. Since *Supervenience* entails nothing about explanation, it is also compatible with the falsity of (c).

Does *Reductionism* entail *Supervenience*? That depends on how we interpret the bi-conditional statements in clauses (a) and (b). If these are necessarily true then *Reductionism* will entail *Supervenience*, but, if they are merely contingent correlations, it will not. I think *Supervenience* essential to physicalism, and to simplify the discussion I intend to construe (a) and (b) as necessary truths. This stipulation means that we do not have to add anything to *Reductionism* in order to get a full-blown physicalist claim.

---

[5] Of course, certain physical conditions may be necessary for the occurrence of a monetary event in specific physical circumstances, but no mention of this physical background is made by the economic law we wish to reduce – only background conditions formulated in economic terms are relevant to the reduction.

None of the problems to be raised for *Reductionism* depend on this feature of my formulation.

On the reductionist view, what makes physics and not economics the fundamental science is the fact that economics can be derived from physics (together with some bridging generalisations) but physics cannot be derived from economics. According to the reductionist, there is nothing of explanatory importance, no laws or nomologically interesting classifications of events which cannot be formulated in the language of physics. But there are many nomologically interesting classifications which can be formulated only in the vocabulary of physics.

Several philosophers have held that a brief consideration of the physical constitution of non-physical objects and events will refute *Reductionism*. Dennett imagines a race of Martians who have all the laws of physics and all the physical facts at their command.

Take a particular instance in which the Martians observe a stockbroker deciding to place an order for 500 shares of General Motors. They predict the exact motions of his fingers as he dials the phone and the exact vibrations of his vocal cords as he intones his order. But if the Martians do not see that indefinitely many *different* patterns of finger motions and vocal cord vibrations – even the motions of indefinitely many different individuals – could have been substituted for the actual particulars without perturbing the subsequent operation of the market, then they have failed to see a real pattern in the world they are observing. Just as there are indefinitely many ways of *being a spark plug* – and one has not understood what an internal combustion engine is unless one realizes that a variety of different devices can be screwed into these sockets without affecting the performance of the engine – so there are indefinitely many ways of *ordering* 500 *shares of General Motors*, and there are societal sockets in which one of these ways will produce just about the same effect as any other. (Dennett, 1987:25–6)

The point Dennett is making in this passage is that physically quite different events may constitute a selling of General Motors shares, just as physically quite different devices may serve as a spark plug. This point is sometimes put by saying that while both share deals and spark plugs must be physically realised, they may be physically realised in many different ways. Call this the multiple realisation point.

The same point can be made by reference to *Fisher's Law*. Quite different physical substances have been, and could be, used as money. Gold, silver, copper, paper and even sea-shells have all been pressed into service. The list of substances that could be used as money is endless. Therefore, the physical predicates true of those things which actually or potentially satisfy the predicate 'is legal tender' are quite heterogeneous

(Fodor, 1981:134). A similar diversity will be found among the physical conditions on which monetary expansions and inflations supervene – some will be printings of paper, others will be minings of precious metals and yet others will be disturbances of the airwaves by people negotiating with their bank managers.

We may infer from all this that there are no bridging generalisations which correlate monetary expansions or inflations with the occurrence of a specific kind of physical event. Since such bridging generalisations are required by *Reductionism*, these banal considerations appear to frustrate those who wish to reduce *Fisher's Law* to physics.

Fodor suggests that a reductionist might attempt to construct suitable physical predicates by disjoining those predicates true of the various substances which are, or might be, used as money (Fodor, 1981:140). But this procedure will not help if it is admitted that the properties referred to by these different predicates are quite heterogeneous. As I have argued elsewhere, a disjunction of heterogeneous physical predicates will not be suitable for mention in a physical law of nature, and thus in any which could underwrite *Fisher's law* (Owens, 1989a).

But, as Fodor and others have noted, we need not reject the claim that physical explanations have a certain primacy just because we have abandoned *Reductionism*. Rather, we may revert to the weaker *Causal Pervasion*. *Causal Pervasion* secures a foundational role for physical explanations while not requiring that every non-physical predicate be co-extensive with some physical predicate. So it is not undermined by the multiple realisation point.

## REDUCTION

In this section, I want to argue that the thought which has led people to adopt *Reductionism* is best expressed by a rather different claim which I call *Reduction*. *Reduction* is not undermined by the multiple realisation point and yet it is, in a certain respect, stronger than *Reductionism*. I shall examine several paradigm instances of reductive explanation in the physical sciences in order to show that *Reduction* describes what is going on better than *Reductionism*. *Causal Pervasion* is best seen as a weakening of *Reduction*.

Some time ago, scientists discovered that water was $H_2O$, that a water molecule was two hydrogen atoms ionically bonded to one oxygen atom. They found they could explain the chemical properties of water (for example the fact that it is a liquid at some temperatures and a gas at others) by supposing that water was composed of molecules with this atomic constitution. In particular, they could explain the way water reacted when combined with other substances once they knew what water was. Given the atomic analysis of water and the atomic analysis of oil, they could account for the fact that oil and water do not mix.

*Reductionism* is an attempt to describe this explanatory success. According to *Reductionism*, the success consisted in the discovery that the chemical predicate 'water' was nomologically co-extensive with an atomic predicate '$H_2O$', and the laws about $H_2O$ enabled us to explain the intrinsic features and the behaviour of water. As a result, explanations which involved the term 'water' and further chemical-substance terms could be restated in terms of '$H_2O$' and other atomic formulae. Thus the chemical laws about water were reduced to atomic laws.

However, *Reductionism*'s description of this explanatory success highlights a quite inessential feature of it, namely that 'water' was discovered to be *co-extensive* with some atomic predicate. What is actually required for a reduction is that physical chemistry be able to *explain* why water has the properties and behaves in the way it does by telling us what *constitutes* water. And finding an atomic predicate which is co-extensive with this physical predicate is neither necessary nor sufficient for this. It is not necessary because one might have provided a constitutive explanation of the presence of water without calling on some atomic description co-extensive with water. And it is not sufficient because finding '$H_2O$' co-extensive with 'water' does not rule out the possibility that the behaviour of water is a coincidence in the presence of $H_2O$ and thus cannot be explained by it.

I have said that co-extension of predicates is irrelevant to reduction, but this might seem inconsistent with my remarks about constitution in chapter 4 (pages 80–1). There I proposed that $x$'s having $P$ at $t$ is constituted by $y$'s having $Q$ at $t$ only if property $P$ = property $Q$. I want to involve the reductionist in making claims about constitution, so it seems he must also make claims about property identity; but if $P = Q$ then surely $P$ must, at the very least, be co-extensive with $Q$, so the reductionist is, after all, out to establish that these predicates are co-extensive. I shall fault this line of reasoning at its last step: property identity statements need not involve simple co-extension of predicates provided the properties are specified in a suitable way.

Water is any substance which satisfies a certain functional specification: boils at 100°C, does not mix with oil etc. It might be that, on earth, the substance which satisfies this specification is $H_2O$ but, in different galaxies, this substance has a quite different chemical formula. I think we, on earth, could still say that 'Water = $H_2O$', could still claim that these properties were identical, despite the existence of water elsewhere which was not $H_2O$. This is no more mysterious than maintaining that the leader of the nation was Margaret Thatcher, in full knowledge that her writ did not run outside the United Kingdom. These identity statements must be suitably contextualised. So neither property identity nor event constitution require co-extension.[6]

Having clarified this point we can reformulate *Reductionism* as follows:

*Reduction*: If the occurrence of an $S(1)$-event explains the occurrence of an $S(2)$-event then there are physical properties $P(1)$ and $P(2)$ such that (a) the occurrence of a $P(1)$-event *both* constitutes *and* explains the occurrence of an $S(1)$-event (b) the occurrence of a $P(2)$-event *both* constitutes *and* explains the occurrence of an $S(2)$-event (c) the occurrence of a $P(1)$ event causally explains the occurrence of a $P(2)$-event.

*Reduction* differs from *Reductionism* in not requiring the co-extension of physical and non-physical predicates in clauses (a) and (b). And it differs from both *Reductionism* and *Causal Pervasion* in requiring that the constituting events in (a) and (b) explain the occurrence of the events they constitute. I shall describe a number of ways in which one might reduce one physical explanation to another without making any claims about co-extension of predicates. But, first, I want to emphasise that both *Reductionism* and *Causal Pervasion* will not give the reductionist what he ought to want in clauses (a) and (b).

All clauses (a) and (b) of *Reductionism* and *Causal Pervasion* guarantee is that there will be a set of atomic conditions which are (necessarily) sufficient for a substance to be water, which constitute its being water. They do not ensure that this set *explains* the fact that our substance is water; for all they say, it may be a complete coincidence that our substance is water relative to this set of conditions. Of course, this set cannot *causally* explain the fact that our substance is water since it constitutes its being water, but it might also fail to explain it *tout court*.

As things actually are, the fact that the substance is $H_2O$ does explain the chemical properties and behaviour which make us call it 'water'. It

---

[6] For a similar view of property identities see Jackson, Pargetter and Prior, 1982. For an opposed view of 'water', see Putnam, 1975:223–35.

may (or may not) be a coincidence that two hydrogen atoms are ionically bonded to one oxygen atom, but these atoms in this arrangement combine to explain the characteristic behaviour and properties of water – they do not separately explain different aspects of it. Therefore, it is no coincidence that the substance behaves like water, given that it is $H_2O$, and the reduction goes through.

But it is quite possible for one set of conditions to constitute a certain phenomenon by being separately relevant to different aspects of that phenomenon. We may find that some of the constitutive conditions are needed to explain one piece of behaviour, while other quite independent conditions are needed to account for another. In this case, the constituting conditions will not combine to explain the phenomenon which they constitute, and a reduction of that phenomenon to its constituents will be impossible.

Take the physical event which is the conjunction of all the motions of struck billiard balls which have occurred on billiard tables across the world in the last five minutes. This event clearly has a set of purely physical constituents, namely its component motions. It also has many physical effects, all the effects of all those different motions. But we cannot explain why this whole event occurred by citing the movement of each of these balls – the fact that these motions occur together is a pure coincidence, and the physical event in question is the logical sum of these events. Nor can we explain why all of the effects of these motions occurred together by citing the independent causes of each effect. Therefore, though physically constituted, our event and its effects are a physical coincidence, and thus are physically inexplicable.

I shall now review two reductive strategies which do not require us to identify relations of co-extension between predicates in the reduced and the reducing science respectively. In the course of this review, I shall establish exactly which conditions are necessary for these strategies to succeed within the physical sciences. This is a prelude to the final section where I shall insist that none can succeed in reducing non-physical to physical science.

One obvious method of reduction is to use laws containing physical determinables to reduce laws containing relatively determinate physical terms. This method may be applied to effect reductions of explanations involving rather different physical determinates to explanations involving a common physical determinable, so it can accommodate the multiple realisation point. Blackburn illustrates this possibility as follows:

Consider (to use an example of Fodor's) the physical process summed up in the geological 'law' that meandering rivers erode their outside banks. A physical process, and one in principle explicable by fluid hydrodynamics. Yet neither river, nor meander, nor bank is a term of physics. All that the 'reduction' of the law to one of physics, in one good sense of the word, requires, is that rivers are each of them some, but not necessarily the same, kind of flowing liquid, that meanders are, each of them some but not necessarily the same kind of curved configuration and banks are (each of them) some, but not necessarily the same, kind of material liable to lose its cohesion under traverse forces. (Blackburn, 1991:219; see also Hooker, 1981:497–500)

The laws of hydrodynamics apply to physical substances with various physical constitutions. For instance, they apply to geological phenomena such as rivers and banks – liquids of quite different types can constitute rivers which erode banks. Nevertheless, one generalises across banks eroded by different kinds of river in the laws of hydrodynamics. Describing something as a 'river full of water' is to give a more determinate specification than that given by 'a flowing liquid' but the less determinate specification is all that is needed to explain those aspects of the river's behaviour relevant to its erosive powers.

The ability of physical science to generalise across items with divergent physical constitutions is well illustrated by the laws of mechanics. The behaviour of any given pair of colliding billiard balls may be explained by invoking the laws of Newtonian dynamics: each billiard ball will be ascribed a certain mass, velocity and direction of motion and their subsequent motions will be explained in terms of these properties. At no point will the physicist worry about the fact that one pair of balls is made of gold, another of wood and a third is full of sand. He will happily ascribe the same mass or velocity to quite differently constituted balls, and there is no reason why the physical explanation of a wooden ball's movement should not be the same as that of a sand ball's movement, provided they have the same mass, velocity and direction of motion (Putnam, 1975:295–7).

Since there is multiple realisation within physics, we cannot halt the reduction of *Fisher's Law* to physics simply by alluding to the physical diversity of the substances which serve as money, nor by pointing out that 'money' occurs nowhere in physical theory. We must demonstrate that a rise in the money supply and a rise in the price level are not the kinds of events which could, when described in slightly more general terms, instantiate a physical law.

The second reductive strategy I wish to describe might be called the strategy of functional analysis (Cummins, 1984 and Hooker, 1981). This strategy is applied to physical systems of some complexity with certain characteristic patterns of input and output. What is to be explained are these characteristic patterns – why we get a certain kind of output given a specific input. We postulate a complex mechanism which mediates between input and output, and set about investigating how that mechanism works, how its various parts combine to explain the production of a given output given a certain input.

Certain conditions must be met if such a functional analysis is to be reductive. Our explanation would not be very illuminating had we to proceed on a case by case basis, describing how a series of perhaps quite different mechanisms effect the same correlation between input and output. Then it might seem a mere coincidence that this one pattern was instantiated in such different mechanisms. We must show that the differences between these mechanisms are irrelevant to an explanation of why they instantiate the required pattern – that rather general conditions, satisfied by all the mechanisms concerned, will guarantee the maintenance of this regularity.

I take the reduction of the heat of a gas to the mean kinetic energy of its molecules to be an example of a successful functional analysis. The input–output correlations which were to be explained in this case are those derivable from the *Boyle–Charles' Law*.

*Boyle–Charles' Law*: For an ideal gas, the product of its pressure and volume equals the product of its absolute temperature and a constant for a given mass of the gas, or, in symbols, $pV = kT$.

From this we know that if we raise the temperature while holding the volume constant (input) then the pressure of the gas will rise (output). So the task is to explain why the *Boyle–Charles' Law* holds of an ideal gas.

This explanation proceeds by formulating some rather general assumptions about the gas. According to these, the gas is made up of a large number of perfectly elastic spherical molecules each of which have the same mass and volume, while their dimensions are negligible when compared with the average distances between them. The molecules are in motion, but it is assumed that the only forces acting upon them are the result of collisions between themselves and the perfectly elastic walls of the container. Given these assumptions, we can use the principles of Newtonian mechanics to calculate the relation of other features of their motion to the pressure exerted by the molecules on the walls of the container by their constant bombardments.

However, it is, in practice, impossible to ascertain the state of all the individual molecules at any given instant and in order to come to grips with the problem, a further assumption must be introduced – a statistical one concerning the positions and momenta of the molecules. This statistical assumption is this: divide the gas into a very large number of smaller volumes, whose dimensions are equal and yet large when compared with the diameters of the molecules; divide the whole range of velocities that the molecules may possess into a large number of equal intervals. A 'phase-cell' is defined as a combination of some volume with some velocity interval and every possible permutation of volumes and intervals is represented by a phase-cell. The statistical assumption then is that (a) the probability of a molecule's occupying an assigned phase-cell is the same for all molecules and is equal to the probability of a molecule's occupying any other phase-cell, and (b) the probability that one molecule occupies a phase-cell is independent of the occupation of that cell by any other molecule.

To deduce that the pressure $p$ is related in a very definite way to the mean kinetic energy $E$ of the molecules, we just need to assume that the pressure $p$ exerted at any instant by the molecules on the walls of the container is the average of the instantaneous momenta transferred from the molecules to the walls. Once this is assumed, we may conclude that $pV = 2E/3$. A comparison of this equation with the *Boyle–Charles' Law* suggests that the law could be deduced from the assumptions mentioned *if* the temperature were in some way related to the mean kinetic energy of the molecular motions.

Thus we can show that any ideal gas, namely any gas which satisfies these assumptions, will fall under the *Boyle–Charles' Law*. We need not strictly *identify* the temperature of a gas with the mean kinetic energy of its molecules in order to provide a molecular explanation of why the gas obeys the *Boyle–Charles' Law*, we just need to suppose that having a certain mean kinetic energy $E$ both constitutes and explains the fact that the gas is at a certain temperature $T$.

The assumptions required for this reduction are general in that they abstract from information about the location of, and velocity of, particular molecules in the gas. If these assumptions hold then, whatever the location and velocity of individual molecules, a rise in pressure where volume is fixed will produce a rise in temperature. So the particular arrangement of the molecules in the gas is actually irrelevant to this functional relationship and gases with quite different molecular arrangements which satisfied these assumptions would also instantiate the *Boyle–Charles' Law*.

Functional analysis is one way in which physics can abstract from the peculiar constitution of physical things while providing a reductive account of regularities which hold across systems with various constituents. Some details of the character of the components of a physical system (the locations of individual molecules) will be irrelevant to an account of those (thermodynamical) aspects of the system's behaviour in which we are interested, and systems whose constituents share those properties which are relevant will be equivalent from that (thermodynamical) point of view.

Raising the temperature of a gas while holding its volume constant will cause its pressure to rise. The functional analysis sketched above accounts for this causal relationship in terms of several rather general properties of the constituents of the gas. What it does *not* do is to explain the increase in pressure by tracing the chain of events at the molecular level which leads up to it. It will not describe the initial distribution of the individual molecules, state how each molecule experienced an increase in its kinetic energy and, as a result, collided with the wall more often, given that it was in a container of the same size and finally conclude that pressure rose because a similar sequence of events happened to occur in the case of every other molecule (Sober, 1983 and Garfinkel, 1981:50–8).

But it is not mere ignorance of the location of velocity of individual molecules that accounts for the omission of these details. Rather, if these details were included the explanation would lose its force. Some have suggested that this is because these details are irrelevant to what we wish to explain, namely why the pressure of the gas went up (Putnam, 1975:295–7). The increase in temperature and stability of volume when combined with our general assumptions will suffice to explain that. But why should introducing irrelevant details undermine our explanation, so long as the relevant ones are there? Surely, if we are told that each individual molecule is in such and such a place and experiences such and such an increase in kinetic energy, then we can explain why it will collide with the container at this place at that time and at that place at this time, and so on and so forth? And, given all these explanations, we can deduce that the total pressure of the gas will rise and thus explain it.

The problem with this deduction is not that it is hideously complex, nor that its premises contain irrelevant details, but rather that the truth of its premises is a coincidence and the deduction represents the rise in pressure as a mere amalgamation of the facts registered in these premises – it represents the rise in pressure as a coincidence and thus cannot explain it. It is a coincidence that the statement 'molecule $x$ hit the container wall at place $p$ at time $t$ and molecule $y$ hit the container wall at place $q$ at time $u$ etc.' is true: the causal factors relevant to molecule $x$'s collision with the wall at that time and in that place (namely its starting position and velocity, kinetic energy etc.) will be separate and independent of those relevant to molecule $y$'s collision.

By contrast, it is no coincidence that the pressure increases if the temperature of the gas is raised and the gas satisfies the conditions for being an ideal gas specified above. These general conditions combine with the increase in temperature to explain the increase in pressure, they are not separately relevant to different parts of that increase. Therefore, if we want to explain the increase in pressure, we *must* leave out the molecular details and stick to general assumptions about the gas.[7]

I set out to demonstrate that even if *Reductionism* and multiple realisation are incompatible, *Reduction* and multiple realisation are not. So have we removed the only obstacle there is to a reduction of the physical to the non-physical sciences? In the next section, I shall argue that *Reduction* cannot adequately describe the relationship between the physical and the non-physical sciences.

## AUTONOMY AND REDUCTION

Recall the economic law introduced earlier:

*Fisher's Law*: If there is an increase in the money supply this will cause a rise in the level of prices.

It seems obvious that there is no physical predicate co-extensive with either monetary or financial predicates, so *Reductionism* is falsified by this law. But what of *Reduction*? Might there be an explanation for the presence of a monetary expansion and of an inflation, one framed in terms of their physical constituents? And might these two constitutive explanations be combined to yield a physical causal explanation of how

---

[7] I think this is the grain of truth in Garfinkel's talk about structural presuppositions preventing the reduction of the whole to a mere sum of its parts, and the sensible thought behind his requirement that causal explanations be stable. Garfinkel, 1981:51–8.

an increase in the money supply brings about a rise in the price level? As we have seen, multiple realisation alone will not rule out this possibility, so let us apply the two reductive strategies outlined in the last section to the case of *Fisher's Law*.

It is not so obvious how every increase in the money supply and every rise in the price level can be brought within the scope of some macrophysical law indifferent to the diversity of their physical constituents. Rivers, meanders and banks slot neatly into the categories of hydrodynamics, but it is hard to see which physical science could deal with an increase in the money supply. Of course, wherever the money supply is increasing, something physical will be going on, but this does not mean that the monetary expansion itself falls under a macrophysical law.

What is it to instantiate a macrophysical law? Two colliding billiard balls clearly instantiate certain laws of Newtonian dynamics, laws which provide a macrophysical explanation of why one ball moved given that the other hit it. But let us take the less salient physical event considered above, the event which consists of all those motions of struck billiard balls which have happened on billiard tables throughout the world in the last five minutes. Does this event have a macrophysical explanation?

If it does have a macrophysical explanation, that explanation must be one derived from the macrophysical explanations of all its constituent movements. This shapeless fusion event is brought within the scope of the laws of mechanics by applying those laws to each of its constituents and then combining the results. By contrast an explanation of the behaviour of an individual billiard ball is arrived at by direct application of the laws of mechanics. A billiard ball is not a mere heap of atoms – we cannot explain what will happen to the whole ball simply by trying to find independent mechanical processes in which its different constituents participate and then summing their outcomes. Rather, we must attend to features of the ball such as its rigidity, features produced by complex interactions among its microscopic constituents.

I would suggest that economic events are, in the eyes of the physicist, to be compared to shapeless fusions of physical events such as our set of billiard ball collisions. They are spatially discontinuous and composed of a plethora of quite independent causal processes. In fact, these economic events have even less physical cohesion then our fusion of billiard ball collisions, since the physical processes implicated in an economic process are physically heterogeneous. There is no reason to believe that this fusion directly instantiates some macrophysical law. If there is a macrophysical explanation of the inflation, it must be one derived from the separate physical explanations of its physical constituents.

To drive this point home, I will describe a possible inflation. Let us say that we have returned to the days when money was backed by gold. One way in which a monetary expansion can take place in such an economy is through an increase in the supply of gold available to the banks. Suppose that several new gold mines are discovered, that merchants start to hoard the gold they have acquired through foreign trade, that people are more inclined to deposit their gold with their bankers. All these factors will contribute towards an increase in the gold reserves available to various different banks and will enable them to issue more currency and make more loans backed by gold.

It should be clear that what will happen on the physical level during such a monetary expansion is a hugely complex array of disparate and mutually independent causal processes. There are the processes caused by the mining of gold, the processes resulting from foreign trade and the processes set in motion by the depositing of gold. These activities are physically heterogeneous and their occurrence has no common physical explanation – they originate and evolve quite independently of one another.

But we have not yet considered the intricate physical causal chain leading from the monetary expansion to the inflation. This chain will have numerous different strands each with innumerable links. It will be composed of the physical processes involved in many different people going into their banks and borrowing the new money which the banks can now lend them; these creditors will go out and spend the money, quite independently of one another, on a diverse range of goods and services and the producers of these goods and services will each note an increase in the demand for their products and will, quite independently, increase the price of their wares.

Think of the length and complexity of the causal chain of physical events leading from any one transfer of paper in a bank to the alteration of some price inscription – and think of the number of such chains needed to bring about a general inflation. The physical conditions relevant to the occurrence of events at different stages of this chain will be different from, and quite independent of, one another, so each of these chains will require a whole series of physical coincidences to keep it going.

However, none of this will affect the cogency of our economic explanation of the inflation. The economist does not concern himself with the vagaries of the physical mechanisms which link the monetary expansion and the inflation. He just formulates some very general macroeconomic background conditions (stability of the velocity of money and of output) under which there will be a functional relationship between the quantity of money in an economy and the level of prices in that economy. The character of the particular causal mechanisms which mediate this functional relationship is just irrelevant – the economist knows that there will always be such a mechanism, however inexplicable the constant appearance of the relevant type of mechanism may be to the physicist, and however unaccountable the physicist may find its production of the required economic result (Dennett, 1987:26–7).

I conclude from all this that if a monetary expansion or an inflation do instantiate laws of physics, then they must do so indirectly, in the way that the fusion of different billiard ball collisions instantiates a law of physics. An increase in the money supply and an inflation are not, from the standpoint of physics, cohesive physical events which might directly instantiate some macrophysical law. Rather they are fusions of the disparate activities of diverse physical objects. If they do fall under a macrophysical law, this is only in virtue of the fact that their physical constituents instantiate such laws.

Given the correctness of this conclusion, *Reduction* cannot be an accurate description of the relationship between economics and physics. For, as in the billiard ball case, the physical components of the monetary expansion and the inflation cannot provide a constitutive explanation for those events, and hence cannot provide a reductive account of how the monetary expansion brings about the inflation. But the reductionist may claim that his second reductive strategy has been left out of account. Why not attempt a functional analysis of the mechanisms which underlie *Fisher's Law*? *Fisher's Law* is, in principle, very like the *Boyle–Charles' Law* in that it lays down a functional relationship between certain inputs and certain outputs, one summed up in the equation $MV = PT$ (which says that the product of the money supply and the velocity of money (the frequency with which each monetary unit gets used in transactions) is equal to the product of the level of prices and the number of transactions made).

Both *Fisher's Law* and the *Boyle–Charles' Law* abstract from the details of the causal processes going on inside the system whose behaviour they regulate, and it is only because these laws abstract from such details and are not embroiled in the coincidences involved that they retain their explanatory force. The *Boyle–Charles' Law* was reduced to more basic physical laws by employing assumptions about the system's molecular constituents, assumptions at the right level of generality, so why could not *Fisher's Law* be dealt with similarly once we have found the right macrophysical assumptions?

If this reduction were effected, we would have a constitutive explanation of the behaviour of our economic system, one which explained why there was a monetary expansion in terms of certain physical conditions constituting that expansion, and why there was an inflation in terms of that inflation's constituting conditions, in the process making clear why the monetary expansion caused an inflation. And this constitutive explanation would proceed independently of assumptions about the positions of individual human bodies and the specific transactions between them, thus avoiding the accusation that it is explaining a coincidence. It would be general features of the constituents which accounted for this functional relationship.

The reductionist is right to say that nothing rules out this reduction. It is just totally unclear what these macrophysical assumptions might be. They cannot be conjunctions of those physical conditions necessary to put each of the physical components of the monetary expansion and the inflation in the right place at the right time for, as we have seen, such conditions will explain the presence of neither. But what else could they be?

Perhaps we should render the problem more tractable by taking things one step at a time. If a straight reduction of economics to physics is too much to hope for, why not instead begin by reducing economics to psychology and then proceed down towards the physical sciences from there, using both of the reductive strategies outlined above? In order to assess this suggestion adequately, I would have to examine every step of the proposed reduction, and this I have neither the space nor the ability to do. But, even in ignorance of all the relevant facts, I can point out two things which darken its prospects.

First, philosophers who have examined in detail some of the steps in the proposed reduction have discovered problems analogous to those which confront the straightforward reduction of economics to physics. For instance, the relationship between the adjacent sciences of Mendelian (or transmission) genetics and molecular genetics is, in the relevant respects, much like that between economics and physics.[8] And yet, presumably, our reductive project must encompass evolutionary biology and its genetic basis on its way towards physics.

Second, even if the reductionist can, by taking small enough steps, negotiate the terrain between the highest and the lowest level in the ontological hierarchy, he will not necessarily have achieved thereby a reduction of the social to the physical. For, as I observed in chapter 1, 'explains' is not a transitive relation. If, in order to reduce psychology to neurophysiology, the scientist had to appeal to background conditions quite independent of those required to reduce economics to psychology say, he could not credit himself with having reduced economics to neurophysiology. More than this is needed for neurophysiological facts to provide a constitutive explanation of economic processes, and *Reduction* requires such an explanation.

Failing this, without any successful reduction, perhaps we can still demonstrate that underlying the economic explanation provided by *Fisher's Law*, there is a physical explanation of how the constituents of the monetary expansion brought about the constituents of the inflation. This explanation will be derived by composing the explanations which link the behaviour of the constituents of the monetary expansion and those of the inflation, thereby constructing one big explanation, much as we intended to do in the case of the billiard balls. I want to round off the present chapter by showing that this hope cannot be realised – *Causal Pervasion* must go the way of *Reductionism* and *Reduction*.

## Autonomy and causal pervasion

*Causal Pervasion* is a weaker claim than either *Reductionism* or *Reduction* in that it does not require a constitutive explanation of the reduced phenomena in terms of the reducing phenomena. All it demands is that every non-physical explanation be accompanied by some physical explanation at the level of constituents. Might this much weaker claim be just what is needed to describe the relationship between the physical and the non-physical sciences?

[8] For the analysis of genetics, see Kitcher, 1984. Some reductionists have concluded that, when a non-physical explanation cannot be reduced to any physical explanation, we should dispense with the ontology and ideology implicit in the non-physical explanation and stick to the physics alone eg. Hooker, 1981 and Churchland, 1986:chapter 9. See in particular the useful example of the virtual governor discussed on pages 508–10 by Hooker, and on pages 364–7 of the Churchland book.

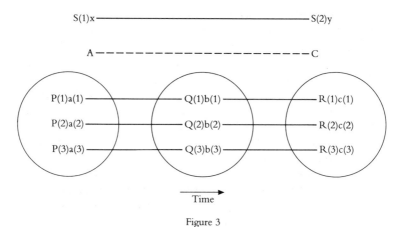

Figure 3

*Causal Pervasion* appears to be a happy compromise between the autonomy of the special sciences and the primacy of physics. It allows that there are nomologically interesting classifications of objects which do not correspond to any physical classification: objects which share some property that appears in the law like generalisations of a non-physical science, may have this property because of quite dissimilar and unrelated subvenient physical conditions. On the other hand, whenever one object explains some feature of another object because of their joint instantiation of some non-physical law, this connection must be underwritten by a physical law. These two things will have their non-physical properties because of the possession of certain physical properties, and so there will always be a physical explanation of why the having of one non-physical property brought about the having of another.

Figure 3 illustrates the relationship between the economic events which instantiate *Fisher's Law* and the physical processes underlying its operation. The capital letters stand for predicates and the small letters for the objects which satisfy those predicates. The solid lines connecting the Ss, and those connecting each of the Ps with one of the Qs, and those connecting each of the Qs with one of the Rs, represent nomological connections. It is an open question as to what is represented by the broken line connecting the set of P-things to the set of R-things.

We should read the diagram as follows: two economic events – $x$'s having $S(1)$ and $y$'s having $S(2)$ – instantiate an economic law. Two sets of physical conditions on which these economic events supervene are denoted by 'A' and 'C'. A contains things with properties $P(1)$, $P(2)$ and $P(3)$ which are denoted by '$a(1)$', '$a(2)$' and '$a(3)$'. C contains things with properties $R(1)$, $R(2)$ and $R(3)$ which are denoted by '$c(1)$', '$c(2)$', and '$c(3)$'.

The bottom half of *Figure* 3 is a much simplified picture of what is happening on the microphysical level during an inflation caused by an increase in the money supply. I am assuming that there is a physical explanation for each of $P(1)a(1)$, $P(2)a(2)$ and $P(3)a(3)$, that is for each of the physical conditions which constitute the increase in the money supply. The explanation will be different in the case of each of these events. The explanations may invoke different physical laws; they will certainly invoke diverse initial conditions, since each event will be explained, in the first instance, by reference to features of its immediate physical surroundings. There is no reason to believe that these surroundings will be similar to, or in any way determined by, the character of the physical surroundings needed to explain the occurrence of other events in the set.

A further feature of the physical situation which should be noted is that each component of the earlier set A is connected by a chain of nomologically related events to some part of the later set C. Therefore, there is a chain of physically explicable events leading from each member of A to some member of C. However, the physical explanation of an event at one stage in a given causal chain is liable to be quite different from the physical explanation of an event at some other stage. The laws invoked in these two explanations might well be different but even if the laws are the same, the physical conditions obtaining at a given stage of the causal chain will, at least in part, be different from, and undetermined by, those obtaining at other stages. Therefore, the initial conditions invoked in the explanations of these two events will be mutually independent.

The question which interests us is whether the broken line in *Figure* 3 which connects the sets of physical conditions A and C can stand for some explanatory link between A and C, as *Causal Pervasion* requires. If the relation 'causally explains' is agglomerative and transitive, then I can see no reason why the A-conditions should not causally explain the C-conditions.

The argument for such an explanation requires two steps. It employs the assumption of transitivity in order to infer from the fact that each member of A explains some member of the set of Q-conditions, which in turn explains some member of C, to the conclusion that each member of A explains some member of C. It then invokes the assumption of agglomerativity in order to infer from the fact that each member of A explains some member of C, the conclusion that the conjunction of the A-conditions causally explains the conjunction of the C-conditions. But, as I argued in chapter 1, neither of these assumptions is tenable. Therefore, the explanation postulated by *Causal Pervasion* is unobtainable (Hornsby, 1980a:84–5 and 87–8).

The laws of many different physical sciences may well be required in order to describe the nomological network connecting these different events, the causal processes happening in the various parts of the physical mechanism which underlies the monetary inflation will be qualitatively different from one another. However, this is not the crucial fact about this physical mechanism. For present purposes, we may assume that all these different physical laws can be derived from some small set of fundamental physical laws, so that the various underlying physical processes are fundamentally similar.

What matters is rather that the physical conditions which are needed to hold the various bits of this physical network together are quite independent of, and undetermined by, one another. The physical conditions which are needed to keep one component causal process going, at a given time, will obtain quite independently of those which are needed to keep other parts of the mechanism going at that time. And, for any given component causal process in the total mechanism, the conditions which are needed to keep that process going at one time will differ from, and be quite independent of, those needed to keep that same causal process going at other times. As we saw in chapter 1, these facts are fatal to the view that A explains C; they ensure there is no physical explanation which could underwrite the economic explanation.

It is not just *Causal Pervasion* which is undermined by this example. *Causal Closure* must also be rejected. For consider the relationship between the increase in the money supply and the set of physical events which constitute the rise in the price level. Surely, if the increase in the money supply renders the rise in the price level no coincidence, it must also render the obtaining of the set of conditions which constitute it no coincidence. So this economic event causes this physical event. Yet there is no physical cause of the conditions which constitute the inflation, for the inflation is a physical coincidence. Therefore, only the economist can explain the physical fact that the conditions which constitute the inflation jointly obtain.

*Completeness* (and thus *Supervenience*) are not threatened. We have assumed that there are purely physical conditions which are both necessary and sufficient for the physical conditions which constitute the inflation to obtain. No physicist should be worried by his inability to explain the arbitrary fusion of physical events which constitute an inflation, and nor should this concern a physicalist. Physicalism is adequately expressed by *Supervenience*.

To sum up, an expansion of the money supply causally explains a rise in the price level. Such a monetary expansion is necessary and sufficient for an inflation. Furthermore, the monetary expansion is a single causal factor which cannot be analysed into component macroeconomic conditions, each of which is separately relevant to a different part of the inflation. Nor are there component macroeconomic conditions which are separately relevant to events at different stages in the causal chain leading from the monetary expansion to the inflation. So, the rise in the money supply causally explains the inflation.

The set of physical conditions which realise the monetary expansion are necessary and sufficient for the set of physical conditions which collectively realise the inflation. However, the former set can be analysed into component physical conditions, each of which is separately relevant to different members of the latter set of physical conditions, and it can also be analysed into component physical conditions, each of which is separately relevant to events at different stages of the physical causal chain leading from the monetary expansion to the inflation. So, the occurrence of this first set of physical conditions does not explain the occurrence of the second set.

It may be objected that, if we can divide the first set of realising physical conditions into components which are separately relevant to different parts of the second set, then we can divide the monetary expansion in a similar way, thereby showing that it does not really explain the inflation. But, while the component physical conditions which constitute these realising sets are perfectly natural physical conditions, and it is the set of them which is the gerrymandered physical entity, there is no way of dividing the monetary expansion into natural economic components which are separately relevant to different parts of the inflation.

If we simply divide the monetary expansion into two halves, we fail to delineate two separate macroeconomic factors operating independently to produce the inflation – we do not thereby show that the inflation was a macroeconomic coincidence. But if we divide the physical set which realises this expansion in certain ways, we do delineate separate physical factors which operate independently to produce different elements of the physical set which realises the inflation – we do demonstrate that the occurrence of this second set is a physical coincidence.

Here, we have one instance in which both *Reduction* and *Causal Pervasion* fail, and there is every reason to believe that the special sciences will furnish us with many such examples. Very often, what must appear an accidental conjunction of events in the eyes of the physicist may be explained if we alter our focus and describe the situation in the language of biology, psychology or economics. This is the source of the explanatory autonomy of the special sciences.

# 7

# *Deviant causal chains*

In the last thirty years, philosophers have formulated analyses of a number of psychological notions, analyses which share the following feature: they stipulate that the psychological analysandum can be applied only if some psychological state and some non-psychological state stand in a causal relation. I shall concentrate on three phenomena which have received this treatment: perception, memory and action.

Causal accounts of all three notions have become part of the received wisdom about the mind but, at the same time, it is widely recognised that these analyses are inadequate. Simply to require that two states of the relevant type stand in a causal relation is not enough for either perception, memory or action, for there are causal chains which link the states in question but which preclude the application of the relevant psychological concepts. These chains have been branded 'deviant causal chains' and conceptual analysts have set about trying to say what they are so that they can be formally excluded.

I believe that the most successful attempts to characterise deviant causal chains all implicitly rely on principles and ideas enunciated in earlier chapters of this book. To eliminate these deviant chains, we must maintain, as I did in chapter 1, that causal explanation is neither transitive nor agglomerative, and we must embrace the idea, broached in chapter 6, that there are distinct and irreducible causal mechanisms to be found on different levels of explanation. In this chapter and the next, I will examine, among other things, Peacocke's treatment of perception and action, and Martin and Deutscher's theory of memory, with a view to demonstrating their tacit reliance on these assumptions.

## THE CAUSAL THEORY OF PERCEPTION

I shall begin by introducing some inelegant but familiar terminology which is necessary to mark important distinctions. When Jane asserts that

Harold sees a tree she might be saying either one of two quite different things. On the one hand she could be saying that there is a tree in front of Harold which Harold now sees, that Harold is having an experience *of* a tree. This remark is one about the *object* of Harold's visual experience, about what he sees and not about how he sees it. It is quite consistent with Jane's remark that Harold is unaware of the presence of a tree and thinks that what he is seeing in front of him is a tall man. On the other hand, Jane may be telling us about the *content* of Harold's experience, about how the world looks to Harold. As I shall put it, she may be telling us that Harold is having an experience *as of* a tree. This remark is quite consistent with the possibility that Harold is suffering an illusion because there is no tree in front of Harold but only a tall man whom he mistook for a tree.

In this chapter I shall be discussing the causal theory of perception. The causal theory of perception is a theory of the *objects* of perception, it is an attempt to answer the following question: what is it for a subject S to perceive an object O? It is not a theory of the *content* of perceptual experience. However, the content and the object of an experience are not unconnected – if S is to see O then S must have an experience E reportable in the words 'I am having an experience as of a such and such thing' where the reported content of E fits O, at least to some extent: a tree might be seen and yet be mistaken for a tall man, but a tree could not be seen while being mistaken for a large sea. So a certain kind of content must be present if a certain type of object is to be seen. I shall not attempt to make this connection more precise, nor shall I provide any account of what it is for an experience to have a given content. I shall simply stipulate facts about the content of experience in the course of discussing how these facts and others fix the object of an experience.

So far we have it that for S to see O, S must have some experience whose content vaguely matches O. But this condition is clearly insufficient for there are veridical hallucinations like this: S, in an alcoholic stupor, has an experience as of a pink rat on the floor in front of him and, quite by chance, a rat which someone has painted pink is running across the floor. S does not see this rat, and he does not see it because it is a pure coincidence that he has an experience as of a pink rat which is, in fact, veridical (Grice, 1967:103–4).

The causal theorist of perception suggests that we add the following condition to our analysis: the experience E must be caused in S by O. And if this condition were satisfied, it would be no coincidence that both E and O occurred. However, it is not enough for O's presence to cause an experience whose content happens to vaguely match O – there could be veridical hallucinations whose content happens to match the scene before the eyes. We must require that it be no coincidence that the content of the subject's experience matches O to the extent required for vision of it, and this is not guaranteed by ensuring that the mere co-occurrence of some E and some O is no coincidence. For example, suppose that S's hallucination of a pink rat was caused, not by alcohol, but by the noxious scent of the rodent – perhaps this scent stimulates a visual image in S which happens to portray a pink rat. Since the same image would have been stimulated by any vaguely noxious smell it cannot be said that S sees the rat, even though the rat causes him to undergo a veridical experience (Peacocke, 1979:55).

Genuine vision requires a causally induced correlation between features of the rat and features of S's experience, a causal link which ensures that if the rat had been a mouse, or had been green rather than pink, S would have had a suitably different experience:

*Causally Induced Correlation*: There is a causally induced correlation between $x$'s being $P$ and S's experience being $Q$ if, and only if, there are causal connections which ensure that if $x$ had not been $P$, S's experience would not have been $Q$ and if $x$ had been $P$, S's experience would have been $Q$. Then, in virtue of having a $Q$-experience, S sees $x$'s being $P$.

The intuition behind *Causally Induced Correlation* is this: there is a rat shaped creature in front of me and it causes an experience with a certain content. If an exactly similar experience would have been caused by a mouse shaped creature, what grounds are there for saying that I see the rat shape? Would it not be better to say that what I see is a small rodent shape or some such thing?

How does *Causally Induced Correlation* fix the objects of experience? In my view, the notion of seeing an object O is to be explained in terms of the prior relation of seeing certain features of O. For me to see O's colour, there must be a causally induced correlation between O's colour and the content of my experience, and to see O *simpliciter* is to see enough of its salient features.

*Causally Induced Correlation* may seem to be too strong as it stands. It is intended as an analysis of what it is for E to be an experience of O's being $P$ yet E may be an experience of O's being $P$ even though E represents O as being $Q$: it may be an experience of the redness of O even if O looks orange to the subject (an orange experience falls within the limits of vague matching). Surely, we must allow for the possibility of illusion: for the fact that experiences are induced by scenes that do not, as well as scenes that do, match their content. But, if illusions are possible, how can there be a one-to-one correspondence between features of the objects I see and features of the content of my experience?

In fact, our analysis does allow for the possibility of illusion, of a mismatch between the features of the content of experience and features of its objects, provided that the mismatched features of the experience are one-to-one correlated, *in the environment which induces the experience*, with those features of the object which they are experiences of. I see the redness of O, even if O looks orange to me, provided the chromatic features of my experience, gross shades like orange, vary in step with chromatic features of the object, gross shades like red. On the other hand, there would be no case for saying that I see the object's vermilion colour as orange, if the change from vermilion to pinkish red made no difference to my orange experience.

*Causally Induced Correlation* is not too strong a demand, in this respect at least. Nevertheless, there are examples which suggest it is too weak, that the presence of such a causally induced correlation is insufficient for vision.

*The Colour Blind*: Suppose that a colour blind person is someone who experiences the world as containing only shades of grey and in whom different colours give rise to a colour experience as of the same shade of grey. Now imagine that our colour blind person has an opaque shield placed over his eyes, a shield which lifts to reveal the scene before him only when some specific array of grey colours is present. There is now a one-to-one mapping from object colour to experienced shade of grey. Must not the causal theorist say that our subject now sees these *specific* grey colours in virtue of the fact that there is a causally induced correlation between colours and features of his experience? (Peacocke, 1979:64)

But the shield surely does not bestow the ability to see the colour of grey things. If the shield were not present, there would be no case for saying that the subject saw the grey shades of certain objects; after all, he can see no difference between these shades and non-grey shades so his eyes must be sensitive to some broader chromatic class than grey. And it is hard to see how restricting the exercise of his visual abilities by installing the shield could improve his powers of discrimination. I do not deny that our colour blind subject experiences a grey shade which happens to match that of the object before him, what I do deny is that he sees the grey colour of that object.

Someone might suggest that the subject fails to see the grey shades of things despite the one–one correlation between grey shade and experienced colour simply because, if the shield were removed the correlation would fail. But we might be able to make people colour sighted by giving them special glasses (as we can make them see very small things by means of microscopes) and, if we could, we would not want to say that the glasses did not really work because their effect wears off upon removal.

Peacocke suggests that there is a crucial difference between the visual mechanism of a colour sighted person and that which operates in *The Colour Blind*. The laws governing the operation of a colour sighted visual mechanism guarantee a one–one correlation between actual colour and experienced colour, while the laws governing the operation of the colour blind visual mechanism guarantee only a many–one correlation (Peacocke, 1979:64–7). But Peacocke faces the following objection: the shield *will* produce a matching between actual and experienced colour in certain circumstances (i.e. when the grey colour array is presented) and favourable circumstances (for example sufficient light) are no less required for a colour sighted visual mechanism to produce the correlation which will ensure colour vision, so why not say that under favourable conditions (namely when the relevant scene is present) the shielded colour blind can also see grey colours?

One might reply that, even when the shield is present, the law governing the colour blind visual mechanism will not guarantee any correlation – it will not ensure any correspondence between the subject's experience and a slightly different scene – it guarantees only a one-off matching. But why should the fact that it is one-off matter? Might not a prosthetic visual device permit a subject to see only one kind of scene, say an intense light which appears in the centre of their visual field, while simply producing no experience at all in other circumstances? What is required of a visual mechanism is that its products be well-correlated with features of the environment *when it produces any experience at all*. This is how the demand for a causally induced correlation should be understood.

As Peacocke suggests, the objectionable feature of *The Colour Blind* is that the laws which govern the visual mechanism concerned *never* explain why there should be a one–one correlation between actual colour and experienced colour – they yield only a many–one correlation. The presence of an extraneous factor, namely the shield, then reduces this many–one function to a one-off matching. But were we to allow that the colour blind mechanism and the shield can be taken together and regarded as a single mechanism with its own law of working, that mechanism would account for the needed correlation. And, undoubtedly, we can derive, from the laws governing the vision of the colour blind and the workings of the shield, a generalisation which says that when the shield is present along with the colour blind mechanism and conditions are normal, the system will deliver a veridical colour experience whenever it delivers any experience at all. What is wrong with this generalisation is that the instantiation of its antecedent does not causally explain the instantiation of its consequent.

What grounds are there for this claim? Here, the intransitivity of 'causally explains' becomes crucial. In chapter 1, I urged that if one needed to invoke different and mutually independent causal conditions at various stages in a causal chain in order to describe how its first stage led to its last, then one's description of the chain would not amount to an explanation of its last member by means of its first: the occurrence of both the first and the last member would be (a partial and singular) coincidence. Suppose we took all the laws connecting the various stages of such a chain to subsequent stages of the chain and derived from them a generalisation which said that if an event of the type that formed the first stage of our chain occurred (in certain complex and mutually independent background conditions each relevant to different links in the chain) then an event of the type that formed the last stage of our chain would occur. The instantiation of this generalisation's antecedent would not explain the instantiation of its consequent.

But much the same is true of the generalisation which covers the working of the colour blind mechanism-with-shield. The presence of the shield and the presence of an intrinsically colour blind visual mechanism are quite independent causal factors operating at different stages of our causal chain. The shield filters out most of the light and then the visual mechanism converts the light into a visual experience. It is an accident that these factors combine so as to produce a correlation between the colours of an object in the subject's environment and the shades of grey experienced by the subject.

To sum up: if we are to see an object's colour, its having that colour must causally explain some feature of the content of our experience. But where the object's colour and the subject's experience are linked by a chain which has the shield at one stage and the subject's colour blind visual cortex at another, the colour of the object will not explain the experienced shade of grey; so the subject cannot see its grey colour, even when he has a matching experience.

*The Colour Blind* shows that the existence of a causally induced correlation between features of experience and features of an object is insufficient for the experience to be a perception of that object. We must require that those features of the experience which made it an experience of O are causally explained by the relevant features of O. There are more examples which suggest such a correlation is both insufficient and unnecessary for vision, but in these others it is the non-agglomerativity rather than the intransitivity of 'causally explains' which matters.

Lewis describes a scenario which he calls *The Censor*.

*The Censor:* My eyes are working normally and I see the scene before me clearly. However, if the scene were to be any different, a Censor would intervene and ensure that I hallucinated in such a way that my visual experience remained exactly the same. Here, my experience is actually caused by the object seen despite the fact that the presence of this object is not, in the circumstances, a necessary condition for such an experience. Yet I clearly do see my environment. So the existence of a causally induced correlation does not seem to be necessary for vision. (Lewis, 1986e:285)

Is the presence of a causally induced correlation even a sufficient condition for vision? An example which Davies calls *The Reverse Censor* suggests that it is not.

*The Reverse Censor:* Here I am hallucinating and (as in the pink rat case) the environment is such as to cause me to have an hallucination which matches the scene before my eyes. However, were that scene to be any different, the Reverse Censor would intervene to stop my hallucinations and I would see normally. I clearly do not see my environment and yet there is a causally induced correlation between my experiences and features of my surroundings – it is a correlation induced by different causal factors in the actual and counterfactual situations. (Davies, 1983:412–23)

According to Peacocke's account, the required causal dependence of features of the experience on features of its object cannot be captured by referring to the content of experiences had in counterfactual situations in which the originating object has different properties. Rather, the required dependence is to be formulated in terms of the kind of law invoked in the explanation of the actual experience event. This law must engender a one–one function mapping the perceived features of the object of vision onto features of the subject's experience.

In *The Reverse Censor*, there is a causally induced correlation between features of the experience and those of the object. But, if we attend to the causal process which is actually operative in the production of the visual experience matching the scene before my eyes, we find that the law invoked in the explanation of the experience does not itself support the relevant counterfactuals. The laws of hallucination do not guarantee a correlation between features of the environment and features of the hallucination. They just stipulate that, in the circumstances which in fact obtain, the two will match. So, in the actual case, I do not see.

If the scene were any different, then a matching experience would be produced. But the law invoked in an explanation of my experience in such a counterfactual situation would be quite different from the law which is invoked to explain the actual experience. It would be the law governing the normal working of the visual system and, as such, would ensure that features of my experience were correlated with features of the object concerned. So, in the counterfactual case, I see.

In *The Censor*, there is no causally induced correlation between features of the experience and those of the object. But the law which covers the actual causal process, namely the law governing normal human vision, does support the relevant counterfactuals. So, in the actual case, I see. If the situation were any different, this law would no longer be instantiated, the law governing the production of hallucinations would have taken over, and this law does not support the relevant counterfactuals. So, in the counterfactual case, I do not see.

To accord with our intuitions, Peacocke must insist that the counterfactuals which matter, in the examples under consideration, are those supported by the laws that are actually instantiated. In *The Reverse Censor*, the counterfactuals which ensure a suitable correlation between object and experience may be true, but they are not underwritten by the operative law, whereas, in *The Censor*, these counterfactuals are false, but they are underwritten by the operative law. Therefore, *The Censor* is a case of vision whereas *The Reverse Censor* is not (Davies, 1983: 413–17).

However, Peacocke faces the following objection. When one says that different laws are instantiated in the actual and counterfactual situations, one is not saying that different laws govern these two situations. Rather, what one means is that the initial conditions of one law are satisfied in the actual world, whereas the initial conditions of the other are satisfied in the counterfactual world. But, since these laws hold in both worlds, why not derive a single generalisation from them, a generalisation instantiated in both the actual and the counterfactual situation?

The generalisation which governs the production of my experience in both the actual and counterfactual environments must be derived from laws of at least two different kinds: firstly, those governing the normal workings of the human visual system, and, secondly, those regulating the production of hallucinations. In *The Reverse Censor*, the derived generalisation will guarantee a correlation between features of my experience and features of the object concerned, whereas in *The Censor*, it will not guarantee such a correlation. Therefore, we will be forced to say, counterintuitively, that *The Censor* is not a case of vision while *The Reverse Censor* is. And where two different laws apply to a given causal set up, surely we should invoke the more specific, derived generalisation to explain what is going on, and not try to ignore it?

Peacocke must respond by denying that this derived generalisation can explain anything. If the law in question were instantiated by the same mechanism in both the actual and the counterfactual environments, there would be a single explanation of what happened therein which applied to both environments. The two elements in the causal set up, namely the visual system and the hallucinatory mechanism, would combine to explain my experiences. But they do not provide a common explanation of those experiences which occur in the actual and the counterfactual situations imagined. Rather, in *The Censor*, the visual system alone determines what happens in the actual situation, while the hallucinatory mechanisms explain what happens in the counterfactual situation, but in *The Reverse Censor* it is the other way round.

As we learnt in chapter 1, you cannot always agglomerate an explanation of $p$ and an explanation of $q$ in order to get an explanation of $p$ and $q$. There may be a perfectly good explanation of the subject's experience in the actual environment, and a perfectly good explanation of his experience in the counterfactual environment. But there will be no common explanation of these experiences so long as the actually and counterfactually relevant factors are mutually independent and operate separately of one another to produce the actual and counterfactual outcome.

Peacocke demands that the operative visual mechanism ensures a correlation between features of the object seen and features of the subject's experience of it. But, if a mechanism does not explain the subject's experience, then it is not the operative mechanism. And the composite mechanism made up of the human visual system and some hallucinatory mechanism will not explain what happens in either the actual or the counterfactual environments. So the correlations it supports or undermines are irrelevant to perception.

I have mounted a defence of Peacocke's solution to the problem of deviant causal chains but any such defence must deal with a purported counterexample to it, constructed by Davies.

*The Discrete Processor*: Consider a person who inhabits an environment rather simpler than ours in which, consequently, only a relatively modest ability to discriminate scenes visually is needed for a full and happy life. Suppose that the ability to discriminate one million different scenes is adequate. In our person, any retinal image activates just one of a bank of one million pulse generators [cells] resulting in a simple pulse being transmitted along one of one million channels to a corresponding one of a bank of one million experience generators which is thereby stimulated and which produces a visual experience which matches the scene before the person's eyes ... The entire mechanism, with its one million discrete pulse generator pairs, is a natural product of evolution. (Davies, 1983:415)

The Discrete Processor is composed of a million sub-mechanisms, and each mechanism works quite independently of the others. When an image hits the eye, only one of the sub-mechanisms is involved in the transformation of the retinal stimulation into an experience. The Discrete Processor resembles the 'visual mechanisms' made from a normal and an hallucinatory component in that the whole mechanism is not involved in production of any given experience. Nevertheless, while we were not tempted to regard these composite mechanisms as visual systems, we *are* inclined to regard the Discrete Processor as a perceptual device.

Why does Peacocke deny that the Discrete Processor is a visual mechanism? After all, there are laws governing the working of the Processor which ensure that the subject's experiences are correlated with his environment. When responding to a similar example, Peacocke says the following:

Given a knowledge of all the details of this mechanism, and of the final kind of experience produced, we can determine what external scene must have produced [the experience]; and such working out determines a function from the surrounding scene to the experience produced. But it is not a function obtained in the right kind of way. I am concerned ... with functions referred to in the laws that cover links in the actual explanatory chain ... The properties of the cells unactivated on this occasion are irrelevant to whether there is such a function. (Peacocke, 1979:85)

152

Peacocke's thought seems to be that different bits of the Discrete Processor would explain the subject's experiences in the actual and the counterfactual environment. We can analyse the Discrete Processor into bits, one of which is relevant to the production of the actual experience, and another of which would be relevant to the production of a given counterfactual experience. Hence, there is no common explanation of his experience under these different circumstances. True, the electro-chemical principles which ensure that each retinal stimulation activates some cell in the Processor are the same in the case of each cell, so the same laws are instantiated in all the different environments which produce an experience. But these laws are instantiated by different parts of the mechanism in these different environments, and therefore there is no common explanation of what happens in all of them.

The suggestion is that, in a genuine visual mechanism, the whole mechanism is involved in the production of each experience. We cannot divide the mechanism into different parts, each of which is relevant on a different occasion. Not only is the same law instantiated by the mechanism in both the actual and the counterfactual environments, but the same initial conditions, the very same features of the mechanism, are invoked to explain the subject's experience.

However, it seems clear that Peacocke is wrong to deny that the Discrete Processor is a perceptual mechanism. I can imagine having much the same experiences as I do now while knowing that my visual system was destroyed in an accident at an early age. The only prosthetic visual mechanisms available at the time were Discrete Processors and I have been seeing by means of one ever since. Neither I, nor anyone else, would be tempted to conclude that I had seen nothing since my accident. The simple fact is that when we ascribe visual experiences to a person, we do not regard ourselves as making any suppositions about the physiological structure of his visual system.

What has gone wrong is that Peacocke has misapplied his criterion for assessing when a single mechanism is being used to explain different experiences. He has descended to the physiological level in order to look for a common explanation of the subject's experiences. But, even in the case of actual visual systems, no common explanation will be found at that level. We must ascend to the level of whole perceptual systems before we can find such common explanations. And, at that level, the demand for a common explanation of the subject's differing experiences will exclude the pseudo-mechanisms which are amalgams of an hallucinatory and a visual system, without excluding genuine visual mechanisms.

But what exactly is 'the level of whole perceptual systems'? Marr introduces the idea of a computational theory of an information processing device. This theory will tell us what the goal of the process is, what information it is attempting to recover, and will give the logic of the strategy by which this task is carried out. He distinguishes a computational description of an information-processor both from an account of how this computational theory is implemented (this will involve specifying how the input and output are represented, and giving the algorithm for the transformation) and from an account of how the implementational algorithm is realised physically (Marr, 1982:22–7).

Now I take it our computational theory of vision will concern itself with the functioning of the whole visual system. For instance, it will describe the stereoptic strategy which the system uses to deliver perceptions of depth to the subject. It will say under what conditions this strategy works, and under what conditions we may expect it to fail and depth illusions to occur. The conditions in question are not physiological, rather they specify constraints which the environment is assumed to satisfy by the system.[1]

It is the business of the perceptual psychologist to formulate computational level descriptions of the human visual system. In so doing he will be discovering laws which specify environmental conditions under which the subject has veridical, or else illusory, experiences of the scene before his eyes. These laws ensure that the presence of an object at a given depth, in certain background conditions (sufficient light etc.), causally explains an experience which is as of an object at that depth. And we cannot undermine such an explanation by conducting a physiological analysis of the processes which realise our computational description of the visual system. Such a physiological investigation might well reveal that, as in *The Discrete Processor*, there is no one physiological factor which ensures a suitable correlation between features of the subject's environment and features of his experience. To someone concerned solely with human physiology, the Discrete Processor is an arbitrary conjunction of distinct mechanisms, but the fact that the apparatus, taken as a whole, secures such a correlation may yet have a psychological explanation.

[1] For example, see Marr's spatial coincidence assumption, a constraint which the stereoptic processes place on the environment. Marr, 1982:70.

We need the hypothesis that perceptual psychology and sensory physiology work on different levels of explanation in order to deal with analogous objections to our treatment of *The Colour Blind*. I said that the presence of the shield between the subject and the object of vision was independent of the other causal factors needed for the object to cause an experience in the subject, and that this made it a coincidence that the experience matched the object in respect of colour. But, it will be pointed out, in the standard case of vision, a whole set of mutually independent physical, optical and physiological factors are necessary to cement different links in the causal chain leading from the object of vision to the subject's experience of it. So why is it not always a coincidence when a subject has a veridical experience of an object?

I reply that these physical, physiological and optical conditions will not appear in a psychological explanation of the experience. The conditions cited by perceptual psychology, which combine to explain the occurrence of a veridical experience, will not become relevant at different stages of the causal chain leading to the experience. Rather, they are those constraints on the environment noted above, standing background conditions relevant at every stage of this causal chain.

So, we must allow that there are different levels of explanation if we are to be able to solve the problem of deviant causal chains. In chapter 6, I provided some account of how these different levels stand to one another. The connections between perceptual psychology and sensory physiology, described above, well illustrate the relationship between other special sciences and the physical sciences. The example confirms that there are explanations and explanatory mechanisms which can be discerned by the economist, the psychologist or the biologist, which would be invisible to the physicist. Therefore, it would be no surprise were psychological explanations to collapse when we insist on analysing psychological mechanisms into their physical elements.

## PERCEPTION AND TELEOLOGY

I have been assuming that it is the mode of operation, the functional structure of a mechanism, which determines whether it can serve as a perceptual mechanism. However, Davies has suggested that what really matters is the teleological background (Davies, 1983). Certain organs have evolved because they made their possessors sensitive to biologically significant aspects of the environment. Other mechanisms were designed by engineers as conduits for information about their environment. Perhaps we should look to these teleological facts, rather than to the details of how the mechanism works for a decision on whether it is a perceptual organ.

In the case of *The Colour Blind, The Censor, The Reverse Censor* and *The Discrete Processor*, we were confronted with the question: what makes a causal set-up into a single perceptual mechanism? Davies will claim that our answer must depend on history, on whether the various parts of the set up have a common aetiology. If the shield in *The Colour Blind* has been designed to rise only when some specific array of colours is present, or had evolved to do so, the subject would see the colour array before him. If *The Censor* were someone who intended that my experience remain the same whatever environment I was in, I would not see the scene before my eyes. If the *Reverse Censor* were someone who intended that my experience match my environment, I would see the scene before my eyes. And *The Discrete Processor* is a perceptual mechanism provided it is either an artifact designed for that purpose or a natural product of evolution.

But Davies is wrong to let his account of what constitutes a single mechanism depend on facts about that mechanism's aetiology. My own intuitions about these examples are quite unaffected by the revelation that the set up was no accident. For instance, if I am asked whether someone who created a subject and put him in the grip of the Censor had created someone who could see, I would answer that he had created someone who could see only in the actual situation. And if I was asked whether an organism which had evolved in an environment governed by the Reverse Censor could see, I would say that it could, except in the actual situation. It is not psychological or biological history which makes a causal set-up into a unitary perceptual mechanism, but something intrinsic to the way the mechanism works.

Furthermore it is unnecessary, as well as insufficient for a mechanism to be perceptual that it have the perception of its environment as its biological function. No one would demand that all perceptual systems be designed for the purpose – many were not designed at all. Nor should we require that every natural perceptual organ have as its biological function the collection of sensory information. Perceptual organs arise from random mutation and are perceptual even before they are selected for. If they go on to survive in the evolutionary struggle, this may be owing not to any advantage they bestow on their host organism, but rather to their being a by-product of some quite different feature of the organism (Snowdon, 1990:148–9). For instance, a creature may be able to get around its environment by smell alone, sight would only give it access to lots of irrelevant and distracting information. Nevertheless, it has sight as well as smell because the two senses happen to be genetically inseparable; the whole package is adaptive in that the advantages of smell outweigh the deleterious effects of sight, but the visual part of the package has no biological function.

Davies might persist and ask us to imagine that the whole causal set up in *The Colour Blind* and *The Reverse Censor* is the product of design. Perhaps the controller of the shield and the Reverse Censor are people who intend to interfere with the subject's vision in such a way as to ensure that the whole set up constitutes a counterexample to *Causally Induced Correlation*. Or perhaps the subject and those who manipulate his vision have evolved 'staying-together' genes because their double-act is somehow advantageous in the environment in which they find themselves. Would this not remove the element of coincidence which was so crucial to my explanation of why neither example is an instance of vision?

Furthermore, there is now a single law instantiated in both the actual and counterfactual situations considered in the counterexamples, either a psychological law or a biological law. Suppose the former. In *The Colour Blind* and *The Reverse Censor*, the law states that, owing to the beliefs and desires of the manipulator, he will act so as to ensure that the subject's experiences and his environment are well correlated. So, in each case, an explanation of what happens in the actual and counterfactual circumstances which invokes the same (action) mechanism is now available. The designs of the Reverse Censor cause the subject to hallucinate veridically in the actual world and see normally in the counterfactual world. Similarly, the intentions of the shield controller ensure both that the subject has veridical experiences when confronted by the grey array and that he has no experience at all when faced with other colours.

Much the same can be said if the causal set-up is a product of evolution rather than conspiracy. Here again, there is a single factor which explains the visual workings of the subject governed by the shield and the subject governed by the Reverse Censor in all the environments they inhabit, namely the fitness-enhancing quality of the overall results. And also, there is a single law which explains why systems like these exist, namely the law which says that fitter mutations will be selected for.

But this is a misapplication of the account of visual experience suggested above. It is not enough that there be a single law which covers all the cases of correlation between object and experience – as I urged at the beginning of the chapter, this law must *in each case* induce the correlation by establishing a direct causal connection between object and experience. And neither the psychological, nor the biological laws in question will induce such a causal connection in all the cases in which the correlation must hold.

Take *The Reverse Censor*. When the subject is veridically hallucinating, there need be no causal connection between object and experience, and the Reverse Censor need do nothing to induce one – he can get his way without bringing object and experience into contact. It is only when the object threatens to get out of kilter with the experience that the Reverse Censor has to induce experiences in the subject, and thus establish an indirect causally induced correlation between object and experience via his own beliefs and desires. Similarly, the manipulator of the shield in *The Colour Blind* engenders the needed correlation precisely by denying the subject any causal access to the colours around him in cases where his experience would not match those colours.

The same points apply if the activities of the Reverse Censor and the shield manipulator are the product of their genetic inheritance rather than their psychological state. So teleological considerations cannot help us deal with the above examples.

## THE CAUSAL THEORY OF MEMORY

Perception is the means by which we acquire knowledge of our environment. However, there is at least one other psychological process, equally crucial and which, it has been argued, conceptually involves a causal link between the subject and his environment: memory. I shall be discussing personal or experiential memory, that ascribed in sentences like 'S remembers the occurrence of event E (because he witnessed it and recalls it)' rather than the factual memory ascribed by sentences like 'S remembers that E occurred (because he was told about it and retained the information)'.

If I am to be said to remember running back home after my first day at school in this experiential sense, at least two things must be true: (a) I must seem to recall running back home on my first day at school and (b) I must have been aware, at the time, of my running back home on my first day at school. As to (a), I need not believe that I ran home in order to remember running home, any more than I need believe that there is a cat in front of me in order to see that there is a cat in front of me – seeming to see and seeming to recall are enough. But I will usually trust my memory, as I usually trust my senses, and believe what it tells me (Martin and Deutscher, 1966:166–71).

As to (b), if I am to remember running home, it must be true that I ran home, just as if I am to perceive that the cat is on the mat, the cat must be on the mat. Further, to genuinely recall my run I must also have been aware of the occurrence of my run at the time it occurred; for if the run made no impression whatsoever on my mind, how can I have remembered it?

However, as Martin and Deutscher observe, these conditions are not sufficient for me to remember – they may be satisfied and yet it be a complete coincidence that I seem to recall what did in fact happen. Suppose that, after I have been at school for several years, I sustain a serious head injury which wipes out all mental trace of my life so far. Some years later a hypnotist, for independent reasons, induces me to believe that I recall running home after my first day at school. Here, I would seem to recall running home from school, but I would not remember it.

The obvious explanation for this is that my past experience of running home from school does not cause some experiential memory of running home from school. So perhaps we should simply require that my memory be caused by the past experience of which it is purportedly a memory. But, as Martin and Deutscher note, I may fail to remember even if my memory is caused by a suitable experience.

Say that after I ran home from school, I told my parents that I had done so. Some years later my parents decided to give me a list of things that happened when I was young, not in a hopeless attempt to stimulate my memory, but just to satisfy my curiosity. Among the things they tell me is that I ran home after my first day at school. Having committed the list to memory, I become a little confused and imagine that I actually remember (in the experiential sense) all the events described on the list (Martin and Deutscher, 1966:180–1).

It is unsurprising that I appear to recall running home – I seem to remember that only because I actually did once remember running home. My parents are honest and they would not tell me a lie, so my running home causes me to seem to recall my running home via a causal chain which includes their memories and honest intentions. This causal chain supports a correlation between the facts about my early childhood and the memories I appear to have in later childhood – if my early childhood had been any different then my parents would have put different events on their list and I would have seemed to recall different occasions. Nevertheless I remember nothing of my early childhood.

What we have here is a correlation between past facts and apparent memories induced by a deviant causal chain. How is this chain to be ruled out? The obvious move is to highlight the various independent background conditions which must obtain if my apparent memories are to be correlated with my past: I must have experienced my run in the normal way and stored it in memory; my parents must have become aware of the run through my testimony and, many years later, have decided to inform me of it; finally I must have confused what I was then told of with what I now remember. This chain requires, at various points, the original normal functioning of my perceptual and memory systems, honest and solicitous parents and the factors which explain my final confusion, in order to knit its stages together. These circumstances are all quite independent of one another and each become relevant at different stages of our deviant chain. So the source of its deviance appears obvious: my running home from school does not causally explain my appearing to recall running home from school. Genuine memories must be explained by the facts of which they are memories.

However, matters are not so simple. Martin and Deutscher point out that a person may remember a past event *upon prompting*. Say that my head injury never occurred but, owing to normal forgetfulness, I cannot presently recall my running home from school. Then I hear my parents regaling some friends with this tale and I suddenly recall the event. Of course, I might be deluding myself when I say 'Now I remember', but I might be right – it is at least possible that my parents' tale has revived a genuine memory. But how is this possibility consistent with the apparent deviance of the causal chain? After all, this chain also requires that I registered the event, that my parents knew of it, recall it and are honest about it etc. (Martin and Deutscher, 1966:183–91).

At this point, we must distinguish two different ways in which the prompt might contribute to my memory-experience. First, it might be the occasion for my remembering the run in much the same way that my opening my eyes may be the occasion of my seeing a blackbird. If I am to have any visual experience at all then I must open my eyes. The fact that I have my eyes open when the blackbird passes overhead may be a coincidence, but it is no coincidence that, given that I see anything at all, I have a veridical experience of the scene before my eyes. Therefore, I see the blackbird despite this coincidence.

If the prompt is just the occasion for my remembering the run, then there must be facts about me which ensure that, if I remember anything at all about that period, I will remember it correctly. The experiences I had at that time must have left traces in my mind which enable me to recall my childhood when my attention is drawn to it by some suitable external prompt. All the prompt does is cause me to have some experience of the relevant period of my life, it does not help to ensure that the content of the experience is veridical. So, even though the occurrence of a prompt of this kind at that moment is a coincidence, it is no coincidence that, if I remember anything at all, I remember correctly. The prompt is no part of the explanation of the *content* of my memory.

However, the prompt can play a quite different role – it can actually be the object of the memory experience. The distinction we want may be introduced as follows: ten years ago, I travelled to school along a certain railway line and if I am now asked to describe the buildings which then lined the route between any two stations I could say relatively little: my recall-memory of the route is poor. However, when I recently took the same journey for the first time in many years, I remembered most of the buildings as I saw them: my recognition memory of the route is good. What we have been discussing so far is recall memory. The occurrence of a prompt may be the occasion of a recall memory; alternatively it may induce recognition of the prompt itself, making the prompt the object of the memory experience, in which case we are dealing with a different kind of psychological state, one which I have called recognition memory (Evans, 1982:285).

The prompt is not merely the occasion of a recognition memory, it provides the object remembered. So the prompt and the circumstances surrounding it are no longer contingent conditions needed to cement links in a rather tortuous causal chain leading from the remembered event to the memory of it, rather they are constitutive of the memory itself – the memory is a recognition of the prompt. So though it may be a coincidence that the object remembered reappears as a prompt, this coincidence does not undermine the assertion that the object is recognised when it does reappear.

To return to recall memory, what exactly is the difference between a prompted recall memory of an event, such as my run, and a mere confusion of what I have been told with what I have remembered? Martin and Deutscher suggest that the crucial point is whether the experience of my run put me into a state which is now operative, together with the prompt, in producing my memory experience. If so, I do remember, given the prompt. If not – if it is just that the experience of the run caused the prompt which caused my belief but did not also cause a state which persisted in me and was necessary, at the time of the prompt, for the recall – I do not remember the run upon prompting.

This conclusion fits neatly into my analysis. It may be a partial coincidence (or even a complete coincidence) that both the prompt and the state caused by the original experience exist but they are individually necessary and jointly sufficient for the memory experience and thus combine to explain this experience. So, given that the state was directly caused by the run and some prompt revives it, I genuinely remember the run.

As Martin and Deutscher note, it is required that the state induced in me by the original experience support a suitable correlation between features of the memory engendered by prompting and features of the past, so that had the past been any different, I would have had a suitably different memory of it. I do not remember my run if my belief in it is caused by a credulous state, somehow induced by the experience of the run, which leads me to believe anything I am told. Further, as I argued in connection with the Censor examples, the needed correlation cannot be induced by different causal factors under different conditions – there must be a non-gerrymandered state of the subject which supports the correlation in all the relevant circumstances. But these qualifications are implicit in the requirement that features of the events which I remember causally explain features of my memory of them.

Of course, my analysis could easily be undermined if we were allowed to look at the fine detail of the causal chain which leads from the remembered event to the memory of it. There will be many mutually independent physical and physiological conditions necessary for the existence of a causal chain connecting my memory experience to the event it is an experience of. But, as I urged in the case of perception, this should not affect our judgment that the remembered event causally explains the veridical memory of it. There are different levels of explanation, and what is a coincidence at one level may easily be explained at another.

# 8

## Causation in action

Perhaps the most fraught application of the concept of causation is to the explanation of our own actions. Many have held it as obvious that our actions are caused by the beliefs and desires which motivate them, while many others have been more impressed by the difficulties which confront any causal theory of action. I'm afraid that the theory of causation advanced in this book does not enable us to arrive at definite conclusions about the role of causation in human action, but it can be used to elucidate some familiar issues and determine what is at stake in some long-running controversies about the causal theory of action. Specifically, I shall formulate several objections to the causal thesis and show that none of them are decisive. I shall also look at the prospects for a causal analysis of the notion of intentional action, at the chances of using causation to distinguish what is done intentionally from what is not. No settled view emerges but certain obstacles to a causal analysis are cleared away.

### THE CAUSAL THEORY OF ACTION

Many philosophers hold that if S does A intentionally then S must have beliefs and desires which make A a sensible thing for him to do. Further they maintain that these beliefs and desires must cause S to do A. Davidson introduces this causal requirement as follows: 'a person can have a reason for an action, and perform the action, and yet this reason not be the reason why he did it. Central to the relation between a reason and an action it explains is the idea that the agent performed the action *because* he had the reason' (Davidson, 1980e:9).

For a given psychological state to explain a certain action, it is not sufficient that the state provide the agent with a rationalisation of the action, the agent must *act on* the reason and there is a difference between merely having a reason which would justify an action and doing something for that reason. Davidson proposes to explicate this difference as follows: the agent acts on those reasons which cause his action.

Imagine that I have a strong desire to strike my father, whom I hate. However, I have not met my father for several years and would not recognise him if I did. I meet an old man on a country lane who gets in my way and I am in such a hurry that I strike the old man to clear my path. In fact, the old man is my father. Here, I have good reason to strike my father, a reason of which I am fully aware and I actually do something which is a striking of my father. But the mere presence of a good reason for striking my father does not ensure that this was the reason on which I acted. I acted out of haste and not out of hate.

The problem is this: there are two distinct reasons which would rationalise what I did under two different descriptions. One would rationalise my hitting the old man who is in my way, while the other would rationalise my striking my father. Since I both struck my father and hit the old man, the question arises: which did I do intentionally? Which set of reasons was the operative set?

According to Davidson, I acted out of haste rather than hate because it was haste rather than hate which *caused* me to lash out. That is why it is true to say that, had I not wanted to walk along the road, I would not have hit the old man and why it is true to say that, had I not wanted to strike my father, I would still have hit the old man. Is there an alternative account of the matter? Can we appeal to the *content* of the agent's mental states to support the relevant conditionals without making suppositions about their causal role?

Perhaps we should look to the content of the agent's beliefs. I do not believe that the man in front of me is my father, so my hatred for my father gives me no reason to strike the old man in front of me: my hatred does not rationalise the action that I take, since I do not believe the action is a striking of my father. Therefore it is not out of hatred that I act, though I would act out of hatred if I knew the truth. Rather, I act out of haste because I believe that the striking will remove an old man from my path. So the non-causal theorist can identify the operative reasons just by attending to the content of my mental states.

Suppose I did know the truth. I now have two independent reasons for striking this old man: one is to remove an obstruction from my path and the other is to express my hatred of my father. Are both reasons operative, or is only one of them operative? Perhaps both are operative but it might well be the case that only one of them is. Davidson may hypothesise that it is the desire for revenge and not irritation at the delay which causes me to strike, and makes that striking an act of revenge rather than an expression of irritation, or *vice versa*, as the evidence warrants; he has the resources to distinguish these possibilities. Since both my impatience and my hatred would rationalise my striking, how can the non-causal theorist accommodate this distinction?

But think of the evidence one would use to determine which motive was operative. Perhaps the agent remarks: 'when I realised it was my father, I just forgot the fact that he was obstructing my path, as memories of my loathsome childhood welled up inside me.' This would incline us to think that I acted out of hatred and not out of impatience, so the fact that the thoughts of revenge were at the front of my mind seems highly relevant. There is also the relative strength of the reasons to take into account. Imagine someone who had long nursed a deep grudge against his father and then meets his father on a road. At first he does not recognise him and impatiently prepares to brush him aside. Then, we see him recognise his father and he strikes. After it is all over, we ask him why he struck out and he tells us that it was purely out of irritation at the delay, his hatred for his father was quite overwhelmed by this irritation. This would seem most strange, unless our aggressor was late for some vital engagement and we would doubt that his account of his own motives was correct.

So, where each of two sets of reasons would rationalise an action, there are several ways of determining whether one or both was operative, and these methods are as open to the non-causal theorist as to anyone else. Davidson will characterise the task before us as one of amassing evidence for a causal hypothesis, but it is quite unclear that this description opens up new sources of evidence, unavailable to the non-causal theorist. Surely Davidson must appeal to exactly the same considerations about what would make most sense of the agent's behaviour given what we know of his state of mind. And where such considerations are not decisive, the causal hypothesis cannot help.

Say that there are two reasons why S might have done A, both are equally strong, equally present to his mind etc. but either would have sufficed on its own to motivate action A. We would then be unable to decide why S did A, our evidential resources being inadequate. Here, Davidson might insist that, nevertheless, there is a fact of the matter about which reasons were causally operative. Davidson will not here appeal to the physiological origins of the subject's bodily movements to decide the issue, since, in both his view and mine, there is no correspondence between types of psychological and types of physical state which might help us to fix the psychological cause of the agent's action.[1] So, given that no psychological evidence is decisive, Davidson will have to admit that the key causal facts are beyond our ken.

But one might equally well hold that there is no fact of the matter about the motive or motives on which our agent acted. Since, given all the evidence we have or might have, either one of several hypotheses would make equal sense of the agent's behaviour, there simply is no answer to the question: what was his motivation? In order to decide between the view I have attributed to Davidson and this behaviouristic alternative, we would have to delve deep into the metaphysics of the mind (Dennett, 1991). No simple observation about the distinction between having a reason and acting on a reason will establish the causal theory.

What happens in a case of irrationality? Do causal notions become essential to the explanation of action? Take weakness of will. I come home late from a party and decide to go straight to bed rather than brush my teeth – I really need the sleep and my teeth can wait. However, the regular brushing of teeth at night was much emphasised by my mother and, soon after I have gone to bed, I duly rouse myself and brush my teeth (Davidson, 1980g:30). Here, in the eyes of the agent, and in fact, he has much better reason to remain in bed than he has to brush his teeth, yet he gets up. The explanation of his getting up cannot proceed by saying that the agent acted on the stronger reason, rather it must cite the weaker reason. And why do we cite this reason, Davidson may ask, if not because it was the reason that caused the action?

However, the non-causal theorist will deal with this case by pointing out that we can make some sense of the action by invoking the weaker reason – invoking the stronger one would make no sense of it at all. This is why we should explain the action by reference to the weaker reason. It is only where there is no reason at all for what the agent does that rational explanation breaks down. But in such cases there is no action to explain, only a bodily movement or physical happening.

My conclusion is this: in so far as we can explain an agent's actions, we

---

[1] Davidson, 1980d:222–3. In chapter 6 I argued that there need be no correspondence between the nomological classifications of a special science such as psychology and a physical science such as physiology.

can explain them simply by stating his reasons, their relative weight and salience to the agent. We need not add that some reasons rather than others caused the action. Notions like strength and salience, applied to reasons, can be explained by reference to the agent's behaviour (eg. the odds he will accept on certain bets) and are not obviously causal notions. The subjunctive conditionals which ensure a dependence of action on reason can be treated as consequences of the canons of rationality. So 'I would not have struck my father if I had not hated him' may be true, not because my hatred caused the striking, but rather because an abatement in my hatred would have deprived me of any reason to strike him.

At this point, the Davidsonian will simply insist that the principles of rationality are themselves causal generalisations, ones which lay down how mental states with a certain content and a certain strength are causally related to behaviour; so the non-causal theorist cannot safely appeal to such principles to support the needed subjunctive conditionals. However, the Davidsonian now requires some further argument for the thesis that the principles of decision theory, for example, are causal generalisations. He cannot base this thesis simply on the fact that there is a distinction between having a reason and acting on that reason. In the next section, I shall consider the status of decision theory.

## IS DECISION THEORY EMPIRICAL?

Taylor puts the following objection to the causal theory of action:

With action, we might say, the behaviour occurs because of the corresponding intention or purpose; where this is not the case, we are not dealing with action. But to use the expression 'because of' here might mislead. For we could not say that the intention was the causal antecedent of the behaviour. For the two are not contingently connected in the normal way. We are not explaining the behaviour by the 'law', other things being equal, intending X is followed by doing X, for this is part of what we mean by 'intending X', that, in the absence of interfering factors, it is followed by doing X. I could not be said to intend X if, even with no obstacles or other countervailing factors, I still didn't do it. Thus my intention is not a causal antecedent of my behaviour. (Taylor, 1964:33)

What Taylor here says about the connection between intention and action could equally well be said of the connection between the reasons which led the agent to form his intention and the agent's action: this link is a logical one and thus cannot be causal.

But Taylor's assumptions about causation are not quite right. In chapter 2, I urged that causes might well be necessarily connected with their effects: only logical connections are problematic. The real question is whether the psychological laws invoked to explain action are part of an empirical theory; to put it another way, do psychological terms like 'belief' and 'desire' have logically independent criteria of application, do they explain logically independent pieces of behaviour? Or is psychology best thought of in the way geometry was before the nineteenth century, as a seamless web of *a priori* truth?

One line of thought which might support the view that psychology is non-empirical is this: the laws of intentional psychology are principles of rationality – they explain human behaviour only in so far as they rationalize it, render it intelligible, make sense of it. If a creature moves in a way which we cannot rationalise, which we cannot make sense of by reference to his beliefs and desires, it is difficult to see this movement as an act rather than a reflex or meaningless physical event. So, we may conclude, in order to count as an action, a physical movement *must* be explicable by reference to the laws of psychology and thus no action could undermine these laws.[2]

Let us see how this line of thought holds up when applied to that branch of intentional psychology which specialises in the explanation of action: decision theory. Decision theorists attribute beliefs and preferences to agents in order to explain their behaviour. These beliefs and preferences come in degrees, one may have stronger or weaker convictions and more or less decided preferences, so decision theorists must establish a measure which will enable them to assign weights to beliefs and desires. Once this measure is established, they affix a value to each of the outcomes available to the agent (its expected utility), a value which is a function of the weights of the relevant beliefs and preferences. Finally they predict that the agent will realise that outcome with the highest value.

In order to construct a measure of preferences and a measure of beliefs the decision theorist must make certain assumptions about these states, assumptions of two kinds: formal and substantial. Let us take preferences. First, there are formal assumptions, assumptions about the structure of

[2] Something like this line of reasoning is present in Davidson, 1980h:266–73. He agrees with Taylor that causal relations must be covered by strict empirical laws, and that psychology cannot provide such laws, but claims that the mental causes of behaviour can be redescribed so as to instantiate purely physical laws. See Davidson, 1980d:223–5 and Davidson, 1980e:13–17.

preferences, such as the assumption that a subject's preferences are transitive: if he prefers an apple to an orange and an orange to a pear, he will also prefer an apple to a pear. Second, assumptions are made about the content of his desires, for instance that an agent will not prefer an apple just when it's raining on the moon and an orange just when it's not raining on the moon, at least without there being some background story that connects the weather on the moon with factors intelligibly related to his taste in fruit. And only when these two kinds of assumption are put together will they constrain the behaviour of a rational agent so the decision theorist may predict it.[3]

Now there is more than one formal constraint on preferences and more than one substantive constraint. On the formal side, expected utility theory constrains preferences with the axiom of independence as well as with the axiom of transitivity. Behaviour has been observed which some have interpreted as a violation of transitivity, and yet other behaviour has been construed as a violation of independence. Non-expected utility theories have been formulated which weaken or dispense with one or other of these axioms. But either or both axioms could be saved from refutation if we were willing to modify our interpretation of the content of the preferences at issue and thus risk undermining some of the substantive constraints on preferences. This all suggests that decision theory is an empirical theory in the sense of chapter 4. The notion of 'preference' gets introduced by means of logically independent formal axioms and substantive constraints, some of which turn out to be empirically inappropriate while others survive. So 'preference' is not to be defined by reference to some one psychological law linking it with action.

Much the same can be said about beliefs. The formal axioms which govern decision–theoretic beliefs are the axioms of the probability calculus. The theorist assigns numbers to propositions which represent the agent's degree of belief in that proposition. These numbers are assumed to behave like standard probabilities, for example the number assigned to a proposition $p$ and its negation add up to 1. Now non-expected utility theorists have proposed that one or other of these axioms should be modified or abandoned for certain purposes, that, though agents might be expected to conform to them in certain circumstances

---

[3] For more about formal and substantive constraints on preferences and the way they interact see Hurley, 1990, chapter 4 and the authors cited therein.

(when betting for instance) they should not be called irrational because they violate them in others (when weighing evidence in a court of law) (Cohen, 1977). So here again we have the possibility that beliefs could satisfy some of the formal constraints they are presently thought to satisfy, but not others, that they might give rise to some of the behaviour they are thought to explain, but not all of it.

So intentional psychology, even if it has principles of rationality at its core, is an empirical theory which can deliver causal explanations of behaviour. To put it another way, our standards of what makes sense, of what constitutes sensible behaviour, is responsible to what people actually do, and we can envisage revising our theories of rationality in the light of experimental inquiry. I conclude that Taylor's objection does not hold water.

However, the demise of Taylor's objection does not leave the non-causal theorist without a defensible position. What an opponent of the causal theory of action can maintain is that decision theory delivers empirical but non-causal explanations of behaviour. According to him, these explanations will be constitutive explanations – states of the human mind stand in a constitutive relation to the behaviour which they explain, and are not something over and above that behaviour, something which might bring it about. Such a position would be a natural consequence of certain forms of Wittgensteinian or Rylean behaviourism. I do not want to pass any judgment on the relative merits of the causalist and non-causalist view of the mind, just to note that there is still an open question here despite the assumption of many that Davidson closed it.[4]

## THE AUTONOMY OF PSYCHOLOGY

There is a further difficulty confronting the causal theory of action which has been much discussed of late.[5] Consider the following propositions:

(1) Psychological factors are essential to the causal explanation of human action and thus to that of the bodily movements which constitute human actions.

(2) Physiology can provide a complete causal explanation of each and every movement of the human body.

[4] For instance McGinn, 1984:110.
[5] This difficulty has been discussed, implicitly or explicitly, for many years. There is a crisp statement of it in Mackie, 1979:20.

(3) Psychological explanations of actions cannot simply be reduced to, or equated with, physiological explanations of their constitutive bodily movements.

Say that I put my hand in the fire and then withdraw it at great speed. If asked to explain my action I will say that pain caused me to withdraw my hand. Yet if the physiologist is required to account for what happened, he will cite a whole series of neurochemical events and will make no mention of the pain. Are these two perspectives on human behaviour consistent?

Faced with this apparent conflict between our three propositions, some have advocated resolving the tension by abandoning one or other of them. Wittgensteinian behaviourists and various latter-day epiphenomenalists have dropped (1); dualist interactions are content to deny (2), while reductionists would favour a rejection of (3).[6] However, I think it fair to say that the majority of philosophers wish to retain all three premises, while giving them an interpretation which removes the impression of inconsistency.

One very popular way of effecting this reconciliation is to claim that the mental causes of behaviour are the very same events as the physical causes of behaviour. In order to state this solution, we must help ourselves to Davidson's two-place predicate 'cause' which I introduced in chapter 3. Recall that if two events are connected by this causal relation, they are so related however described. So if the pain causes me to jerk my arm away from the fire and the pain is identical with some neurophysiological state, that neurophysiological state also causes me to jerk my arm away from the fire. Far from there being a conflict between the causal efficacy of the pain and that of the brain state, the one's being a cause entails that the other is also a cause, once these states are identified.

On this view, there are no causal factors in aetiology of behaviour which the psychologist highlights and the neurophysiologist ignores, rather the psychologist and the neurophysiologist simply supply different descriptions of the same causal process. So there is no real competition here – the pain is just a neurophysiological state in a mental guise. To

---

[6] For a Wittgensteinian response to the problem see Malcolm, 1982:132–6. Many philosophers who do not share the Wittgensteinian intuition that psychological explanations are of a kind different from physiological explanations are nevertheless forced into a more or less explicit epiphenomenalism by their acceptance of (2); see for example Kim, 1984b.

assert that the pain causes the movement is not to imply that a purely neurophysiological explanation of the movement must be incomplete – for the physiological explanation will cite the very same psychological cause, albeit under a different description (Davidson, 1980d:223–5 and Peacocke, 1979:134–9).

However, (1) to (3) do not speak of causation, a relation between particular events, rather they concern causal explanation and, as I urged at the end of chapter 3, what causally explains and is causally explained are the havings of properties by objects (or events). Once we are clear about this, the problem can be restated even while granting that the pain is the same event as the neurophysiological cause of pain behaviour. For the question remains: which properties of the cause of the hand movement causally explain that movement's occurrence, its physical properties or its mental properties? Our neurophysiologist will say that in citing the neurophysiological properties of the cause he has done enough to explain the subsequent movement – the occurrence of an event with those physical properties is a condition necessary and sufficient for the occurrence of the movement. And this does appear to contradict the psychologist's assertion that the occurrence of an event with the property of being painful was at least necessary to explain why I moved as I did (Mackie, 1979:22).

How are we to negotiate this trilemma? I am inclined to think that we can resolve the apparent tension between (1), (2) and (3) by making a distinction first introduced in chapter 6 (page 119). There I distinguished *Completeness*, the thesis that every state, physical or non-physical, has a purely physical necessary and sufficient condition, from *Causal Closure*, the thesis that every state, physical or non-physical, has a purely physical causal explanation. I endorsed *Completeness* while rejecting *Causal Closure*. (1) tells us that psychological factors are essential to the causal explanation of action, that a non-psychological causal explanation of action is not to be had. This is inconsistent with the thesis that actions have a purely physical causal explanation, but it is in no way inconsistent with the thesis that actions have a purely physical necessary and sufficient condition, for, as we know, to cite a necessary and sufficient condition is not always to deliver a causal explanation.

Applied to the case before us, the idea is this. When a human action is described in the fine-grained vocabulary of the neurophysiologist, we get a physical phenomenon of great complexity. Each part of this physical phenomenon can be given a purely physical causal explanation, from which it follows that there is a purely physical condition necessary and sufficient for the occurrence of the action which these physiological events constitute. But this does not imply the existence of a physical explanation for the constituted action. In order to explain why these physiological elements occur together in such a way as to constitute a human action, we must introduce psychological factors, factors which are themselves doubtless constituted by further complex physiological phenomena. And only these psychological factors can make sense of the co-occurrence of all the elements of that neural *mêlée* which form a human action. (O'Shaughnessy, 1980:1–2 and Hornsby, 1980a).

Of course, I have no *a priori* argument for the thesis that physiology will (always) be unable to explain the co-occurrence of the physical movements which constitute a human action. My aim is only to outline one possible way in which our belief in the autonomy of psychology might be reconciled with a commitment to the completeness of neurophysiology. But I shall remark in passing that recent empirical research is not wholly inhospitable to this possibility. The considerable literature on connectionism suggests that the mental causes of behaviour are constituted by a multitude of extremely simple interactions between different physical elements. The psychological regularities which govern the workings of the mind and the way it brings about linguistic and other behaviour arise out of these simple interactions. But the lack of isomorphism between neural and psychological regularities frustrates any reductive explanation of one in terms of the other. So it may well be that psychological processes derive from a whole lot of quite independent physiological phenomena.[7]

## DEVIANCE IN ACTION

Those who hold that the existence of a causal relation between reason and behaviour is a necessary condition for intentional action might reasonably hope to turn this necessary condition into a sufficient condition, that is to provide a causal analysis of the notion of intentional action. But any such analysis must successfully distinguish what was done intentionally from what was not. The possibility of deviant causal chains shows that the

[7] For instance, see Smolensky, 1988. The view of the mind adumbrated in Dennett, 1991 arises naturally out of the connectionist research programme, and is congenial to my own approach.

causal connections acknowledged by most causal theorists are insufficient for intentional action. A more discriminating notion of causal explanation is needed before the causal analysis can succeed.

Here are two examples of deviant causal chains in the aetiology of human action.

*The Killing*: A sets out across town with the object of killing his uncle. The excitement generated by his plan causes him to drive fast and carelessly. As a result, he knocks down and kills a pedestrian whom he does not see. It turns out to be his uncle. A's attempt to murder his uncle brought it about that he killed his uncle. But his killing was not intentional. (Armstrong, 1980:76)

*The Fraud*: A bank clerk wants more money and knows that he could without detection write some accounts financially favourable to himself and who is so distracted by this desire and belief that he absent-mindedly writes his own rather than another's name on a line, which action will result in a large payment of money to himself. (Peacocke, 1979:55)

In each case, it is clear that the agent did not intentionally commit any crime, and yet he intended to commit a crime and the thing which he intended came about as a result of this intention.

Armstrong proposes to deal with *The Killing* by looking to the agent's plan of action. The killing was not intentional because it was brought about in a way that the agent did not intend. At no point did A plan to kill his uncle by running him over in the street on his way across town. His desire to kill his uncle did not rationalise his running over the old man, since he had no belief that the old man was his uncle. Therefore, his beliefs and desires cannot explain what he did in the way necessary for what he did to be intentional.

At first glance, Armstrong's suggestion might seem to dispose of *The Fraud* also. After all the bank clerk did not plan to defraud his customer absent-mindedly. But the sense in which he 'did not plan' this is quite different from the sense in which A did not plan the killing. While A planned to kill his uncle in a way inconsistent with what actually occurred, the bank clerk's action conformed to the plan he had formulated; it is just that there were certain aspects of the causal chain between his decision and the desired outcome which the bank clerk had not envisaged because he simply did not consider them.

The bank clerk planned to defraud the customer by filling in a form, and that's exactly what happened. He had no plan for the causal chain between his decision and the action of writing on the form. And, in this, he was no more than a normal agent. We cannot require that the internal, psychological or physiological stages of a causal chain which leads to action conform to some plan of the agent's, since agents usually do not have intentions about these matters. So it is hard to see how Armstrong's suggestion can deal with *The Fraud* (Davidson, 1980f:78–9).

Peacocke offers an account of why the bank clerk does not intentionally defraud his client: there is no law which guarantees that if the bank clerk had had a slightly different intention, his nervousness would have interacted with that intention to produce the intended outcome, therefore his action is not a function of his intention in the way required for intentional action (Peacocke, 1979:69–70). But might there not be a mechanism which permitted only one action? A paralysed person might be fitted with a prosthetic device which enabled him to summon help but nothing else. If he had intended something different, this mechanism would not have worked, nevertheless it enables him to summon help intentionally.

In both *The Killing* and *The Fraud* there is an element of coincidence which is essential to the production of the desired outcome. It is a coincidence that my uncle was crossing the street at exactly the moment when I was driving past towards his house. The factors which caused me to be at that place, my desire to kill him etc., were quite independent of those which caused him to be there, perhaps his desire to go shopping. In *The Fraud* it was a coincidence that the desire to defraud a customer by filling in a certain form led to the filling in of just such a form. The factors needed to make the clerk nervous – his belief and desire, were quite independent of those physiological conditions needed to ensure that his nervousness would lead him to write in the way required.

This observation leads me to make the following proposal:

(I) S does A intentionally if, and only if, A is no coincidence given S's beliefs and desires.

It may be objected that many different and independent factors are required for S's reasons to cause his actions, even in a quite normal case of action: think of the physiological conditions inside the agent which are relevant at different stages of the intricate causal chain leading from decision to bodily movement. So it will always be a coincidence when his designs are implemented.

In order to deal with this objection we must make a move analogous to that made in chapter 7 when dealing with perception and memory – we must introduce the idea of an action mechanism which, in normal conditions, enables the agent to move his body as he wishes. It is no coincidence when the normal working of this mechanism ensures the realisation of the agent's plans. The level of explanation appropriate to intentional action is not one which would reveal different causal factors at different stages of the causal chain between intention and bodily movement. Rather, what exists at that level is an action mechanism which combines with certain (coincidentally but normally coexisting) background conditions (for example the fact that gravitational forces are within certain limits), to produce the desired movement.

But it will be said that, whenever the agent wants to do more than move his body, the success of his action will depend on factors well beyond his body. Say that I go into a bank in order to draw money from my account. My pen must be working, the bank clerk must be willing to serve me, the bank's computer must not be down, and these are quite independent factors relevant at different stages of the chain between my entry with the intention of drawing cash and my exit with the cash. Nevertheless, I may intentionally draw out money from my account.

However, where I intend to bring about a certain outcome by means of an apparent coincidence, that outcome is, in fact, no coincidence. I reasonably believe that the bank clerk will help me and the computer will not be down, and I believe this because of past experience of factors relevant to them now working, for example the past reliability of the computer or the past helpfulness of the clerk. These factors help to cause my decision and my movement by affecting my beliefs, so they are a common cause of my decision and that decision's success. It is no coincidence that my action succeeds given these factors.

This point is relevant to other examples. Say that I intended to run my uncle over while he was on a shopping trip. Would it not still have been a coincidence that he was crossing the road as I passed – after all, his reason for being on that road is quite different from mine? But, provided I were aware of his intention to cross that road in the course of his shopping trip, our collision would be no coincidence. His intention to go shopping would (by influencing my beliefs) have become a common cause of his crossing that road and my driving along it, so the killing would be intentional.

Similarly, our bank clerk may know that the only way he can persuade himself to defraud the customer is to contemplate the fraud in an effort to make himself nervous. Here, there is a causal chain from the conditions which ensure that the nervousness will result in a suitable action to the agent's knowledge of this fact and thence to his acting on that knowledge. Therefore, the fact that he acquires a belief and desire which makes him nervous at the very moment at which the nervousness will result in fraud is no coincidence, and the fraud is intentional.[8]

(I) provides us with a common explanation of the deviance in both internal and external causal chains considered above. I can think of no deviant causal chains which do not contain a crucial coincidence, so I commend (I) as an essential part of any causal account of intentional action.

[8] Peacocke, 1979:72–4 discusses such cases of 'planned deviance'. These cases should be distinguished from those where the agent has an unconscious intention to defraud his client and implements it by means of his nerves. These Freudian examples are not cases of intentional action in the strict sense but they are intentional in some broader sense. I cannot go into these matters any further here.

# Conclusion: Whither Causal Realism?

Does the analysis of causation laid out in the last eight chapters have any relevance to wider philosophical issues? One area in which the word 'cause' makes a regular appearance is in the contemporary debate about realism. Realism, crudely put, is the view that the character of the world is independent of the character of the human mind. Philosophers have understood various things by 'realism' and have sought to argue for it in many different ways, but one particular strategy has achieved something of a vogue. The idea behind it is that one should use notions like 'cause' and 'law' along with other 'naturalistically acceptable' notions to construct an account of problematic mental and linguistic phenomena. So, rather than starting one's theorising, as in former times, with facts about our experience of the world, or features of our language, the causal realist analyses both mental notions, such as 'experience' and 'belief', and linguistic notions, such as 'meaning' and 'reference', in 'naturalistic' terms. By means of this reduction, the causal realist exhibits the natural constitution of mind and language, how they are composed of nothing more than the causal and nomological relations between non-psychological and non-linguistic entities. He will thus undermine the anti-realist opinion that the direction of explanation goes the other way – mental or linguistic phenomena can hardly explain nature's most general features if they themselves are to be accounted for in 'naturalistic' terms.

Philosophers involved in the realist project have produced causal theories of truth, reference, representation, property, knowledge, belief and the direction of time – this in addition to the causal treatment which I myself handed out to perception, memory, action. Now these attempts at a causal analysis may, or may not, have come off, but none of them will serve the purposes of the realist unless the notion of causation is itself 'naturalistically acceptable'. The realist must be certain that he can say what it is for one event to be causally related to another event without alluding to mental or linguistic phenomena. The realist may feel inclined

178

to take 'cause' as a primitive, but he must be in a position to rule out theories of causation which query the mind-independence of causal facts.

Unfortunately for him, there is no shortage of philosophers who have asserted the mind-dependence of causation. Many of these philosophers take themselves to be following Hume, who allegedly denied that the world contains any necessary connections between distinct events, while admitting that such necessary connections are essential to causation. Hume resolved this problem by arguing that the impression of necessity originates in those expectations which the regular succession of events generates in the mind and which the mind then projects onto the world: so causation involves a mental element essentially.

Now, in presenting my own theory of causation, I did not endorse Hume's view that causal facts can be analysed into an objective constant conjunction between events and a subjective feeling of necessity. Indeed, I completely failed to resolve the issue of whether the world contains necessary connections between logically distinct events. Nevertheless, the realist may be worried by my repeated insistence that causation is a form of explanation. 'Explanation' sounds as if it is bound up with the human mind, with what makes sense to us and what we find intelligible. My equation of causation and causal explanation creates no Humean division between a subjective and an objective aspect of causation, but it might make the whole relation look rather mind-dependent.

At two points in the book, this realist worry will have been particularly acute. Firstly, I grounded the distinction between causal and logical relations on the epistemic division between what can be known *a priori* and what cannot. I said that causes resolve apparent coincidences, and apparent coincidences are combinations of events where there is no *a priori* connection between the events combined – events whose components are, as I put it, logically independent of one another. But the causal realist would not be inclined to delineate the class of causal relations by reference to their role in our thought. He would object to the idea that relations of causal necessity are to be distinguished from other modal relations by asking how we can find out about them. At best, the realist would treat this epistemic difference as an indication of some more fundamental metaphysical divide between the causal and the logical, a divide which I failed to locate.

A second source of realist concern may be my account of the direction of causation. In several places, I rejected causal hypotheses on the *a priori* grounds that they served no explanatory purpose. For example, I argued that, in a world in which there was no asymmetry of overdetermination, there would be no explanatory gain to be had from postulating causal relations and thus we should conclude that such a world is devoid of causation. Here, a realist might wish to ask why we should suppose there to be no causation in a world just because such causal relations as there were would not fulfil our epistemic ambitions? Perhaps causal suppositions may be true even where they are useless to rational beings. In my view, the tie between causation and explanation is too close for there to be one without the other, but the realist may think this savours of allowing the mind to shape the world.

I have left these difficult matters until now because I am quite uncertain of what to think about them. I am unclear about the terms of debate, unsure of the contrast between a mind-dependent and a mind-independent world and of what the causal realist should demand from a theory of causation. As a result, I shall confine myself to making a few relevant, but inconclusive, points.

First, I have eschewed analyses of causation which make explicit reference to intelligent beings and their perceptions, thoughts or actions. For instance, in chapter 5 (pages 108–10) I rejected a theory of the direction of causation based on the thought that a cause is something one has to bring about in order to get its effect. I also argued that there could be a systematic mismatch between the perception of causation and causation itself since, while our theory of perception laid it down that, if two events seemed to be causally related, the apparently earlier had to seem to cause the apparently later and not *vice versa*, our theory of causation left open the possibility that causation might run against the grain of time (pages 102–5). The perception of causation is necessarily connected to the apparent direction of time, while there is no corresponding link between causation and the actual direction of time. So it would be hard for the realist to claim that my analysis was explicitly anthropocentric.

As to the intrusion of explanation into my account, whether this worries you will depend on your view of explanation. I have urged that the type of explanation which ought to interest the theorist of causation is that which works by resolving coincidences. Now someone might think that whether a certain event was a *prima facie* coincidence or not was a matter about which rational beings might disagree. Say it is obvious to one party that the conjunction of two events would be an accident if there were no third factor to tie them together; another party might be unable to see these two events as accidentally conjoined, regarding them instead as *a priori* connected, as not standing in need of any third factor to bring them together. In chapter 1 (page 10), I dismissed the notion that explanation is in the eye of the beholder simply because people's explanatory needs may diverge, owing to differences in what they already know and in what they wish to know. But what of the more radical possibility that people with exactly the same background information and exactly the same interests in life might disagree over what required explanation and what did not? Could we come across someone who regarded the fact that I grew a beard soon after my voice broke as no more in need of explanation, as no more of a *prima facie* coincidence, than the fact that you ended up on my right when I moved to your left? I doubt it, but I have no argument to offer. Were this possibility realised, this would give the lie to the assertion that it was up to nature whether one event causally explained another.

Furthermore, even if all rational beings must agree on what counts as a *prima facie* coincidence, the realist may still complain that this consensus is a product of the necessary mental constitution of the rational person, rather than of some feature of the non-mental world to which we are all properly sensitive. Any relation between events which was such that it necessarily made one event intelligible by reference to another in the way a causal explanation does, would, on this view, be mentally constituted in an unacceptable way. I have little insight into whether this complaint is well grounded or not. All I can say is this: here is my theory of causation which ties causation to causal explanation and, if the realist does not like it, he must provide us with another which serves his metaphysical purposes better.

# Bibliography

Achinstein, P. (1983) *The Nature of Explanation*, Oxford University Press.

Anscombe, E. (1981a) 'Whatever has a Beginning of Existence Must have a Cause', in her *From Parmenides to Wittgenstein*, Oxford, Blackwell.

(1981b) 'Causality and Extensionality', in her *Metaphysics and the Philosophy of Mind*, Oxford, Blackwell.

Armstrong, D. (1973) *Belief, Truth and Knowledge*, Cambridge University Press.

(1980) 'Acting and Trying', in his *The Nature of Mind*, Brighton, Harvester.

(1983) *What is a Law of Nature?*, Cambridge University Press.

Bennett, J. (1988) 'Farewell to the Phlogiston Theory of Conditionals', *Mind*, 97.

Blackburn, S. (1990) 'Filling in Space', *Analysis*, 50.

(1991) 'Losing One's Mind: Physics, Identity and Folk Burglar Prevention', in ed. Greenwood, J. *The Future of Folk Psychology*, Cambridge University Press.

Bunzl, M. (1979) 'Causal Overdetermination', *Journal of Philosophy*, 76.

Carnap, R. (1949) 'Logical Foundations of the Unity of Science', in eds. Fiegl, H. and Sellars, W. *Readings in Philosophical Analysis*, New York, Appleton, Century and Crofts.

Churchland, P. (1979) *Scientific Realism and the Plasticity of Mind*, Cambridge University Press.

Churchland, P. (1986) *Neurophilosophy*, Cambridge Mass., MIT Press.

Cohen, L. (1977) *The Probable and the Provable*, Oxford University Press.

Cummins, R. (1984) 'Functional Analysis', in ed. Sober, E. *Conceptual Issues in Evolutionary Biology*, Cambridge Mass, MIT. Press.

Davidson, D. (1980a) 'Causal Relations', in his *Essays on Actions and Events*, Oxford University Press.

(1980b) 'The Logical Form of Action Sentences', in his *Essays on Actions and Events*, Oxford University Press.

(1980c) 'Agency', in his *Essays on Actions and Events*, Oxford University Press.

(1980d) 'Mental Events', in his *Essays on Actions and Events*, Oxford University Press.

(1980e) 'Actions, Reasons and Causes', in his *Essays on Actions and Events*, Oxford University Press.

(1980f) 'Freedom to Act', in his *Essays on Actions and Events*, Oxford University Press.

182

(1980g) 'How is Weakness of the Will Possible?', in his *Essays on Actions and Events*, Oxford University Press.

(1980h) 'Hempel on Explaining Action', in his *Essays on Actions and Events*, Oxford University Press.

(1984) 'Truth and Meaning', in his *Essays on Truth and Interpretation*, Oxford University Press.

Davies, M. (1983) 'Function in Perception', *Australasian Journal of Philosophy*, 61.

Dennett, D. (1987) 'True Believers', in his *The Intentional Stance*, Cambridge Mass, MIT. Press.

(1991) 'Real Patterns', *Journal of Philosophy*, 88.

Ducasse, C. (1951) *Nature, Mind and Death*, La Salle, Illinois, Open Court.

Dummett, M. (1964) 'Bringing about the Past', *Philosophical Review*, 73.

Eells, E. (1991) *Probabilistic Causality*, Cambridge University Press.

Evans, G. (1982) *The Varieties of Reference*, Oxford University Press.

Fodor, J. (1981) 'Special Sciences' in his *Representations*, Cambridge Mass., MIT Press.

(1990) *A Theory of Content*, Cambridge Mass., MIT. Press.

Garfinkel, A. (1981) *Forms of Explanation*, Yale University Press.

Goldman, A. (1970) *A Theory of Human Action*, Princeton University Press.

Goodman, N. (1983) *Fact, Fiction and Forecast*, fourth edition, Harvard.

Grice, P. (1967) 'The Causal Theory of Perception', in ed. Warnock, G. *The Philosophy of Perception*, Oxford University Press.

Grunbaum, A. (1973) *Philosophical Problems of Space and Time*, Dordrecht, Reidel.

Hart, H. and Honore, A. (1959) *Causation in the Law*, Oxford University Press.

Hart, W. (1988) *The Engines of the Soul*, Cambridge University Press.

Hempel, C. (1965) *Aspects of Scientific Explanation*, New York, Free Press.

Holt, P. (1976) 'Causality and our Conception of Matter', *Analysis*, 37.

Hooker, C. (1981) 'Towards a General Theory of Reduction: Part III – Cross-Categorial Reduction', *Dialogue*, 20.

Hornsby, J. (1980a) 'Which Mental Events are Physical Events?', *Proceedings of the Aristotelian Society*, 81.

(1980b) *Actions*, London, Routledge.

Horwich, P. (1987) *Asymmetries in Time*, Cambridge Mass, MIT Press.

Hume, D. (1948) *Dialogues Concerning Natural Religion*, New York, Hafner Press.

(1975) *Enquiry Concerning Human Understanding*, third edition, Oxford University Press.

(1978) *Treatise of Human Nature*, second edition, Oxford University Press.

Hurely, S. (1990) *Natural Reasons*, Oxford University Press.

Jackson, F. (1977) *Perception*, Cambridge University Press.

Jackson, F., Pargetter, R. and Prior, E. (1982) 'Functionalism and Type–Type Identity Theory', *Philosophical Studies*, 42.

Jackson, F. and Pargetter, R. (1988) 'Causal Statements', *Philosophical Topics*, 16.

Jackson, F. and Pettit, P. (1988) 'Functionalism and Broad Content', *Mind*, 97.

Kim, J. (1969) 'Events and their Descriptions', in ed. Rescher, N. *Essays in Honour of Carl Hempel*, Dordrecht, Reidel.

(1973) 'Causes and Counterfactuals', *Journal of Philosophy*, 70.

(1974) 'Non-Causal Connections', *Nous*, 8.

(1984a) 'Concepts of Supervenience', *Philosophy and Phenomenological Research*, 45.

(1984b) 'Epiphenomenal and Supervenient Causation', in eds. French, P., Uehling, T, and Wettstein, H. *Midwest Studies in Philosophy*, Volume IX, Minnesota.

Kitcher, P. (1984) '1953 and All That', *Philosophical Review*, 43.

Lewis, D. (1973) *Counterfactuals*, Oxford, Blackwell.

(1983a) 'Mad Pain and Martian Pain', in his *Philosophical Papers*, volume 1, Oxford University Press.

(1983b) 'New Work for a Theory of Universals', *Australasian Journal of Philosophy* 61.

(1986a) 'Causation', in his *Philosophical Papers*, volume 2, Oxford University Press.

(1986b) 'Events', in his *Philosophical Papers*, volume 2, Oxford University Press.

(1986c) 'Causal Explanation', in his *Philosophical Papers*, volume 2, Oxford University Press.

(1986d) 'Counterfactual Dependence and Time's Arrow', in his *Philosophical Papers*, volume 2, Oxford University Press.

(1986e) 'Veridical Hallucination and Prosthetic Vision', in his *Philosophical Papers*, volume 2, Oxford University Press.

Lowe, E. (1980) 'For Want of a Nail', *Analysis*, 40.

Mackie, J. (1965) 'Causes and Conditions', *American Philosophical Quarterly*, 2.

(1973) *Truth, Probability and Paradox*, Oxford University Press.

(1974) *The Cement of the Universe*, Oxford University Press.

(1979) 'Mind, Brain and Causation', in eds. French, P., Uehling, T., Wettstein, H., *Midwest Studies in Philosophy*, volume 4, University of Minnesota Press.

Malcolm, N. (1982) 'The Conceivability of Mechanism', in ed. Watson G. *Free Will*, Oxford University Press.

Marr, D. (1982) *Vision*, New York, Freeman.

Martin, C. and Deutscher, M. (1966) 'Remembering', *Philosophical Review*, 75.

McGinn, C. (1984) *Wittgenstein on Meaning*, Oxford, Blackwell.

Mellor, D. (1971) *The Matter of Chance*, Cambridge University Press.

(1974) 'In Defense of Dispositions', *Philosophical Review*, 83.

(1981) *Real Time*, Cambridge University Press.

(1987) 'The Singularly Affecting Facts of Causation', in eds. Petit, P., Slyvan, R., Norman, J. *Mind, Morality and Metaphysics*, Oxford, Blackwell.

Michotte, A. (1963) *The Perception of Causality*, London, Methuen.

Mill, J. (1906) *A System of Logic*, eight edition, London, Longmans.

Nagel, E. (1961) *The Structure of Science*, London, Routledge.

Neander, K and Menzies P. (1990) 'David Owens on Levels of Explanation', *Mind*, 99.

Nozick, R. (1981) *Philosophical Explanations*, Oxford University Press.

O'Shaughnessy, B. (1980) *The Will*, volume 2, Cambridge University Press.

Owens, D. (1989a) 'Disjunctive Laws', *Analysis*, 49.

(1989b) 'Levels of Explanation', *Mind*, 98.

(1989c) 'Causes and Coincidences', *Proceedings of the Aristotelian Society*, 90.

Papineau, D. (1985) 'Causal Asymmetry', *British Journal for the Philosophy of Science*, 36.

Peacocke, C. (1979) *Holistic Explanation*, Oxford University Press.

(1983) *Sense and Content*, Oxford University Press.

(1985) 'Imagination, Experience and Possibility', in eds. Foster, J. and Robinson, H. *Essays on Berkeley*, Oxford University Press.

Popper K. (1956) 'The Arrow of Time', *Nature*, 177.

(1960) *The Poverty of Historicism*, second edition, London, Routledge.

Putnam, H. (1975) *Mind, Language and Reality*, Cambridge University Press.

Reichenbach, H. (1956) *The Direction of Time*, Berkeley, University of California Press.

(1958) *The Philosophy of Space and Time*, New York, Dover.

Robinson, H. (1982) *Matter and Sense*, Cambridge University Press.

Russell, B. (1953) 'On the Notion of Cause', in *Mysticism and Logic*, London, Penguin.

Salmon, S. (1984) *Scientific Explanation and the Causal Structure of the World*, Princeton University Press.

Shoemaker, S. (1984) 'Causality and Properties', in *Identity, Cause and Mind*, Cambridge University Press.

Sklar, L. (1974) *Space, Time and Spacetime*, London, University of California Press.

Smolensky, P. (1988) 'On The Proper Treatment of Connectionism', *Behavioural and Brain Sciences*, 11.

Snowdon, P. (1990) 'The Objects of Perceptual Experience', *Proceedings of the Aristotelian Society, Supplementary Volume*, 64.

Sober, E. (1983) 'Equilibrium Explanation', *Philosophical Studies*, 43.

Sorabji, R. (1980) *Necessity, Cause and Blame*, London, Duckworth.

Stalnaker, R. (1984) *Inquiry*, Cambridge Mass., MIT Press.

Swain, M. (1980) 'Causation and Distinct Events', in ed. Van Inwagen, P. *Time and Cause*, Dordrecht, Reidel.

Taylor, C. (1964) *The Explanation of Behaviour*, Henley, Routledge.

Thomson, J. (1977) *Acts and Other Events*, Cornell University Press.

Tooley, M. (1987) *Causation*, Oxford University Press.

Van Fraassen, B. (1980) *The Scientific Image*, Oxford University Press.

(1989) *Laws and Symmetry*, Oxford University Press.

Von Wright, G. (1971) *Explanation and Understanding*, London, Routledge.

Williams, B. (1973) 'Imagination and the Self', in his *Problems of the Self*, Cambridge University Press.

# Index

Achinstein, P., 80
Action, 74–5, 108–10, 163–77, 180
Anscombe, E., 30n, 74
Armstrong, D., 37, 112n, 174–5

Bennett, J., 26n
Blackburn, S., 63n, 128
Bunzl, M., 98

Carnap, R., 114
Causal theory of,
    action, 163–77
    memory, 158–62
    perception, 143–52
    time, 101–2, 106–7
Causation,
    and action, 74–5, 108–10, 170–3, 180
    analysed, 23–6, 70–1
    asymmetry of, 82–4
    and causal explanation, 23, 42–3, 48,
        60–2, 84, 107–8, 171–2, 179–81
    causal loops, 82n
    distinguished from common cause,
        50–1, 97
    as extrinsic relation, 108
    and laws, 24–7, 48–9, 63, 77–9
    and logical form, 42–3, 50, 53, 60–2
    cause as necessary and sufficient
        condition, 1–2, 24–7, 82–4
    between object and itself, 45–6, 74–5
    objectivity of, 10, 179–81
    and overdetermination, 85–102
    between part and whole, 45, 57–60,
        72, 75
    perception of, 102–5, 107
    and preemption, 97–8
    probabilistic, 5, 24, 96n
    regularity theory of, 82–3
    as relation between event-objects,
        42–9, 51–60, 75, 171–2
    and symmetrical processes, 105–10

subjunctive theory of, 49–51, 57–60,
    82–4, 91–4
Churchland, P., 31
Churchland, P., 137n
Closure of physics, 119, 140, 170–3
Cohen, L., 170
Coincidence,
    asymmetry of, 94–6
    defined, 5–10, 24–6, 70–1
    come in degrees, 8–9
    can explain, 11–13
    inexplicable, 11–22
    and levels, 137–42
    objectivity of, 10, 180–1
Conditionals,
    backtracking, 83, 91–3
    subjunctive, 32–6
    subjunctive and indicative, 24–6
Constitution, 78–81, 116–18, 124–37
Cummins, R., 129

Davidson, D., 41–9, 61–2, 73n, 74–5,
    118n, 163–7, 168n, 171–2
Davies, M., 149–50, 152, 155–8
Dennett, D., 123, 135, 166
Dispositions, 35–7, 63, 67–71
Dormitive Virtues, 68–9
Dummett, M., 98–102, 108
Dummett Processes, 98–102, 105–10
Ducasse, C., 42, 63n, 83n

Eells, E., 18n, 83n
Evans, G., 161
Events,
    and actions, 74–5, 171–2
    essential and inessential properties of,
        51–7
    whether objects, 7–8, 42–9, 51, 75
    as possessing parts, 45, 57–60, 72, 75,
        78–9
    real and unreal, 7–8, 45, 54–5, 71

Explanation,
of action, 74–5
not agglomerative, 11–15, 20–1,
139–40, 149–51
causal and non-causal, 20, 26–7,
41–9, 51–60, 71–81
constitutive, 77–81, 124–37
context-relativity of, 9–10
and laws, 20–2
levels of, 114–15, 153–5, 175–6
matter of degree, 13
objectivity of, 10, 179–81
of similarities and differences, 14–15,
76–7
not transitive, 15–19, 20–1, 137,
139–40, 148
transparency of, 73–5

Fodor, J., 31n, 118n, 124
Functional analysis, 128–32

Garfinkel, A., 131, 132n
Geometry, 64–6
Goldman, A., 74–5
Goodman, N., 21
Grice, P., 144
Grunbaum, A., 101

Hart, H., and Honore, A., 7
Hart, W., 29
Hempel, C., 16n, 21, 22n
Holt, P., 63n
Hooker, C., 129, 137n
Hornsby, J., 16n, 74–5, 140, 173
Horwich, P., 93, 110
Hume, D., 3, 14, 27–32, 83n, 179
Hurley, S., 169n

Jackson, F., 72n, 78n
Jackson, F., Pargetter, R. and Prior, E.,
126n
Jackson, F. and Pargetter, R., 45
Jackson, F. and Pettit, P., 76–7

Kim, J., 43n, 46n, 61, 73–5, 115n, 116,
118n, 171n
Kitcher, P., 137n
Knowledge,
of possibility, 28–31
and scepticism, 39
and time, 110–13

Laws,
a posteriori, 31, 48–9, 63–8, 167–70,
179
causal and non-causal, 25–7, 79–81,
107–8
contingent or necessary, 27–40,
117–18
not deductively closed, 22
not disjunctive, 124
must explain, 21–2
involve non-observational predicates,
31
regularity theory of, 32–7
support subjunctive conditionals, 21,
25, 32–4
Lewis, D., 22n, 33–6, 49–60, 80, 88–94,
100n, 105, 117–18, 149
Lowe, E., 15n

Mackie, J., 35, 74, 83n, 85–8, 97, 109,
170n, 172
Malcolm, N., 171n
Marr, D., 154
Martin, C. and Deutscher, M., 158–62
Martin, M., 61n, 91n
McGinn, C., 170n
Mellor, D., 36, 53, 66–70, 73n, 101, 103
Michotte, A., 102
Mill, J., 8, 15n, 83n
Multiple Realisation, 123–4, 127–8

Nagel, E., 121
Neander, K. and Menzies, P., 20n
Nozick, R., 39

O'Shaughnessy, B., 173

Papineau, D., 86
Peacocke, C., 29, 30n, 31n, 118n, 145–53,
172, 174–5, 177n
Popper, K., 19, 100n
Properties,
and causal powers, 38–41, 70, 80–1
dispositional, 35–7, 63, 67–71
identity between, 80–1, 125–6
relational, 47, 76–7
Putnam, H., 65n, 126n, 128, 131

Recording machines, 110–13
Regularity theory of,
causation, 82–3
law, 32–7

Reichenbach, H., 69n, 101, 106–7, 110
Robinson, H., 63n
Russell, B., 26n

Salmon, W., 70
Shoemaker, S., 38–40, 69–71, 81
Sklar, L., 107
Smolensky, P., 173n
Snowdon, P., 157
Sober, E., 131
Sorabji, R., 11, 12n, 22, 23
Stalnaker, R., 36n
Supervenience, 115–22
Swain, M., 45, 57

Taylor, C., 167–70
Teichmann, R., 61n
Thomson, J., 45, 57
Time,
    apparent direction of, 102–5
    causal theory of, 101–2, 106–7
    knowledge and, 110–13

Tooley, M., 37, 105

Van Fraassen, B., 9–10, 32n
Von Wright, G., 109

Williams, B., 30n